NO
STRAIGHT
LINES

SMALL CITIES SUSTAINABILITY STUDIES IN COMMUNITY AND CULTURAL ENGAGEMENT

SERIES EDITORS:

Will Garrett-Petts, Professor of English and Associate Vice-President of Research and Graduate Studies, Thompson Rivers University

Nancy Duxbury Carreiro, Senior Researcher, Centre for Social Studies, University of Coimbra, Portugal, and Co-coordinator of its Cities, Cultures, and Architecture Research Group

Published with the support of Thompson Rivers University.
ISSN 2561-5351 (Print) ISSN 2561-536X (Online)

This series is interested in discovering and documenting how smaller communities in Canada and elsewhere differ from their larger metropolitan counterparts in terms of their strategies (formal and informal) for developing, maintaining, and enhancing community and cultural vitality, particularly in terms of civic engagement, artistic animation, and creative place-making.

No. 1 · *No Straight Lines: Local Leadership and the Path from Government to Governance in Small Cities*
Edited by Terry Kading

UNIVERSITY OF CALGARY
Press

NO STRAIGHT LINES

LOCAL LEADERSHIP AND THE PATH FROM GOVERNMENT TO GOVERNANCE IN SMALL CITIES

Edited by
TERRY KADING

THOMPSON
RIVERS
UNIVERSITY

Small Cities Sustainability Studies
in Community and Cultural Engagement

ISSN 2561-5351 (Print) ISSN 2561-536X (Online)

University of Calgary Press
2500 University Drive NW
Calgary, Alberta
Canada T2N 1N4
press.ucalgary.ca

LIBRARY AND ARCHIVES CANADA CATALOGUING IN PUBLICATION

No straight lines : local leadership and the path from government to governance in small cities / edited by Terry Kading.

(Small cities sustainability studies in community and cultural engagement, ISSN 2561-5351, ISSN 2561-536X ; no. 1)
Includes bibliographical references and index.
Issued in print and electronic formats.
ISBN 978-1-55238-944-7 (softcover).—ISBN 978-1-55238-945-4 (Open Access PDF).—ISBN 978-1-55238-946-1 (PDF).—ISBN 978-1-55238-947-8 (EPUB).—ISBN 978-1-55238-948-5 (Kindle)

1. Quality of life—British Columbia—Kamloops. 2. Community leadership—British Columbia—Kamloops. 3. Social participation—British Columbia—Kamloops. 4. Kamloops (B.C.)—Social conditions. I. Kading, Terrance William, 1962-, editor II. Series: Small cities sustainability studies in community and cultural engagement no. ; 1

HN110.K36N6 2018   361.6'10971172   C2018-901695-7
                                               C2018-901696-5

The University of Calgary Press acknowledges the support of the Government of Alberta through the Alberta Media Fund for our publications. We acknowledge the financial support of the Government of Canada. We acknowledge the financial support of the Canada Council for the Arts for our publishing program.

This book is published with financial support from Thompson Rivers University.

 Canada   Canada Council   Conseil des Arts
                                                    for the Arts   du Canada

Printed and bound in Canada by Friesens
This book is printed on 100% PCW FSC paper

Cover image: Radomír Režný, June 2011, *Graffiti captured on a San Francisco building*, photograph. Image courtesy of the artist.
Copyediting by Peter Enman
Cover design, page design, and typesetting by Melina Cusano

CONTENTS

ACKNOWLEDGEMENTS

We would like to thank all the community organizations and local leaders identified in this collection for their time and support in providing us with a remarkable education about the diverse challenges and opportunities in the City of Kamloops. Without their openness and patience we would not have been able to understand the complexity of their efforts, and we hope that we have been able to capture the richness of their endeavours through this work. We would also like to acknowledge and thank all the students at Thompson Rivers University who over the years have participated in the various research opportunities that inform many of the important outcomes and insights in our chapters. Through their own interest in our community, they have enhanced our teaching skills and heightened our attentiveness to local opportunities for community-engaged research for more undergraduate researchers. Notable recognition goes to the various anonymous reviewers of this collection who have all provided critical but supportive examinations, and deepened the quality of the insights and evaluations by helping us to better frame and integrate the varied themes and issues in this collection.

Special credit is due to Dr. Will Garrett-Petts for recognizing early on the value of a "leadership and local learning perspective" as a means to organize quite disparate themes into a cohesive work. His resolute support for this project has kept us engaged and committed to completing this collection, and he has offered, over many years, critical insights and lessons on how a university can be an active supporter of community initiatives and a better community partner. In addition, we would like to thank all the staff of the Office of Research and Graduate Studies for their support and advice in promoting community-engaged research and the early outcomes from this collection. To this end, we would like to acknowledge the support of the Social Sciences and Humanities Research Council of Canada (SSHRC) through the Community-University Research Alliances (CURA) grants that made the outcomes of this collection possible, and continue to generate enduring results in our city. Lastly, we would like to thank all the family and friends who have provided their own observations and insights on "life in the small city" that have further served to enrich this collection.

Leadership, Learning, and *Equality of Quality of Life* in the Small City

Terry Kading

As soon as several of the inhabitants of the United States have conceived a sentiment or an idea that they want to produce in the world, they seek each other out; and when they have found each other, they unite. From then on, they are no longer isolated men [sic], but a power one sees from afar, whose actions serve as an example; a power that speaks, and to which one listens.

—Alexis de Tocqueville

The city is ultimately a shared project, like Aristotle's polis, a place where we can fashion a common good that we simply cannot build alone.

—Charles Montgomery

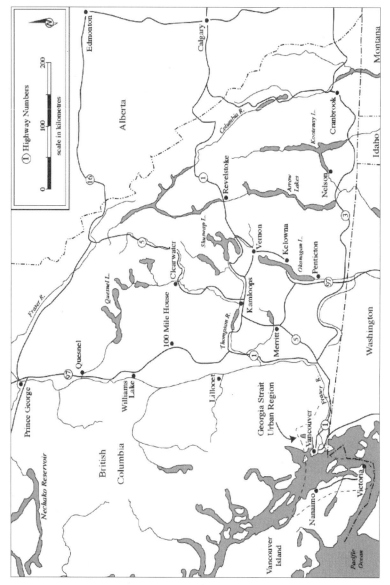

FIGURE O.1. Southern British Columbia. From *The Small Cities Book: On the Cultural Future of Small Cities*, edited by W.F. Garrett-Petts (Vancouver: New Star Books, 2005). Courtesy of W.F. Garrett-Petts.

TERRY KADING

The insights from this collection reveal and challenge present understandings of *quality of life* in the small city, thus opening up new opportunities for local initiatives and research on "leadership and learning" at the local level, with the goal of maximizing joy, minimizing hardship, increasing empathy and cooperation, instituting fairness for all residents, and building lasting bonds between friends, families, and strangers. How the needs and aspirations of residents of the small city are addressed, who foments these changes, and what accounts for the success of certain initiatives over others is the focus of our collection.

As in all urban centres, there are in Kamloops the most visible forms of leadership and the less visible forms—all of which contribute to the diversity of urban life. The most visible forms of leadership are understood as being driven by the local "pro-growth coalition," a combination of developers, property owners, professionals, tradespeople, and businesses acting in concert with the local government to ensure the continuous expansion of the city. From this leadership we witness the appearance of housing developments, shopping districts, and various business and industrial ventures, enhanced and augmented by the range of services and amenities provided by the local government. With this dynamic emerges a particular *quality of life* (or *quality of place*)—generated by the need to perpetuate increases in the population by attracting investment and employment—as one important measure of municipal success. For the small city, as a more diverse urban setting, "growth imperatives" have been challenged and supported by broader notions of *quality of life* beyond employment and consumer needs—resulting in less visible forms of leadership and learning to address local needs and aspirations. These less visible forms of leadership reveal the intricate and diverse types of network collaborations that foster unique contributions to our *quality of life* in the small city—or what we identify as *equality of quality of life*—as a new perspective on *quality of life* issues.

The purpose of this collection is to expose how these leadership initiatives have and continue to fortify—often unknowingly—the *equality of quality of life* in one small city, Kamloops, British Columbia. With a population of 90,000, and as the largest urban centre within a regional district of some 132,000+, the City of Kamloops has an important profile as a small to mid-sized regional city offering a range of professional, industrial, retail, government, and educational services not available in the smaller towns within a much larger catchment area. With this diversification in economic opportunities and employment, the City of Kamloops has engaged in new types of planning, moving beyond basic land-use planning to encompass social, cultural, recreational, and sustainability plans that express a more comprehensive and inclusive process than in the past (Kading and Walmsley 2014; Walmsley and Kading 2017). *Quality of life* has become a powerful idea in establishing collective goals for urban centres and assessing the effects of proposals or change in our communities, and as the Chief Administrative Officer of Kamloops has affirmed, "Collectively we are committed to a goal of building a beautiful city and a quality of life that is one of the best in Canada" (City of Kamloops 2017).

But what is *quality of life*? Generally this is understood in terms of expanding a set of local amenities or services to enhance health and leisure opportunities (e.g., sports facilities, cultural and educational venues, parks, festivals, and bike paths) expressed through municipal community planning documents. *Quality of life*, in this regard, tends to be seen through the quite visible appearance of facilities and services to achieve this optimal state, or urban ambience, and may be used to promote the attractiveness of the urban centre in soliciting investment, tourism, and residential growth. This collection expands on the concept of *quality of life* to encompass *equality of quality of life*, a new perspective comprised of less recognized but critical components that ensure the health and vitality of urban life—particularly in the small city, where the structures and capacities of local government are more circumscribed than in large urban centres. The themes we will explore include engagement with urban social challenges, an aging population, sustainability, and local heritage. Leadership initiatives and local learning are much more pronounced in addressing these issues, generating certain services and conveniences, and fostering an improved urban experience for all residents. As academics with both a professional and a personal attachment to the local initiatives under review and discussion, we can further attest to the distinctive institutional role the *small university* in the small city can play in initiating, supporting, or promoting these *equality of quality of life* features. The strength and novelty of our collection, we feel, lies in the way we provide an overview of the multiple ways in which this community-university engagement may occur, and the wide variety of outcomes and opportunities that may emerge from this collaborative context. The aim of this collection is to acknowledge and account for these dynamics—the active engagement between the university and the local community in the City of Kamloops—offering insights for other small to mid-sized cities and small universities where *equality of quality of life* issues have become more prominent.

Quality of Life Debates and Equality of Quality of Life

Important features of the *quality of life* debate have generally been framed around the contrasting views of two influential thinkers on community and urban life—Robert Putnam and his focus on the precarious state of social capital, and Richard Florida on the urban requirement to develop creative capital. Putnam is renowned for his research on and lament over the decline in "social capital," or "social networks and interactions that keep us connected with others," captured in his famous reference to *bowling alone* (Montgomery 2013, 53–54). For Putnam, social capital allows citizens to resolve collective problems more easily, allows communities to "advance smoothly" due to trust, widens "our awareness of the many ways in which our fate is linked," and provides "conduits for the flow of helpful information that facilitates achieving our goals" (Putnam 2000, 288–89). Lives rich in social capital exhibit significant mental and physical benefits as well as better outcomes in child welfare and education, healthy and productive neighbourhoods, economic prosperity, health and happiness, and democratic citizenship and government performance. Putnam presents the evidence that social capital "makes us smarter, healthier, safer, richer, and better able to govern a just and stable democracy" (290). The decline in social capital, or "civic / community engagement," is attributed to the pressures of time and money, suburbanization (increased commuting and urban sprawl), the effects of electronic entertainment (privatizing leisure time), and, most significantly, generational change—"the slow, steady and ineluctable replacement of the long civic generation by their less involved children and grandchildren" (283). Putnam's remedies for this "civic malaise" and "breakdown in community" consist of general prescriptions, calling on professionals and leaders in various fields to make the workplace substantially more family-friendly and community-congenial, create more integrated and pedestrian-friendly areas with public spaces, foster new forms of electronic entertainment and communication that reinforce community engagement, and introduce ways to ensure more participation in cultural activities, public life, and our communities. While Putnam does not make a specific appeal to a "university role" in addressing these trends, the strength of his work is in highlighting the academic research on the decline of community engagement and the negative effects on our quality of life.

The decline in social capital has been viewed by Richard Florida as less an issue of concern than as an opportunity for the revising of urban amenities to attract the new "creative class" of the 21st century (Florida 2002; Dubinsky 2006). The significance of Florida's research is to identify the successful urban centres in the United States that were well prepared for the emerging trends in the global economy in the face of rapidly declining prospects in the manufacturing and resource industries that had been bases of urban prosperity in the 20th century. For Florida, the cities that are gaining in prosperity and population are the ones attracting a new "creative class"—highly educated and innovative individuals who choose where they want to live based on the amenities and the unique atmosphere of a particular urban environment. *Quality of place* becomes critical, then, in order to establish an urban context that will attract this creative class and preserve the local growth and investment prospects in a global economy. Florida places a premium on higher education, and on the arts, culture, and diversity in generating "creative capital," with a university as a necessary component to "quality of place" in fostering a "creative community." Florida's sense of how the university contributes to this dynamic is through "technology, talent, and tolerance," in which collaborations between the discoveries of the hard sciences and the investment of private companies are the critical facet (Florida 2002, 291–93). Thus, not only is a particular urban context a necessary ingredient, but a particular type of university and university role is required within this urban context. From this it is not hard to imagine the advantages for larger urban centres with corporate and financial head offices and several large universities with established research programs in the sciences, technologies, engineering, and medicine (STEM) in capturing this "creative capital." An added downside of Florida's prognosis is that not all urban centres (even those with a university or college) would be able to "retool" to benefit from these global trends:

> Florida considers many small communities to be "hopeless" cases. In particular, he suggests that small communities, especially those tainted with the residue of resource extraction or noxious industries, cannot go head-to-head in the global competition to attract postindustrial firms: they lack the diversity and cultural capital necessary to attract the creative class. (Nelson 2005, 92)

Thus, rather than offering a general prescription for reviving the fortunes of communities, Florida suggests there will be "winners" and "losers" in this competition for "creative capital"—with limited prospects for many smaller urban centres. Despite this prognosis, Florida does identify the critical role a university has, or may have, in contributing to or even shaping the prospects for a given community, even if the "small university" in a small city may be disadvantaged relative to larger urban centres.

A significant contribution to this debate has been the work of Charles Montgomery, not just in bridging this debate on social versus creative capital but in redefining the meaning of *quality of life / quality of place* and deepening our understanding of the relationship between leadership, learning, and *quality of life* in the small city. Montgomery provides a rich account of local leadership initiatives and learning aimed at enhancing social interaction and community engagement through access to nature, greater choices in mobility, and redesigning urban spaces for conviviality, while simultaneously reducing the costs to residents and local governments, generating new economic and social opportunities and addressing concerns over urban sustainability. Most importantly, these initiatives extend beyond our largest urban centres as ideals for all urban centres irrespective of size. It is evident from Montgomery's examples that the "small university" can play a decisive leadership and creative role in forging *quality of life / quality of place* that generates a creative community while directly addressing declining "social capital" concerns in achieving the goals of a "happy city." Building on Putnam's observations, Montgomery further expands on the negative effects of increased isolation and a solitary existence by increasing numbers of citizens:

> Social isolation just may be the greatest environmental hazard of city living—worse than noise, pollution, or even crowding. The more connected we are with family and community, the less likely we are to experience colds, heart attacks, strokes, cancer, and depression. Simple friendships with other people in one's neighborhood are some of the best salves for stress during hard economic times. . . . Connected people sleep better at night. They are more able to tackle adversity. They live longer. They consistently report being happier. (Montgomery 2013, 54–55)

Backed by research from psychology, economics, philosophy, sociology, and urban planning studies, Montgomery argues that the design of our largest urban centres is making us sick—mentally, emotionally, and physically—while fostering isolation and mistrust and undermining family and community life. The prevailing model of urban design, which is built to accommodate automobiles rather than citizens, is increasingly expensive, inequitable, and unsustainable for both residents and local governments. The roots of this "broken social scene" lie in continuing urban sprawl, where longer commute times and the heavy reliance on automobiles to get to and from work and to access all services and amenities leads to less time for family, friends, and community engagement—the very ingredients of a happy and fulfilling life. Montgomery's work highlights communities and individuals who have contested these negative trends. He quotes Enrique Peñalosa (a community leader and former mayor of Bogotá): "One of the requirements for happiness is equality . . . Maybe not equality of income but *equality of quality of life* and, more than that, an environment where people don't feel inferior, where people don't feel excluded" (235; emphasis added). With this ideal of happiness in mind, Montgomery makes an appeal for new ways of thinking, planning, and building—in essence, proposing a new creative project of reimagining both physical and social spaces in our urban environment and transforming them through local leadership initiatives.

Montgomery's analysis offers a unique view on what comprises *quality of life / quality of place*, establishing the following principles for a *happy city* that will generate a more inclusive, affordable, diverse, and sustainable urban experience:

- The city should strive to maximize joy and minimize hardship

- It should lead us toward health rather than sickness

- It should offer us real freedom to live, move, and build our lives as we wish

- It should build resilience against economic or environmental shocks

- It should be fair in the way it apportions space, services, mobility, joys, hardships, and costs

- Most of all, it should enable us to build and strengthen the bonds between friends, families, and strangers that give life meaning, bonds that represent the city's greatest achievement and opportunity

- The city that acknowledges and celebrates our common fate, that opens doors to empathy and cooperation, will help us tackle the great challenges of this century. (43)

Montgomery offers a specific antidote to the decline in social capital highlighted by Robert Putnam while simultaneously highlighting the creative capital—the university research, academic studies, understanding of local challenges, and the leadership initiatives that are necessary to achieve these outcomes. It is from this framework that we may assess both the small city context against that of larger urban centres fraught with the challenges Montgomery identifies, and the extent to which leadership initiatives in the small city can reverse or prevent the negative trends evident in these larger centres. Notable from these *happy city* principles, or goals, is the congruence with the raison d'être (or very purpose) of the contemporary university, highlighted in university mission statements and institutional plans: diversity, equity, inclusion, tolerance, addressing societal challenges, and engagement with new ideas and peoples.

However admirable this confluence of ideals, though, Montgomery highlights the varied power structures and forces that have shaped our largest urban centres and mitigate against change, noting their tendency to seem overwhelming. "It is easy to feel small in the face of the monumental power of the real estate industry, the tyranny of zoning codes, the inertia of bureaucracy, and the sheer durability of things that have been built" (295). Recognizing that we have made mistakes, Montgomery observes that "we let powerful people organize buildings, work, home, and transportation systems around too simplistic a view of geography and of life itself" and that it is "not too late to rebuild a balance of life in our neighbourhoods and cities and, in so doing, to build a more resilient future (316). While he identifies political figures, specific individuals, neighbourhoods and cities that have challenged the status quo, what is less apparent from Montgomery's account are the types of leadership initiatives that have, or may develop, the social-creative capital needed for equality of quality of life outcomes, particularly as we transpose these challenges and ideals onto a smaller urban setting. Whereas "bonding" social capital is highlighted as a virtue and a goal (connections between people who know each other quite well, e.g., family, friends, neighbours), "bridging" social capital (links to people outside one's own group) and "vertical" social capital (links to power and decision-making authority, such as government) have been recognized as critical to enabling overall social capital and establishing the bases of real community development, resilience, and adaptability that support sustainability (Dale and Newman 2010, 7–9; Emery and Flora 2006, 21). These forms of social capital are seen as necessary to move from the supportive "bonding" capital that may just allow a community to "get by" to forms of capital that support "getting ahead." Further, communities "are based on networks, both personal and professional, and the density and diversity of network formation vary tremendously within and between communities. As well, networks appear to be crucial in any one community's ability to access more diverse kinds of capital, particularly social capital linking ties" (Dale and Newman 2010, 8). Thus, in assessing the capacity of a small city to build social-creative capital and adopt *equality of quality of life* standards, it is necessary to understand (1) the types of effective leadership critical to developing bridging and/or vertical capital, (2) where this city is situated within the broader range of urban settings, and (3) the city's particular resources and challenges in terms of achieving *equality of quality of life* outcomes.

Leadership and Learning under the New Governance Model

At an international level, new forms of local or "place-based" leadership have increasingly been recognized as an important factor (or "missing link") in accounting for regional growth, economic and social performance, achieving environmental sustainability, the development and well-being of particular places, or the success of certain local cultural industries (Beer 2014; Sotarauta, Beer, and Gibney 2017; Sotarauta and Beer 2017; Bentley, Pugalis, and Shutt 2017; Wellbrock et al. 2013; Dubinsky 2006; Emery and Flora 2006). A shared quality of this leadership is the move from traditional hierarchical relationships of leadership to collaborative relationships between institutional sectors (public, private, and community sectors)—based on mutual trust and cooperation—and having "a distinctive long-term time horizon" (Beer 2014, 255). Pivotal contributors to local leadership are that "it should involve the sharing of power; it should be flexible and it should be rooted in entrepreneurialism" (255). Studies of leadership have also contrasted *transactional leadership* (a "top-down" process targeted to the realization of a limited number of specific objectives) with *transformational leadership* that emphasizes "processes that transcend organizational, environmental, and human limitations in order to guide a process of change" and is "broad ranging and strategic" (255). Australian research on rural communities identified effective local leadership in building community resilience and helping to secure an economic future for a region or community, and having a "pivotal role in providing ideas and a vision for the future, and thus provided a focus around which community identity and belonging could be fostered" (255). Four key qualities of effective rural leadership were found to be "the formulation of a realistic vision of the community's economic and social development; the achievement of a high level of community approval of, if not active commitment to, that vision; motivating key persons and groups to achieve the vision; and leading by example" (255). In a study of six rural European development initiatives,

> visionary leaders made the difference. They enjoyed considerable trust and generated inspiring, bounding ideas. They were also capable of bridging diverging interests and transcending (at least temporarily) actual conflicts, and could access additional resources by means of their wider networks. . . . These visionary leaders did not operate alone; in fact they enacted collaborative leadership. They initiated and enabled the participation of residents in low threshold meetings, networks, collaborative (private-public) partnerships and wider collaboration in employing development activities (Wellbrock et al. 2013, 427)

The authors note the ability of these leaders to "adopt" and "mediate" the "complex interplay of power, resources and people," and observe that "collaborative leadership thus provides an incentive for joint reflexivity, building collective agency and institutional reform" (427). An important caveat to this new focus on leadership is that "discussions of local leadership inevitably raise questions of power and the ability to influence either others within a community or government processes. This means that the leadership of places cannot be examined in isolation; any thorough account also needs to consider the relationship between local leaders and governmental or other power" (Beer 2014, 256). Thus, the success of collaborative leadership initiatives is contingent on a range of local and non-local factors, and an understanding of the conditions that have fostered or prompted the move to more collaborative leadership in more areas.

Dubinsky (2006), in examining the success of cultural initiatives in Kamloops, BC, identified five kinds of collaborations in the "new organizational paradigm" that had become the rule in achieving goals,[1] thus providing a rough framework as to the motivations for establishing new collaborative networks:

- *Organic collaboration*—arising from evolving or emergent conditions or opportunities (often serendipitous) in which organizations recognize that there are ways to "work together more effectively to accomplish goals than going it alone"

- *Self-interested collaboration*—may have emergent or serendipitous qualities "but one or more parties will be specifically self-interested from the outset—on the lookout, as it were, for possible partnerships and alliances" (100)

- *Mimetic collaboration*—"based on emulation, whereby an organization thinks collaboration is a good idea or is needed . . . with the expectation that the collaboration will be fruitful and satisfy what has been missing, since others have benefited from it"

- *Normative collaboration*—"happens as a result of, or in response to, standards or conventions in a given field or sector that require or recommend cooperation of some sort. . . . [and] may be the basis for emergent collaboration or more formalized alliances and partnerships."

- *Coercive collaboration*—"forced cooperation, whether an organization coerces another to collaborate or whether an organization feels compelled to collaborate. . . . Coerced organizations occasionally turn out to be the most cooperative" (101).[2]

What Dubinsky was capturing in this discourse of collaboration has become understood generally as a larger and highly uneven process of moving from *government* to *governance* taking place across Western nations. Seen as rooted in the adoption of neoliberal ideals of "smaller government," and the disruptive and unequal effects of technological changes and globalization, *governance* refers to a range of governing styles which "imply a shift from state sponsorship of economic and social programmes and projects . . . towards the delivery of these through partnerships involving both governmental and non-governmental organizations and perhaps other actors" (Shucksmith 2010, 3). Shucksmith states

> Features of this style include a new role for the state as co-ordinator, manager or enabler rather than as provider and director; the formation of tangled hierarchies, flexible alliances and networks through which to govern (often to the confusion of most citizens); the inclusion of new partners, notably from the private and voluntary sectors; and indeed 'governing through community' or 'government at a distance' (4).

Assessments of the local effects and results of this shift to "governance" have generated highly contradictory positions. Some researchers see this as an abdication of state roles and responsibilities, leading to increased competition between places, resulting in new forms of inequalities and exclusions in society and an increased burden on those who participate, within a context of a more "confused set of accountabilities"—rather than fostering a general revival or local resilience (Beer 2014, 256). In addition, in this discourse of decentralization, increased local self-government, and "local empowerment," serious questions remain about the extent to which there has been a meaningful devolution of power and resources. Other researchers have seen within this process the opportunity for participation and real empowerment, "leading to capacity building" and the ability to challenge, resist, negotiate, or mediate the relationship of "the local" with the central government / state authorities to acquire resources or affect policy changes to the benefit of the community or region (Beer 2014, 256; Shucksmith 2010, 4–5). Success in capacity building has also resulted in a stronger sense of community, identity, and local purpose.

Research outcomes by nation-locality have been mixed, but have generally affirmed that leadership *and learning* within this collaborative network approach to addressing local challenges have been critical to achieving some measure of success within these new state-endorsed governance arrangements, and have involved the ability of particular figures or local organizations to facilitate both bridging and vertical forms of social capital

(Wellbrock et al. 2013; Clark, Southern, and Beer, 2007; Herbert-Cheshire and Higgins 2004; Emery and Flora 2006). For instance, in Northern Ireland, a European Commission program to promote local development resulted in enhanced local networks and horizontal links between public, private, and community sectors "with the involvement of statutory and key local agencies" (Scott 2004, 56). Most evident was that "a significant degree of mutual learning had developed between the stakeholders in the development process," leading to "new ways of working," "changing styles of discussion" and through "communication and interaction, increasingly a shared understanding of the local area" (56–57). Partnership capacity was enhanced, as "there appeared to be an increasing level of rural development know-how" such that autonomous strategizing replaced a reliance on outside consultants, indicating "increased confidence and leadership of the groups, in addition to the development of strategic planning skills," an outcome contingent on "the ambit of the individuals involved" (57).[3] And although there may be a natural tendency to assume that "bottom-up / grassroots" (or *organic*) collaborations have greater prospects for success than "top-down—government-directed" (or *normative/coercive*) collaborations, research suggests that leadership has been the key quality for determining the success or failure in either type of collaboration (Clark, Southern, and Beer 2007, 263 and 265). In a study of a rural economic development strategy in Nebraska, an initial emphasis on "leadership development," with a focus on local youth, and the effort to "increase skills, create awareness of leadership opportunities, and expand their understanding of the County," was "still identified" two years into the project as "the most critical element for success" (Emery and Flora 2006, 24). "Working to increase the number of people committed to building a new future for Valley County, as well as their skills to do so effectively, was the cornerstone upon which other strategies depended" (24). Evaluations of government "leadership development programs" in Australia have added important insights, suggesting that the transactional leadership skills imparted to participants through these programs "limited themselves to a process-driven role, tended to have one-off success, but lacked longevity as a leader. By contrast, those who stepped beyond the bounds of their training and engaged with their broader community were more likely to emerge as transformational leaders, build social networks, and contribute to socio-economic aspirations" (Beer 2014, 257). Also evident was that "context is fundamental to leadership and effective leadership needs to be generated internally, rather than imposed via an externally-funded program. Critically, leadership needs to be given the opportunity to be practiced, which in turn implies some form of mobilization or exercise of power" (257). Thus, the potential for effective and successful local leadership collaborations is about both local and vertical learning, in which "bottom-up versus top-down" or "grassroots versus government-led" may be categories of limited value for understanding the potential for local capacity building and developing social-creative capital. Rather, there is a complex interplay of accumulating local and vertical knowledge to support the development of bridging and vertical social capital to foment creative activities, solutions, and outcomes to economic, social, and sustainability challenges (Beer 2014, 260).

Although we can identify particular qualities and features of effective leadership, and highlight the importance of particular leadership styles within collaborative networks, far more complex processes and variables need to be considered in order to fully understand the context in which these may be effective. While holding out the hope that from within these new forms of governance "the state exercises generative power to stimulate action, innovation, struggle and resistance, to release potentialities, to generate new struggles and to transform governance itself," Shucksmith (2010, 12) cautions that

> while this should be founded upon deliberative processes
> and collective action, the mobilization of actors (especially
> the least powerful) to develop strategic agendas in such a
> context of diffused power where nobody is in charge will
> be a crucial challenge. And strategies, once agreed, will en-
> counter the unexpected: for innovation to be successful, it
> is likely to be multiple, non-linear, complex and continually
> emergent rather than conforming to a rigid development
> plan. This will present a huge challenge of cultural change
> to actors in rural development, and its realisation will de-
> pend partly on the institutional capacity of these actors in

terms of knowledge resources, relational resources and mo-
bilising capabilities (12).

This insight is shared by Montgomery (2013) with regard to large urban
centres, observing that

> the struggle for the happy city is going to be long and dif-
> ficult. The broken city lives in the rituals and practices of
> planners, engineers, and developers. It lives in law and
> code, and in concrete and asphalt. It lives in our own habits,
> too. Those of us who care about the living city are going to
> have to fight for it in the streets, in the halls of government,
> in the legal and social codes that guide us, and in the ways
> we move and live and think. . . . There have been victories
> in thousands of neighbourhoods where people have chal-
> lenged the written and unwritten rules of how we move,
> live and share space. . . . Victory is not guaranteed, not in
> every fight, but every time one of us stands up to dispersal,
> we chip away at its power and get a chance to find new life
> within ourselves (317).

These insights reinforce the recognition that the power of local / place-
based leadership and collaborative efforts are practised within particular
and quite varied contexts with regard to the sets and types of resources
available to affect change. Bryant and Marois (2010) have constructed a
conceptual frame-work—"the dynamic of localities"—to capture the complex environment affecting developmental outcomes, beginning with the
actors (local and non-local) with different interests and objectives, capacities, resources, and degrees of power and influence. Actors utilize and
construct networks to help mobilize support, resources, and information
for their actions, and these networks represent the formal and informal
organization of the particular place under study (338):

> The dynamic of community change is linked to the na-
> ture of the power and social (or informal) relationships in
> a community and how they are articulated through the

networks both internal and external to the community. In short, communities can be characterized by different community cultures with respect to the management of change and the recognition and inclusion of the legitimate interests and segments present in the community in the management of change. Inevitably, this leads to the hypothesis that as a result of these differences, different local communities will experience different trajectories in the transformation of their space (Bryant 1995, 261).

The resulting *profile* of a place leads to each place or locality having different orientations: *observed orientations* that "reflect the cumulative effects of all these actions, including any public planning and management effects" (often expressed through public documents and plans), and *latent orientations* that "have not yet been recognized or acted upon by the actors in place" (Bryant and Marois 2010, 339). A combination of these orientations "can be identified and acted upon by the community and local players. They then become central to the management and planning of development in the community or territory; as such, they become strategic orientations which in turn become the framework within which actions are pursued to achieve the community's objectives" (339). Nevertheless, "the actors function in context, which can be defined at different scales that include economic, legal, administrative, cultural and political dimensions" (339), which serves to highlight how these new forms of *governance*, such as governing "through community" or governing "at a distance," may take markedly different forms depending on the country. It has been observed that "leadership at the regional or local scale is a more challenging proposition in highly centralized systems of government when compared with nations—such as the United States—where powers are devolved" (Beer 2014, 260; and see also Sotarauta and Beer 2017, 213 and 221).[4] For instance, with the more centralized system in Australia, and in a top-down effort to advance a particular "entrepreneurial" model of governance, communities and regions deemed "healthy" (receptive to government efforts) enjoyed more support and resources than those deemed "unhealthy" (confrontational), introducing new inequalities and greater "risk of exclusion from decision making, and potential for the imposition of solutions by external agencies" (Beer 2014, 260; and see also Herbert-Cheshire and Higgins 2004). Such examples attest to the need for both local leaders (formal and informal) and researchers to be cognizant of the "orientations" of higher levels of government if they are to effectively negotiate and mediate on behalf of the community. This is most evident within federal systems (as in Canada), where "governance is marked by both horizontal connections but also hierarchical, competitive and co-op-erative modes of interaction . . . with both positive and negative outcomes" (Beer 2014, 256). In examining communities in Canada through the lens of these new forms of governance, it has been observed that "it is important to understand how the different contexts, especially at the provincial level, affect local and regional decision-making processes of local actors (public, private and community or associative actors)" (Bryant and Marois 2010, 339). Given the devolution of powers and responsibilities from the feder-al to provincial levels throughout the 1990s, the unequal capacities and resources among the provinces, and the often conflictual, changing, and unclear role of the federal government vis-à-vis the provinces (resulting in a "confused set of accountabilities"), developing vertical social capital can be difficult, with each province offering a different set of challenges and opportunities. Despite what may be many constraints "from above," the importance of local leaders has been affirmed "even under circumstances where they appear to have little influence. This often unseen power of lead-ers and communities should make us reconsider how rural communities can shape their future, even in environments where their formal powers appear muted" (Beer 2014, 260). This is a particularly apt insight for sit-uating and assessing communities and community dynamics in Canada, where the centralized forms of power practised at the federal and provin-cial levels have often left local governments and community groups feeling frustrated, rather than empowered, over the downloading of responsibil-ities to the local level without the necessary or commensurate financial resources to address various challenges (Duffy, Royer, and Beresford 2014; Federation of Canadian Municipalities 2014).

From this overview it is evident that the specific qualities for effec-tive "leadership"—that may generate social-creative capital under the new forms of governance in achieving *equality of quality of life* outcomes—are difficult to affirm. At one level we do know that these collaborations need

to be about sharing power, being flexible, and developing trust and cooperation in establishing strong linkages and bonds. However, the ability to
learn and accumulate knowledge at the local level is a critical component
of this process, and one from which flow the skills to create realistic initiatives, goals, and plans; to foster awareness of local and non-local resources
and their potential; and to develop the local capacity to recognize and
act on "serendipitous" opportunities as they emerge locally or externally
(Herbert-Cheshire and Higgins 2004, 290). The capacity of "key figures"
within organizations (as public, private, or community-based entities) to
learn and continually acquire knowledge of the local and the non-local
underlies the ability to discuss and "work in new ways" with other partners; to increase local levels of confidence in taking actions, challenging
conventions and established forms of thinking and power; and to progress
from transactional forms of leadership to transformational leadership and
outcomes. As recognized, this process of developing local / place-based
leadership is highly contextual, and requires an understanding of the local
resources and dynamics in determining the potential opportunities and
trajectories in advancing *equality of quality of life.*

Situating "Kamloops" as a Small City—Challenges
and Opportunities for Leadership and Learning

In emphasizing that neither central governments nor the research community across Canada have effectively or systematically addressed the challenges of small towns and rural communities, Bryant (2009) observes that
"the challenges range from rapid population growth in the context of our
major urban and metropolitan regions to continued decline or stagnation
in resource peripheries because of changes to their economic bases. Even
within these two broad regional types, there is considerable heterogeneity of circumstances—demographic growth versus stagnation, economic
revival versus economic collapse, conflict versus harmonious transformation" (142). Within these extremes, small to mid-sized regional cities (and
Kamloops in particular) demonstrate a combination of urban strengths
and rural vulnerabilities under the new forms of governance that may be
contrasted against our large metropolitan areas and rural small towns in
exploring the bases for effective leadership initiatives. We have utilized the

term *small city* in recognition of the different views as to what constitutes a small city versus a mid-sized or medium-sized city, while drawing on literature from both perspectives. Small to mid-sized cities have become subject to increased examination as growth in local population, public and private services, residential accommodations, and occupational diversity has generated urban centres that are no longer "towns" but are clearly not "big cities" in terms of size, resources, and complexity (Bell and Jayne 2006; Garrett-Petts 2005; Brennan, Hackler, and Hoene 2005; Garrett-Petts, Hoffman, and Ratsoy 2014; Walmsley and Kading. 2018b). In this nebulous context, where there is little consensus on the parameters—population or otherwise—in defining a small to mid-sized city,[5] these urban centres have acquired a heightened level of sophistication that is often expressed in the emergence of municipal plans addressing a broad range of issues—culture, social, environment and sustainability, heritage, downtown revitalization, and economic development—that match practices in our largest urban centres. However, depending on provincial support and local financial conditions, the capacity to implement the laudable goals enshrined in these plans may be quite circumscribed in comparison to large cities (Cleave, Arku, and Chatwin 2017, 4). Recognized in Canada for the valuable role they "play as regional hubs and economic engines in their respective regions," economically, mid-sized cities have had quite varied and unpredictable growth experiences. In a study of 31 mid-sized cities across Canada, between 2005 and 2015 only 12 posted levels of economic growth stronger than the national average of 1.8% a year (Conference Board of Canada 2016). With the collapse of commodity prices in late 2014 reducing national economic growth levels to 1.2%, only 10 mid-sized cities were able to "match or beat the Canadian benchmark" in 2015. Such data continues to affirm an earlier observation that "depending on the historical evolution, location and asset base of the community, mid-sized cities can face significant economic development challenges presented by global, national or regional economic change—whether structural and/or cyclical in nature" (Seasons 2003, 67), and demonstrates the continued and significant effects of rural resource and agricultural industries on the economic health of many mid-sized cities. Unlike small towns, small city "social issues often parallel those of large metropolitan centres" (67), which is evident in the high numbers of visible and hidden homeless (Kading 2012; Walmsley and Kading, 2018b). Small and mid-sized cities markedly lack the advantages that the large metropolitan centres have in maintaining the benefits of continued population growth from immigration. The vast majority of new immigrants remain attracted to Canada's largest metropolitan areas due to the presence of friends, family, and established immigrant groups in these centres, with only a small fraction moving to small and mid-sized regional hubs outside of the largest metropolitan areas (Hyndman, Schuurman, and Fiedler 2006). Even within the category of mid-sized cities, those with the largest population benefit disproportionately from immigration compared to small or small mid-sized cities. Given this combination of factors affecting the local prospects for economic and population growth, local municipal efforts in revitalization, redevelopment, and building resilience are often constrained by the lack of "fiscal resources to intervene to guide the future of their core areas" (Seasons 2003, 69). For small to mid-sized cities, comprised of a complex mix of urban and rural qualities, there is considerable variation in local resources that affect their respective capacities, trajectories, and orientations. While they do not face the stagnancy or decline that confronts many small towns and rural areas, there are still significant limits in their capacity to respond to a variety of urban challenges under the new forms of governance, all of which are evident in the City of Kamloops.

As a small regional centre in British Columbia, Kamloops is a city partially defined by its resource-based past, but striving to establish a new urban identity based on *quality of life* features. Long affected by the vagaries of the agriculture, forestry, and mining industries, which remain important generators of local investment and employment, the city has maintained a persistent strength from its status as a regional centre since the late 1970s. This has ensured the placement and expansion of a range of provincial and federal government offices and services, with the ongoing government investment contributing to the growth in retail, commercial, transportation, education, health, and tourism-related services. Since the late 1990s there has been a steady increase in population (of about 1% a year) and a notable diversification in forms of employment, suggesting a move toward a "post-industrial" economy comprised of professional and service sector careers (MacKinnon and Nelson, 2005).

This has generated a strong emphasis by the local government on advertising emergent strengths in high-tech, green energy, manufacturing, retail, and healthcare industries (Venture Kamloops 2017). And while the city had long experienced notoriously high rates of unemployment from the 1980s into the 21st century, even with the global economic crisis of 2008 and the falling commodity prices of 2014, Kamloops has retained an unemployment rate at or below the national average (Kading and Bass 2014; Venture Kamloops 2017). What has been less recognized in this recent phase of local economic and employment stability is the significant change in the employment profile of the city, with Interior Health, School District 73, and Thompson Rivers University (TRU) becoming by far the dominant employers in the city—the combined employment rising from 3,732 employees in 2000 to 6,865 in 2017, with a notable doubling of TRU and Interior Health employees (Kading and Bass, 2014; Venture Kamloops 2017; TRU 2017). Increased provincial and federal spending on high-paying professional jobs, with related spinoffs from capital expenditures and consumption, has been evident in the expansion of facilities, home building, the increase in big-box and local retailers, and the measured revival of the downtown core. Prospects for growth in all three of these major employers appear strong, with a recognized local shortage of doctors and other healthcare professionals, an aging population, and commitments by the provincial government to capital spending and program expansion at TRU and the hiring of more teachers in the school district to reduce class sizes. Thus, the overall context suggests both a gradual strengthening of important conditions for developing bridging and vertical forms of social capital—not inhibited by a shrinking economy and out-migration that would "weaken social relations and vitality by creating 'voids' and posing severe obstacles for initiating a collaborative spirit and uptake of joint development activities" (Wellbrock et al. 2013, 427)—and the continual expansion of knowledge-support structures that may act as "facilitating agents and agencies" (422) such as the City of Kamloops, School District 73, Interior Health, and TRU. The other less recognized but critical feature is the presence of both well-established and emerging community organizations that have sought to address a range of local challenges. Involving individuals from the public, private, and non-profit sectors, increasing collaborations among these organizations have generated numerous services, conveniences, and opportunities that may serve to alter and redefine the small city urban landscape. It is the identification of these entities, their relationship to the various knowledge-support structures, and their ability to forge transformational leadership collaborations, that is the central focus of our collection.

Our collection seeks to situate and understand leadership, local learning, and the role of the university in the small city against the challenges and the goals outlined by Montgomery and his contribution to understanding *equality of quality of life*. Having a much smaller population has not exempted small cities from having to confront the same challenges in homelessness, addictions, poverty, isolation, discrimination, and exclusion for numerous residents that afflict large urban centres. In other words, a smaller community does not guarantee the high levels of community engagement or a "natural solidarity" that will ensure *equality of quality of life* as per Montgomery's principles (as is evident in several of our chapters). It is because of this insight that we have placed an emphasis on "leadership"—as recognized as a critical ingredient for success in other initiatives and locales—and on revealing both the origins of various local initiatives and the type of leadership required to be effective in this particular urban environment. Our focus on "learning" is to demonstrate how this critical quality of effective leadership is created and utilized to develop community awareness, increase skills and confidence, and recognize constraints, challenges, and opportunities. Thus, our effort is not only to bring attention to how these specific leadership initiatives have contributed to the local *equality of quality of life*. It is also to convey to a wider audience the collective understanding or experiences that have developed within the community and the university from these initiatives, and the lessons they hold for undertaking or evaluating similar initiatives in other urban centres. The collection comprises research themes as varied as adult learning, community gardens, heritage preservation, and the marginalized in Kamloops (from disciplines as varied as English, Anthropology, Sociology, History, Tourism, and Political Science), and seeks to reveal leadership initiatives and local collaborations that play an important role in forging the present *equality of quality of life* in the City of Kamloops. The collection reveals the quite unlikely alliances that have emerged, generating unique forms of bridging social-creative capital to address particular needs or generate new opportunities for residents. As university researchers, each with quite varied connections to these leadership initiatives, we highlight the social and creative capital that has surfaced as small groups envision particular goals or outcomes with respect to local social issues, sustainability, heritage, or education. These creative acts, though, are not without challenges and constraints, which further shed light on the unique qualities, both positive and negative, of leadership initiatives within a small city setting.

This collection of original research on *leadership* and *learning* in the small city serves a variety of purposes. First, the collection draws attention to existing and emerging community initiatives under the new forms of governance, identifies formal and informal network linkages, and other forms of local support, that have been forged through leadership, and expands our understanding of how these collaborations/partnerships play a critical role in improving *equality of quality of life* for the community. This diversifies and enriches our understanding of what *quality of life* is comprised of within the small city. Second, these articles highlight the "collective understanding / local knowledge" outcomes that have emerged from these initiatives—exposing the particular political, social, or resource challenges that have accompanied and perhaps altered, limited, or redirected these initiatives. Third, as community-engaged research outcomes, these articles are intended to help in understanding the knowledge-support and leadership capacities of the small university in fostering initiatives here in Kamloops, with potential appeal for other urban centres in enhancing *equality of quality of life* in small to mid-sized cities.

Three of the contributions address social challenges and the needs of the marginalized in the small city. Terry Kading examines and assesses the local response to homelessness in the City of Kamloops, focusing on the context (local and federal) that gave rise to this leadership initiative, the achievements to date, and the multiple challenges that have arisen as a result of increased knowledge about local homelessness. Drawing on government documents, local plans, press reports, interview materials, and active observation, the chapter assesses the accomplishments in improving *equality of quality of life* to date, highlights what has been learned about the local homelessness situation, and details the challenges in the effort "to end homelessness" in Kamloops. Lisa Cooke tells the story of a shower, the people who built it, and those who now use it, providing a compelling example of a community-based initiative that has not only changed the ecosystem of street-involved life in Kamloops by providing a much-needed service but has also shifted the ecology of giving and community compassion in Kamloops. Tracking the politics and poetics of the giving of this gift—a shower facility—shows how a group of individuals came together to address a gap in services, what obstacles they encountered along the way, and how this act of community leadership has affected not just the lives of those who now use the shower but the very terrain upon which such acts can occur. Dawn Farough focuses on the nature of and possibilities for collaboration between academics (representing the disciplines of theatre, literature, and sociology), community workers, and artist/activists as they work with a group of homeless and marginally housed individuals who will create and then perform a play about their lives and their experiences of homelessness. Interviews with members highlight the diverse views of group members regarding the strengths, weaknesses, and challenges of their project as they design a very ambitious and somewhat unconventional method of tackling homelessness in the small city. Farough also draws upon existing literature in theatrical studies and the social sciences in order to ask what this group can learn from previous theatrical projects involving marginalized community members. Combined, these articles reveal the depth, variation, and novelty in the local response and the university role with respect to social challenges in the small city.

Significantly broadening and enhancing our understanding of creative collaborations are critical assessments covering themes of local sustainability, adult education, and heritage preservation in the small city. Robin Reid and Kendra Besanger examine how a grassroots community group in Kamloops bridged partnerships across the community to create the city's first fully accessible, free public produce garden (the Kamloops Public Produce Project). In addition to successfully transforming a dead space in the downtown core into a vibrant, arable, and entirely public space, the project successfully raised awareness of food security issues at both the community and municipal government levels and provided a platform for social and political discourse surrounding the role of edible landscaping and the potential for community-driven food security initiatives to transform the urban landscape. Ginny Ratsoy focuses on how local seniors, out of a need for affordable and flexible education, established the Kamloops Adult Learners Society, a non-profit, independent organization dedicated to improving the community's *quality of life* by furthering the education of the growing demographic of citizens in their retirement years. The article examines the motivation behind the creation of this resource for lifelong learning, situates it among programs for seniors in other locations in Canada, explores the distinct challenges and successes of the group, and concludes with the role of the Kamloops Adult Learners Society in knowledge dissemination and community outreach in the small city. Tina Block reflects on the development of a public history project—the Tranquille Oral History Project (TOHP)—which involves representatives from private industry, academia, and the non-profit sector. Despite varied backgrounds, participants in the project share a mutual interest in Tranquille, a site of historic significance located west of Kamloops, and Block reveals how this oral history project offers a lens on the challenges common to collaborative research, particularly multiple stakeholders with varied motivations and expectations.

The final article in our collection is, in the spirit of the themes under discussion—and perhaps not surprisingly—a collaboration by all the contributors entitled "Leadership Initiatives and Community-Engaged Research—Explorations and Critical Insights on "Leadership and Learning" in the Small City of Kamloops." We offer an assessment on the varied initiatives and how they have contributed to *equality of quality of life* in the small city, as well as reflections and insights on the practice of community-engaged research. Drawing on researcher experiences, and their various forms of engagement with these local initiatives, this chapter first evaluates small city specificity—notably the issues of urban size, resources and capacities, orientations and trajectory, identity, and other small city features that may limit or expand opportunities for initiatives and the development and sustaining of collaborative networks—reviewing these leadership initiatives in meeting Montgomery's goals for urban happiness. A second set of evaluations focuses on the outcomes and challenges for leadership and learning from the various formal and informal network linkages identified in each chapter, in determining the bridging and vertical social capital in place, the qualities and features necessary for success, and the small city context in supporting these transformational ends. A final set of evaluations situates and exposes the significance of Thompson Rivers University as both a knowledge-support structure and a transactional/transformational leader in achieving *equality of quality of life* outcomes in a small city, and as an emergent and integral feature of local learning and creativity at the local level. This includes reflections from contributors on the practice and challenges of research, writing, and interrogating local leadership, offering insights on community-engaged research—a flexible and emergent research model based on our understanding of the local limitations in resources and capacities confronted by existing and potential community partners in this small city.

NOTES

1   "One can hear the language of collaboration in the corridors of governments—and this includes granting agencies and programs—and one can also hear it in the corporate sector, in universities, in the cultural sector, and in other non-profit areas. Strategic alliances, shared resources, co-productions, co-sponsorships, and cross-sectoral partnerships are some of the key concepts and arrangements that govern, if not determine, the organization of many activities" (Dubinsky 2006, 99).

2   "The initial two categories are derived from the author's work in 'The Cultural Future of Small Cities' project. The third, fourth, and fifth are inspired by the work of Paul J. DiMaggio and Walter W. Powell on the increasing sameness of organizational forms. See in particular DiMaggio and Powell, 1991. Extensive discussions with Catherine Cole, heritage consultant, Edmonton; Wendy Newman, director of ArtStarts in Schools, Vancouver, BC, and Linda Schohet, Director of the Centre for Literacy, Montréal, also contributed to the formation of the framework as a result of our work on collaborative models and community facilitation for linking literacy and the arts." (Dubinsky 2006, 104).

3   Scott (2004) highlights the challenge of "institutionalizing" this dynamic within successful leadership initiatives for long-term impact—an issue we return to in the Conclusion in understanding how the university may support this process of institutionalization.

4   Sotarauta and Beer (2017) identify the United States and Germany as "highly favourable to the emergence of local leaders, while centralized systems of government, such as Australia or the UK, generate adverse conditions for local leaders" (213).

5   Our classification of Kamloops as a "small city" comes from Ofori-Amoah (2007), who defines a small city as a population of 100,000 or less (3). In contrast, see Cleave, Arku, and Chatwin (2017): large cities—population greater than 350,000; mid-sized cities—population between 75,000 and 350,000; small cities—population less than 75,000 (4).

References

Beer, A. 2014. "Leadership and the Governance of Rural Communities." *Journal of Rural Studies* 34:254–62.

Bell, D., and M. Jayne. 2006. *Small Cities: Urban Experience Beyond the Metropolis*. New York: Routledge.

Bentley, G., L. Pugalis, and J. Shutt. 2017. "Leadership and Systems of Governance: The Constraints on the Scope of Leadership of Place-Based Development in Sub-National Territories." *Regional Studies* 51 (2): 194–209.

Brennan, C., D. Hackler, and C. Hoene. 2005. "Demographic Change in Small Cities, 1990 to 2000." *Urban Affairs Review* 40 (3): 342–61. doi:10.1177/1078087404269161

Bryant, C. 1995. "The Role of Local Actors in Transforming the Urban Fringe." *Journal of Rural Studies* 11 (3): 255–67.

Bryant, C. 2009. "Co-Constructing Rural Communities in the 21st Century: Challenges for Central Governments and the Research Community in Working Effectively with Local and Regional Actors." In *The Next Rural Economies: Constructing Rural Place in a Global Economy*, edited by G. Halseth, S. Markey, and D. Bruce, 142–54. Oxfordshire, UK: CABI International.

Bryant, C., and C. Marois. 2010. "The Management and Planning of Communities in the Rural-Urban Fringe." *The Rural-Urban Fringe in Canada: Conflict and Controversy*, edited by K. B. Beesley, 337–47. Brandon, MB: Brandon University Press.

City of Kamloops. 2017. *City of Kamloops: City Hall*. Accessed June 10. http://www.kamloops.ca/departments/index.shtml.

Clark, D., R. Southern, and J. Beer. 2007. "Rural Governance, Community Empowerment and the New Institutionalism: A Case Study of the Isle of Wight." *Journal of Rural Studies* 23 (2): 254–66.

Cleave, E., G. Arku, and M. Chatwin. 2017. "Cities' Economic Development Efforts in a Changing Global Economy: Content Analysis of Economic Development Plans in Ontario, Canada." *Area* 49 (3): 359–68. doi:10.1111/area.12335.

Conference Board of Canada. 2016. *Mid-Sized Cities Outlook*. http://www.conferenceboard.ca/topics/economics/mid-size-city.aspx.

Dale, A., and L. Newman. 2010. "Social Capital: A Necessary and Sufficient Condition for Sustainable Community Development?" *Community Development Journal* 45 (1): 5–21.

Dubinsky, L. 2006. "In Praise of Small Cities: Cultural Life in Kamloops, BC." *Canadian Journal of Communication* 31:85–106.

Duffy, R., G. Royer, and C. Beresford. 2014. *Who's Picking Up the Tab? Federal and Provincial Downloading Onto Local Governments*. Columbia Institute: Centre for Civic Governance. http://www.civicgovernance.ca/wordpress/wp-content/uploads/2014/09/Whos-Picking-Up-the-Tab-FULL-REPORT.pdf.

Emery, M., and C. Flora. 2006. "Spiraling-Up: Mapping Community Transformation with Community Capitals Framework." *Community Development: Journal of the Community Development Society* 37 (1): 19–35.

Federation of Canadian Municipalities. 2014. *The State of Canada's Cities and Communities 2013: Opening a New Chapter.* http://www.fcm.ca.

Florida, R. 2002. *The Rise of the Creative Class.* New York: Basic Books.

Garrett-Petts, W., ed. 2005. *The Small Cities Book: On the Cultural Future of Small Cities.* Vancouver: New Star Books.

Garrett-Petts, W., J. Hoffman, and G. Ratsoy, eds. 2014. *Whose Culture Is It Anyway? Community Engagement in Small Cities.* Vancouver: New Star Books.

Herbert-Cheshire, L., and V. Higgins. 2004. "From Risky to Responsible: Expert Knowledge and the Governing of Community-Led Rural Development." *Journal of Rural Studies* 20 (3): 289–302.

Hyndman, J., N. Schuurman, and R. Fiedler. 2006. "Size Matters: Attracting New Immigrants to Canadian Cities." *Journal of International Migration and Integration/Revue de l'integration et de la migration international* 7 (1): 1–25.

Kading, T. 2012. *The Politics of Social Planning in the Small City.* Canadian Political Science Association. http://www.cpsa-acsp.ca/papers-2012/Kading.pdf.

Kading, T., and E. Bass. 2014. "Can You Build an Open Pit Mine in an Urban Centre?" *Alternate Routes* 25:181–206.

Kading, T., and C. Walmsley. 2014. "The Politics of 'the Arts' in the Small City: Contexts and Prospects." In *Whose Culture Is It Anyway? Community Engagement in Small Cities,* edited by W.F. Garrett-Petts, J. Hoffman and G. Ratsoy, 38–59. Vancouver: New Star Books.

MacKinnon, R., and R. Nelson. 2005. "Urban and Economic Change in Kamloops: Postindustrial Adjustments in a Staples Economy." In *The Small Cities Book: On The Future of Small Cities,* edited by W. F. Garrett-Petts, 23–48. Vancouver: New Star Books.

Montgomery, C. 2013. *Happy City: Transforming our Lives through Urban Design.* Toronto: Doubleday Canada.

Nelson, R. 2005. "A Cultural Hinterland? Searching for the Creative Class in the Small Canadian City." In *The Small Cities Book: On the Cultural Future of Small Cities,* edited by W.F. Garrett-Petts, 85–109. Vancouver: New Star Books.

Ofori-Amoah, B. 2007. *Beyond the Metropolis: Urban Geography as if Small Cities Mattered.* Toronto: University Press of America.

Putnam, R. 2000. *Bowling Alone: The Collapse and Revival of American Community.* Toronto: Simon & Schuster.

Scott, M. 2004. "Building Institutional Capacity in Rural Northern Ireland: The Role of Partnership Governance in the LEADER II Programme." *Journal of Rural Studies* 20 (1): 49–59.

Seasons, M. 2003. "Indicators and Core Area Planning: Applications in Canada's Mid-Sized Cities." *Planning Practice & Research* 18 (1): 63–80.

Shucksmith, M. 2010. "Disintegrated Rural Development? Neo-Endogenous Rural Development, Planning and Place-Shaping in Diffused Power Contexts." *Sociologia Ruralis* 50 (1): 1–14.

Sotarauta, M., and A. Beer. 2017. "Governance, Agency, and Place Leadership: Lessons from a Cross-National Analysis." *Regional Studies* 51 (2): 210–23.

Sotarauta, M., A. Beer, and J. Gibney. 2017. "Making Sense of Leadership in Urban and Regional Development." *Regional Studies* 51 (2): 187–93.

TRU (Thompson Rivers University). 2017. *Facts and Figures*. Accessed June 10. https://www.tru.ca/about/facts.html.

Venture Kamloops. 2017. *Kamloops: Invest in Our City*. Accessed June 12. http://venturekamloops.com.

Walmsley, C., and T. Kading. 2018a. "Social Planning and the Politics of Small City Governance." In *Small Cities, Big Issues: Community in a Neoliberal Era*, edited by C. Walmsley and T. Kading. Edmonton: Athabasca University Press.

Walmsley, C., and T. Kading. 2018b. *Small Cities, Big Issues: Community in a Neoliberal Era*. Edmonton: Athabasca University Press.

Wellbrock, W., D. Roep, M. Mahon, E. Kairyte, B. Nienaber, M. D. D. García, M. Kriszan, and M. Farrell. 2013. "Arranging Public Support to Unfold Collaborative Modes of Governance in Rural Areas." *Journal of Rural Studies* 32:420–29.

Promoting "Community Leadership and Learning" on Social Challenges: Government of Canada Homelessness Initiatives and the Small City of Kamloops, British Columbia

Terry Kading

Introduction

Kamloops, British Columbia, is one of many urban centres across Canada engaged in an effort to "end homelessness" in their communities. The impetus for this effort lies in the federal government's *National Homelessness Initiative*, launched in late 1999 to "partner" with communities across Canada in addressing the immediate needs of the homelessness crisis emerging on the streets of Canada's cities (Smith 2004; Graham 2011; Kading 2012). While first proposed for the ten largest urban centres in Canada, the initiative was expanded in 2001 to include another 51 designated communities confronting evident homelessness. This federal initiative was, and remains, a response to the withdrawal by this very same

THE PATH TO
HOME

Join us on a "Seeing is Believing" tour to learn
about the path from homelessness to finding a home

**Friday, November 3
1- 3 PM**

 Canadian Mental
Health Association
Mental health for all

 ASK
Wellness Centre

 KAMLOOPS AND DISTRICT
Elizabeth Fry Society

 **THOMPSON
RIVERS
UNIVERSITY**

**RSVP to office@unitedwaytnc.ca
or 250.372.9933**

 **United Way**

FIGURE 1.1. "The Path to Home," poster by Geralyn Alain, 2017. Courtesy of Geralyn Alain and the United Way Thompson Nicola Cariboo.

level of government from some 40 years of direct funding and support for low-income and social housing, in an effort to balance budgets and reduce the national debt. With an inadequate response from the provinces to this off-loading of responsibility in housing and social support, the Government of Canada returned with a new and revised funding model to address homelessness—a model that placed the onus on local communities to assume a leadership role in addressing an emerging homelessness crisis. This leadership role compelled designated communities (of which Kamloops is one) to enter into a complex area of urban planning for which many small cities lack both the experience and the resource capacity (Kading 2012).

This chapter examines the local response to homelessness in the City of Kamloops, focusing on the context that gave rise to this local leadership role, the achievements to date, and the multiple challenges that have arisen as a result of increased knowledge of local homelessness. Drawing on government documents (local and federal), local plans, press reports, interviews, and observations from participation in a local anti-poverty network—*Changing the Face of Poverty*—the chapter assesses accomplishments in improving *equality of quality of life* in this area, highlighting what has been learned about the local homelessness situation and detailing the challenges in the effort to end homelessness in Kamloops. This study is unique, as it examines the increased responsibility of local communities and local governments in addressing homelessness and the distinctive politics of the small city in adjusting to this devolution of responsibility. There is little doubt that the local response was initially a *coercive collaboration*—the Kamloops Community Committee—as a condition of accessing federal monies to address the immediate needs of the local homeless population. However, from this would emerge the Changing the Face of Poverty network, a *mimetic collaboration* that would ensure that housing the homeless and addressing poverty would be the local priorities.[1] The tension between the numerous limitations inherent in this devolution of responsibilities and partnership with higher levels of government, along with the positives—notably the gathering of detailed information on *lived realities* in this particular community—is the central focus of this chapter, and confirms the worst and the best qualities of the new models of *governance* and "governing through community" (see Introduction). This

Kamloops Community Committee (KCC) & Kamloops Working Group on Homelessness (KWGH) (2000)

Change the Face of Poverty (CFP) (2004)
Kamloops & District Elizabeth Fry Society, City of Kamloops, The United Way, Interior Community Services, ASKWellness, Kamloops Food Bank, Canadian Mental Health Association, Boys & Girls Club, Thompson Rivers University, Kamloops & District Labour Council, Phoenix Centre, Faith-based organizations, Salvation Army, JUMP Program, Ministry of Children & Family Development, Interior Health, Kamloops Brain Injury Association, HomeFree Lived Experience Committee

HomeFree Collective (2014)

Chairs Committee

Policy & Governance

Housing Supports

Aboriginal Committee

Funding Task Force

HomeFree Council

Lived Experience Committee

Sub-Committee on Anti-Poverty Strategies (2013)
Elizabeth Fry, School District #73, Ministry of Children & Family Development, City of Kamloops, ASK Wellness, Boys & Girls Club, Thompson Rivers University

A Way Home Committee to End Youth Homelessness (2014)
120 members from all sectors including non-profits, Indigenous organizations, businesses, landlords, youth, and community members
19 different organizations have identified one Youth Homelessness Champion who would connect youth to the WrapForce

Informal Network Linkages
Various local businesses (providing supplies and services for yearly Homeless Awareness Week, the Out of the Cold program, New Life Mission, and JUMP Program), concerned citizens, Credit Union, Kamloops Immigrant Services, TRU Social Work program, TRU Nursing Program, TRU Law School, Kamloops Food Policy Council

FIGURE 1.2. Changing the Face of Poverty Network by Terry Kading. Design by Moneca Jantzen, Daily Designz.

chapter details the benefits of the transactional leadership resulting from this devolution, along with the myriad of constraints in moving toward transformational leadership outcomes in achieving *equality of quality of life* for our most marginalized residents.

Fomenting Community Leadership and Learning

After decades of federal government dominance in social and housing policies, this critical leadership role was rapidly devolved to the local level in initiating solutions to complex social problems—notably the homelessness crisis. The required community planning process would involve broad consultation with numerous agencies, non-profit organizations, business groups, and the local community on multiple themes related to homelessness. At another level this process would include the contracting of consultants for research, the creation of an official "social planning / community development" position, new program budgeting, and substantial monetary commitments in city property, tax and development cost exemptions, and non-profit grants to fulfill these various social planning goals. This section examines the terms of the new model advanced by the Government of Canada in 1999 in addressing homelessness, and the local and provincial dynamics as communities assumed an awkward leadership role that had been thrust upon them by higher levels of government. Since 1999 the Government of Canada has established a firm position on addressing these social issues through what it refers to as *The Power of Partnerships*:

> The basic theory behind partnerships is that working together and leveraging assets and resources is more effective than working in isolation. A partnership draws its strength from coordinating resources so that two or more individuals or groups can work toward a common goal. Partnerships are especially important in addressing issues such as homelessness and poverty. Because they are multi-dimensional, these issues require multi-dimensional responses (such as affordable housing, employment, justice, training, child care, mental health, addictions, etc.). (Government of Canada 2008)

What is noteworthy in this statement is the extent to which areas of jurisdiction understood as responsibilities of only the federal or provincial levels of government are passed down to the local level—with the justification that "no one level of government, sector or organization can claim to be able to address these issues in isolation. . . . Community-based approaches to addressing social issues like homelessness seek to empower local organizations and individuals through an atmosphere of dignity and participation, with the goal of achieving durable results" (Government of Canada 2008). It is against this understanding of the benefits of collaboration, both vertical (local, provincial, and federal) and horizontal (community level), that we will evaluate this devolution of leadership and learning.

By the end of the 1990s there were only a very small number of public housing units being built at the provincial level, and the majority of subsidies needed to promote the construction of low-income rental or housing units had been whittled away in a drive to rein in federal and provincial spending (Murphy 2000; Layton 2008).[2] These federal and provincial actions did not go unnoticed at the local level, as homeless issues (often linked to cold winter deaths) garnered media attention in Canada's largest urban centres (Schwan 2016). By late 1999 the federal government had decided to re-enter the "housing" arena, but with a considerably narrower field of attention—support for emergency shelters and transitional housing, through the creation of the National Homelessness Initiative (NHI). The NHI initially invested $753 million over three years to "help alleviate and prevent homelessness across Canada" (Human Resources and Skills Development Canada 2011). More than a renewed collaboration with provincial governments, the focus of the NHI was on a direct federal government partnership with communities with a demonstrated homeless problem. The NHI had the goal to "facilitate community capacity by coordinating Government of Canada efforts and enhancing the diversity of tools and resources," "foster effective partnerships and investment that contribute to addressing the immediate and multifaceted needs of the homeless and reducing homelessness in Canada," and "increase awareness and understanding of homelessness in Canada" (HRSDC 2011). The NHI was composed of three components: the Supporting Communities Partnerships Initiative (SCPI)—"a demonstration program, aimed at encouraging communities to work with provincial, territorial and municipal governments and the private sector and voluntary organizations to address the immediate needs of homeless people"; the Youth Homelessness Strategy; and an Urban Aboriginal Strategy (NHI n.d., 2–5). Of the three the SCPI was the most important component. SCPI established nine criteria for an acceptable planning process as the bases for accessing available funds:

- designated Geographic Area
- *Objectives*—"to be achieved by March 31, 2003"[3]
- *Community Plan Development Process*—with particular attention to "involving Aboriginal, youth and homeless persons throughout"
- *Assets and Gaps* reports—updated on a regular basis
- Priorities
- *Sustainability*—ability to secure other sources of funding
- *Evaluation*—"that should be an annual process"
- Communication Plan
- Community Financial Contributions

These funding conditions compelled not just a local collaboration but considerable documentation as to existing resources and services and a commitment to ongoing local consultation, reporting, and promotion. Notable is the original short time frame in which to establish and meet all objectives, with only two years, including the completion of proposed projects. With no certainty of continued funding after 2003 despite local efforts to meet these criteria, and the fact that the Government of Canada was only committed to funding a portion of the overall initiative, it is clear that there was no comprehensive and long-term plan to empower local organizations.

Access to funds required a "Community Plan" that directly addressed the issue of homelessness, establishment of "Community Planning Groups" that had demonstrated broad consultation and inclusion, and a

"City Homelessness Facilitator." The Community Plan was expected to "provide community service organizations with a framework in which to work together to achieve common goals; assist the community to make the best possible use of scarce resources by reducing overlap and duplication; enable the community to evaluate its progress in reaching its objectives; and identify other sources of funding that the community will use to meet its 50% matching requirement" (NHI n.d., 12). Further, "the plan must reflect the needs of the key groups at risk—Aboriginal peoples, women and their children, youth, immigrants, refugees, substance abusers and the mentally ill—and involve them in the planning process" (12). Of these, the clear identification of *Assets and Gaps* was the most important, as "research has shown that homelessness is most effectively reduced by implementing a seamless underpinning of support services that helps people—over time—move from a situation where they are without permanent shelter or in danger of becoming homeless, to one of self-sufficiency" (14). It was expected that the community "list the supports and services that currently exist in your community—programs, services, human resources, equipment, buildings, land, etc." and use "this list to quantify the supports and services that are required to meet the needs of the homeless—the gaps" (14). In addition, an official *Community Entity* to administer funds needed to be in place, along with a *Community Advisory Board* to oversee the application process and the allocation of funds. Thus, this local leadership role comprised quite onerous demands in determining service assessments, matching funding, evaluations and reporting, and community engagement and outreach.

A renewal of the NHI would be introduced, extending initiatives and funding commitments until 2007. Government of Canada feedback from community partners on the usefulness of the NHI was generally positive. The main problem remained that there was no long-term commitment by the federal government to these communities. This situation not lost on community partners engaged in developing community plans, as the "duration of funding for these programs has been limited to only two to three years at a time. This lack of predictability and sustainability has led to uncertainty and inefficiency in delivering an adequate response to the homelessness crisis" (Kelowna Committee to End Homelessness 2009, 9).

More importantly, it was apparent to these partners that the NHI was only addressing the homeless crisis at a surface level.

> Despite the progress that has been made as a result of the NHI, most communities identified gaps in their continuum of supports and services, particularly in the area of affordable housing. Although not within the mandate of the NHI, the continued gap in availability of independent, affordable housing at the final stage of the continuum was identified by evaluation respondents as having a detrimental impact on establishing the overall continuum of supports and services. (HRSDC 2008, 5)

In response to these shortcomings the NHI was reintroduced as the Homeless Partnering Strategy (HPS) in 2007. By 2009 the HPS would commit to a longer funding horizon, with financial commitments until 2014, ending the 2–3 year renewal process that had generated so much uncertainty within communities. It also included the encouragement of a Housing First approach, recognizing that little could be achieved for the most visibly street-entrenched individuals until stable housing was assured, and completing the "seamless underpinning of support services" earlier affirmed in the NHI as necessary to achieve self-sufficiency for many homeless individuals. There was also financial commitment of over $1.9 billion to affordable housing and homelessness over five years, in which the transfer of funds and terms of use would be negotiated with the provinces (not with the local partners).

Despite these improvements, the HPS re-emphasized that it is a "community-based program that relies on communities to determine their own needs and develop appropriate projects" (HRSDC 2011), reaffirming that the municipal level must continue to take the lead and will only receive HPS funding if this is matched at the local level.

> Designated communities must have an approved, up-to-date and comprehensive community plan before they can receive funding. The plan must identify long-term solutions to address homelessness and how the community intends

to continue these activities. Designated communities have to demonstrate in their plan that other partners will provide a contribution of at least $1 for every dollar of the Homelessness Partnering Strategy allocation to the designated community (HRSDC 2011).

Even though the HPS funding involved a far more comprehensive approach to the homeless crisis, the continuation of past conditionality on funding meant a significant increase in the social responsibilities and financial commitments at the local level. Whereas the NHI had focused on front-line support such as emergency shelters and improving transitional housing, the HPS now placed the local level in the lead role in the provision of affordable housing. Not only did this require a considerably higher level of specialized planning (moving from community plans to "homeless action" plans), it also involved a sizable increase in the upfront local resource commitment to initiate projects. This created considerable uncertainty as to the long-term financial implications at the municipal level with respect to social housing and in-house social support (particularly in housing for addictions and mental illness).

As an exercise in effective planning, these conditions established clear criteria to maximize the benefits of funding, but there was minimal consideration for the disparities in preparedness of the various communities eligible for NHI/HPS funding to meet these criteria. Recognizing these limits within the NHI, the City of Kelowna, which had created a social plan in 1995 and a position to oversee implementation, moved instead to petition the province over a reliance on the NHI—"our senior management staff sat down with the Premier and with BC Housing people that were there (at an annual meeting of the Union of British Columbia Municipalities) and said look, we have a huge problem with homelessness and very little resources to deal with it, we need it to be a priority" (Walmsley & Kading, 2018). Shortly after this meeting the premier announced the formation of the Task Force on Homelessness, Mental Illness and Addictions at the Union of British Columbia Municipalities (UBCM) in 2004, and initiated ongoing consultation with select cities in BC.[4] Through 2005 the Provincial Housing Strategy that was emerging emphasized "the importance of partnerships to leverage provincial resources to maximize the number of households who can be provided with assistance," thus adopting the federal model with communities (Patterson et al. 2008, 26). At the end of 2006 the provincial government announced the creation of *BC Housing Matters*, with a priority being establishment of affordable housing and income support for those homeless with the most pressing care needs. In the case of British Columbia the broader HPS mandate served to further integrate the local government level into a far more complex leadership and planning role in the provision of affordable housing, as the local-provincial partnership with BC Housing became linked to the federal initiative on affordable housing. In 2008 the province stipulated that "municipalities with populations over 25,000 identify and zone appropriate sites for supportive housing and treatment facilities for persons with mental illness and addictions" as part of the local planning process (UBCM 2008). As noted by many observers, most local governments in Canada are subservient to provincial government dictates, financially dependent on upper levels of government to even meet basic infrastructure needs, and are treated as administrative extensions of provincial-level policy decisions (Haddow 2002, 101–4; Kelly and Caputo 2011, 37–42). Thus, the prospects of local governments realizing these social planning goals are highly contingent on the conditionality and discretion of upper levels of government, now integrated into a complex three-level intergovernmental collaboration that to date has been fraught, as we will see, with uncertainty and unclear lines of jurisdictional authority and financial resolve. It is within this context that we examine the local leadership initiatives and learning in addressing the challenge of homelessness in Kamloops.

The Community of Kamloops and Federal Homelessness Initiatives

The experience of Kamloops as a designated city eligible for initial NHI funding reveals the complex planning process that quickly emerged, beginning in 2001, and the new demands on this small city as it became thrown into a complex social planning role. This account of the early years establishes a baseline as to issues, knowledge, and leadership capacity in this city from which to measure and evaluate Government of Canada homelessness initiatives and the accomplishments, constraints, and limitations in ending homelessness at the local level. Representatives from the Government of Canada (Human Resources Development Canada), City of Kamloops planning department, the Elizabeth Fry Society, the Kamloops Women's Resource Centre, provincial agencies (health and social services), the Kamloops Indian Band, the John Howard Society, the AIDS Society (later ASK Wellness), youth outreach organizations, and the Phoenix Centre (addictions counselling), formed the Kamloops Community Committee (KCC). They quickly established committees, planning sessions, initial assessments, and priorities and practices to establish eligibility for federal funding. What this early period discloses is the general understanding of the dimensions of the local homelessness challenge, but also a need to rapidly adjust to the program criteria and requirements of the Government of Canada in order to ensure the maximum available funding.

KCC minutes from 2001 attest to the dearth of detailed information available to fulfill the federal government criteria for funding, but also to a committed leadership and network that emerged in response to the short timelines to access funding. While the City of Kamloops put together an initial inventory of "gaps and assets" based on existing service providers at the time, the KCC worked on a definition of "homelessness," a communications strategy, and a procedural model for adjudicating projects under the SCPI. While KCC consultants conducted focus groups and interviews to enhance the report on assets and gaps, the KCC Working Group developed the mandatory Community Plan on Homelessness. Conclusions from the initial Assets and Gap report emphasized:

- Need for housing at all levels (short-term, transitional, affordable, supported, etc.)

- Need for additional services such as life skills, self-esteem building, employment programs and drop-in multi-purpose centres that provide a wide range of services

- Location of housing and services as a key consideration when developing services/housing because travel is challenging for low-income earners

- Increased coordination of services and better information on existing services

- Importance of recognizing that some individuals will choose a particular lifestyle (e.g., to live on the street) and may not want to access any services. However, there should be appropriate choices available for people when they are ready to make lifestyle changes (KCC June 4, 2001).

With minimal financial commitments, suggested local improvements included "better coordination of services and communication between agencies; respectful treatment of homeless people; more accessible information on services available; advocacy for the homeless, especially for monitoring standards of housing; support and education for landlords; and community education." Concerted efforts were made to have the plan approved by the federal government within two months in order to receive proposals by early fall, with the goal of having "funding out to the Community in early fall before the cold weather hits" (KCC June 4, 2001). By July 2001, Kamloops had been allocated total funding of $1,769,000 for 2002 and 2003, to be disbursed as set out in Table 1.1.

Funds would be provided by the provincial government to meet this critical NHI matching funding requirement, and the City of Kamloops would assume the role of *Community Entity*. In addition, committee members travelled to Vancouver for workshops on completing federal government requirements on the community plan, ran training sessions for potential local applicants seeking SCPI funding, and were active in writing articles and appearing on local news shows to increase community awareness on homelessness issues and funding opportunities. Initial monies were used to renovate and upgrade facilities for the homeless and at-risk youth, including the purchase of equipment for dental services (in which 12 local dentists came forward to volunteer their time), the purchase of a home to provide emergency and transition space for women, and mobile outreach services for at-risk youth. Only six months later it was reported that from these funds some 100 individuals had received dental care, 50–70 youth were being assisted each night, and at the new

TABLE 1.1. Kamloops Allocation of Federal Funding from the National
Homelessness Initiative, 2002-2003

Apportioned	2002	2003	Total
Community	740,000	370,000	1,110,000
Aboriginal	243,000	164,000	407,000
Youth	126,000	126,000	252,000
Total	1,109,000	660,000	1,769,000

emergency shelter for women "demand had been overwhelming." Thus results of these achievements demonstrated the potential power of collective action in the community. What had emerged in a short period of time was an impressive and complex partnership between three levels of government and local community groups and professionals supporting a range of critical new services and facilities for those in need. However, it was evident that the local leadership had to contend with the multiple vicissitudes of the other partners, provincial and federal, in addressing local gaps and establishing goals.

From the beginning, uncertainty surrounded the NHI itself, as the first three-year mandate would have a one-year extension before then being renewed for another three years. The KCC never knew until near expiration whether the NHI would continue or whether the level of financial commitment would change. Other federal partnership issues revolved around compliance with processes, as it was unclear how to evaluate, for reporting purposes, programs that had been funded, and there was a need for someone with "program evaluation experience" (KCC February 11, 2002). Another concern was the lengthy project approval times at the federal level, which had eroded project-life from three years down to one and also resulted in costs (e.g., for renovations) being different from those originally proposed. Perhaps most significant, "for unincorporated or volunteer organizations the application process was seen to be onerous and perhaps some SCPI projects that would have served the community well were abandoned because of the resources required to apply" (KCC February 11, 2002). The bigger problem that emerged, though, was from the "provincial partner" providing matching funds, which began to engage in extensive spending cutbacks, thus affecting the sustainability of initiatives and creating a sense of lost ground in addressing homelessness due "to recent adjustments to provincial funding for social programs" (TRUE Consulting Ltd. 2003, 12). Thus, services and facilities that were originally deemed assets became vulnerable and emerged as new gaps in serving homeless residents. At the local level, issues included the lack of hard facts as to the homeless population, and concerns over an onerous compliance and reporting process that had further deterred local groups from applying despite innovative ideas. Other problems revolved around local partnership arrangements and a sense that the committee lacked broad enough representation (e.g., from seniors, business community, churches, immigrants, and at-risk families), and that the time commitments on various committees were taking staff away from actual service delivery for the homeless. Overall, the sense was that SCPI funding had allowed for the short-term priority issues for the homeless to be addressed, but that longer-term projects (i.e., creation of supportive and transitional housing) were less successful. At the time, then, local bridging links and social capital were weak within the KCC, a situation no doubt fuelled by the unclear resolve of the Government of Canada.

With the formal announcement in 2003 of the renewal of the NHI for another three years, the KCC and its Working Group on Homelessness (KWGH) became more formalized, with the Working Group establishing a clear mandate and set of responsibilities: attendance requirements, conflict of interest guidelines, satisfying reporting requirements of the federal government, advising city council, oversight on the application process for funding, developing links to the private sector, and overseeing research (e.g., homeless counts).[5] Under this new structure the City of Kamloops would remain as the Community Entity that would administer funds, the KWGH would be the official Community Advisory Entity responsible for the allocation of NHI funding, and the KCC would only serve to ratify decisions by the KWGH (with KCC meetings to be determined by the KWGH).

With this more formal structure the KWGH would oversee the funding of a number of important research initiatives that would significantly enhance the local understanding of homelessness in Kamloops. The first was the 2005 Kamloops Homeless Count, comprising both a numerical count and an extensive survey of willing participants, using a definition of "those who do not have a place (room, apartment or house) of their own and not paying rent" (TRUE Consulting Ltd. 2005, 7). From the 168 counted, 134 provided invaluable survey information about the age, living conditions, use of local facilities and services (shelters, meals, and supplies), needs, and most importantly the length of time and reasons for being homeless. Of note, findings found that the majority were not transient, and the largest group surveyed—in an age range of 13 to 68—were between 40 and 60 years of age (suggesting an older homeless population than in larger centres). Only two respondents chose to live without a home—and thus less than 1% were homeless as a "lifestyle choice." This report provided a baseline count on visible absolute homeless from which to inform government and community-based policy makers about the extent and makeup of homelessness in the Kamloops area (TRUE Consulting Ltd. 2005, 2). This report would be the basis for the *Homelessness Awareness Guide*—a document that combined local research with "best practices" from across North America in advising concerned citizens and organizations on potential initiatives to increase community awareness of the gravity of the challenge and/or support the needs of the local homeless population (with information about local organizations that may be contacted to support initiatives).

The KWGH then produced the most significant report on homelessness, with the *Inventory of Service Assets and Gaps For the Homeless— Kamloops, B.C.—2007* (TRUE Consulting Ltd. 2007). This report adopted a definition of homelessness recognizing both "absolute homelessness" ("a situation where an individual or family has no housing at all or is staying in a temporary form of shelter, or in locations not fit for human habitation") and "relative homelessness" ("a situation where people have a home but are at risk of becoming homeless; those living in accommodations that are inadequate, unsafe, and unaffordable; and those who face multiple social economic barriers"). In Kamloops, those affected by "relative homelessness" constituted the largest homeless subpopulation, in which "significant attention must be given to preventative measures which can have a major impact on keeping people from becoming homeless" (4). The report contained community stats demonstrating that rental vacancy rates had declined from nearly 8% in 2000 to below 1% in 2006—making the transition out of homelessness "more challenging." In addition, provincial income assistance did not reflect the reality of housing costs, insufficient affordable housing existed through the current economy, and more and more working poor were ending up homeless. With an inventory of housing (emergency shelters, transitional and supportive housing, and independent subsidized housing) the report provided an extensive list of service delivery gaps for homeless youth, Indigenous peoples, women, men, senior citizens, offenders released from correctional facilities, and people with substance misuse issues. The report concluded with the position that the highest local priority was affordable housing.

Within a short period of time the KCC and KWGH were able to progress from just a general understanding of the local homelessness problem to a very detailed and sophisticated understanding of the economics and policies that generated homelessness, the local capacities and limits in services and facilities to address targeted groups, and the priorities necessary to address immediate needs and reduce local homelessness. This initiative was complemented by the City of Kamloops initiative in 2006 to develop a Social Plan for the city (which would be adopted in 2009), in which housing and homelessness would be a primary theme. With the adoption of the Social Plan, the city committed to the long-term goal to "continue to position the City of Kamloops as a leader in addressing the social issues in the community by serving a partnership building and information sharing role" (City of Kamloops 2009, ii), supported by the hiring of a Social Development Supervisor to undertake the implementation of the plan. This period, then, is marked by two features: a solid determination of local gaps and needs based on comprehensive and extensive research; and the consolidation of critical local community entities buttressed by a social planning position within the municipal government. With this consolidation, though, it was evident that the broad community and government dynamic of the original KCC had been pared down as federal and provincial funding to manage the immediate needs of local homeless residents had become more stable. It was within this context that a new network emerged, with experience within the KCC, to advance a more comprehensive and aggressive approach to addressing local homelessness.

New Leadership and Learning in the Drive to "End Homelessness"

The Changing the Face of Poverty network (CFP), which emerged in 2004, "is a network of community and faith based organizations, individuals, and businesses working collectively to coordinate, connect, and create resources and solutions related to the issue of poverty in Kamloops" (CFP). Notable goals have included: developing creative solutions for poverty-related challenges; building partnerships to create long-term solutions; increasing access to safe and affordable housing; developing funding supports through partnerships and collaboration; expanding the current network of partnerships; engaging partners in solution-based action planning; and liaising with community decision makers on strategies to reduce poverty. By 2006 the CFP moved to a more aggressive strategy, going beyond managing and alleviating homelessness to solving the local homeless problem through services and advocacy for the building of transitional and affordable housing. It is these efforts that are credited with the more detailed knowledge, solution-oriented services, and coordinated plans with the City of Kamloops that now exist in advancing long-term solutions (Personal communication). By 2008 the CFP had linked with the United Way on initiatives, and in 2009 created a Homelessness Action Plan Steering Committee that had approached the city and the mayor directly in making the case for more affordable housing. This led to the hiring of a Homelessness Action Plan Coordinator and the development of the *Kamloops Homelessness Action Plan—2010* (HAP 2010), comprising the following goals and strategies:

> GOAL 1—Assess the local housing situation, enhance the stock of acceptable housing, and respond to changes in the housing market
>
> • Strategy—establish a local housing board
>
> GOAL 2—Provide greater housing stability and reduce evictions
>
> • Strategy A—promote housing support agreements
>
> • Strategy B—establish a Homeless Resident Program

GOAL 3—Connect people with the help they need

- Strategy A—improve outreach
- Strategy B—adopt a network approach to support services

GOAL 4—Build the basic skill that people need to maintain housing and financial independence

- Strategy—improve access to life skills coaching

GOAL 5—Improve fairness, accessibility, and responsiveness

- Strategy—create changes to laws, procedures, regulations, and protocols

GOAL 6—Help people build and maintain employment

- Strategy—improve workplace supports

The approach adopted to end homelessness in Kamloops was a comprehensive model that went beyond just the creation of new housing to the development of a broader system of supports, education, and training while maintaining a strong role for advocacy with respect to the provincial and federal levels of government (i.e., Goal 5). This model also involved a range of tasks to deepen engagement with the City of Kamloops and to expand links with local landlords, property developers, the university, and employers as partners in addressing homelessness. Endorsed by the City of Kamloops (particularly the mayor), the Homelessness Action Plan created the framework within which the city proceeded to allocate four parcels of land zoned for social housing initiatives advanced by community organizations, and for the creation of the Kamloops Housing Authority as a municipal government entity to formulate policies to support the goals of the plan. The plan also made possible two years of HPS funding of $75,000 to support a Life Skills network and the development of a plan to improve life skills training in the community. (Personal communication; HAP 2012), which has since continued on with the support of established and new member organizations within the CFP.

The CFP has also significantly increased our understanding of the extent of the homelessness challenge in Kamloops and determined the extent of the local housing needs. In 2010, in collaboration with community groups from four other small cities (Kelowna, Prince George, Nanaimo, and Nelson), and overseen by the Social Policy and Research Council of BC, researchers investigated the number of "hidden homeless" in each of these small cities. The results revealed a significant discrepancy between "street counts" (in which it is often assumed that the larger homeless population is roughly three times the size of the visible homeless) and those confronted by ongoing housing insecurity in which the street or a shelter were utilized on an occasional basis. For Kamloops the projected hidden homeless over the previous year (2010–11) were 1,167 (range of 808–1,631) (SPARC BC 2011, 23). Interviews with hidden homeless revealed both the broader dynamics of homelessness and the complex housing needs of many of those who are "sometimes" visible on our streets. Some 80% were staying with friends or acquaintances for various lengths of time, and then forced to find "other" arrangements (45). The most common "other" arrangement was couch surfing, camping, a rental suite, or sleeping in the streets. Some 64% included the use of emergency shelters or transition housing in the last year, and 82% had used community or government services to try to get their own place. The majority of hidden homeless were 25–45 years of age, with a higher percentage female than the visible homeless—53% female and 47% male (46). Some 65%+ reported having mental health challenges, while over 52% had substance use challenges, and 48% had physical challenges—with 22% reporting having all three challenges (47). Of note, 74% already relied on income assistance—either social assistance or provincial disability benefits (45). The vast majority identified "low income" and the "lack of affordable housing" as the two most significant barriers preventing them from getting their own place (51). While the numbers were not a surprise to CFP participants, the data was seen as critical in demonstrating the depth of the challenge and in advocating for funding from various levels of government (Personal communication with participant in research for report).

TABLE 1.2. Kamloops Affordable Housing Needs Assessment 2013

Type of Housing	Additional Units Needed (as of 2013)
Temporary Supported Housing *transitional housing—120 units at present*	99
Permanent Subsidized Housing *social housing—448 units at present*	120
Private Market Rental *affordable rents—7,421 at present*	1,632
Entry Level Ownership *less than $240,000—695 at present*	371
Total Number of Affordable Housing Units Needed	**2,222**

This research would be followed by an in-depth investigation of the specific housing needs of the homeless and at-risk citizens based on an inventory of housing options at the time. The *Kamloops Affordable Housing Needs Assessment* (HAP 2013) captures the spectrum of housing needs for the homeless and at-risk and the appropriate housing units that need to be constructed, as set out in Table 1.2.

Prominent in the assessment is the focus on transitional and social housing as opposed to any discussion of emergency shelter—in an effort to move beyond managing and toward resolving local homelessness. Projections of population growth in the report also showed that if these housing needs did not begin to be addressed, the numbers in each category would only continue to increase. With these two reports, the knowledge and understanding of the dimensions of homelessness in Kamloops had never been more complete. However, the local leadership needed to rapidly address these needs is severely compromised by the partnership model—particularly as the provincial and federal partners control the critical funding components.

Key figures in the CFP network recognize the general merits of the "partnership" model originally proposed by the federal government in addressing homelessness (Personal communication). Strengths of the model include the local research component focused on understanding the extent and character of homeless/at-risk residents and determining the particular needs of these varied residents to ensure that specific services and the appropriate housing are provided. Thus, there is agreement with the federal government that homelessness is a complex challenge in which needs and responses will vary from community to community based on the findings from local research. Weaknesses of the model involve the highly bureaucratized nature of the relationship with respect to reporting and the disbursement of funding, characterized as "stringent and ridiculous." Even small amounts of funding for locally approved proposals required multiple reviews and signatures by senior officials of the city (as the *Community Entity*) before approval could take place. This is viewed as a demeaning level of accountability for this partner in light of the large budgets for infrastructure and other services the city is responsible for on an ongoing basis. The increased pressure for "evaluative measures / measured outcomes" linked to applications and ongoing funding was also becoming a large administrative burden, one that needed to be accepted, as these requirements were becoming a standard adopted by other sources of funding outside of government. However, "they also haven't added any funding to accomplish that with, so it actually takes away from providing the service." The effect of these onerous application and reporting procedures was seen as discouraging proposals and participation by smaller community organizations with limited staff and resources, as "you've got to jump through all these hoops and if you are not ready to go, if you are not a big enough organization with your poop in a group enough, then you are SOL" (Personal communication). The hiring by the city in 2012 of a *Project Manager—Housing and Homelessness* (a position funded by the Government of Canada), responsible for the implementation, administration, coordination, and financial monitoring of programs and services funded under the HPS, has served to narrow the communication gap between community organizations at the CFP and funding opportunities for new collaborations. And one initiative has led to Kamloops being only one of two communities selected for a five-year pilot program to develop a plan to end youth homelessness, "a model that is [to be] shared with communities across Canada in the coming years" (City of Kamloops 2014).

The largest concern though, was that there was still too much focus by the federal and provincial partners on emergency/temporary shelters and services rather than long-term housing solutions. Present levels of HPS and provincial funding directed at the development of new housing units would have to be at the expense of ongoing facilities and services, as the majority of services were still unsustainable without federal monies and would always remain vulnerable to losing their ongoing funding:

> The federal government's approach to addressing homelessness and working with local groups . . . is totally disrespectful. It has no sense of the legitimacy of running programs and how long it takes to build an effective, solid program. They chunk them into these little sections and they go, "Okay, here it is for two years" . . . and we don't know what the new one is going to look like. Up until now, every operating agreement had to have an exit clause, meaning "how will it be sustainable once we pull the money out?" Social issues just don't disappear, right? I mean do a renewal. Have a sense that you have to meet certain expectations by the end of it, but if you've got to write a contract to say you are going to resolve the issues that you've encountered, such as homelessness, in a two or three year span, and you have to write a sustainability plan, I don't know how you do that. (Personal communication with executive director of community organization)

There was also a sense that provincial and federal funding was becoming more difficult to access, not easier, despite ample local research confirming the extent of needs. Notable was the feeling that the local Member of Parliament, Members of the Legislative Assembly, and local federal and provincial staff from various government entities (e.g., BC Housing), had all played a supportive and constructive role but were themselves limited by the administrative procedures and the priorities that had already been established at the top. There was also an awareness that the "city here is very clear that it doesn't want to be a social housing provider or housing provider of any kind." From a municipal perspective, homelessness and related social issues were regarded as a "grey area," "tricky," and in "limbo" until the jurisdictional issues between the federal, provincial, and local levels were resolved. Observing that most social issues are "health-related," the sentiment was that the provincial level should assume responsibility, as "that would be a much simpler, more effective way for social issues to be addressed" but "that's not clearly defined now" and "no level of government wants to take on new responsibilities" (Personal communication with member of city council).

The author's participation in the monthly CFP meetings revealed the multiple initiatives in place to provide and enhance services for the homeless and at-risk residents in Kamloops (food, meals, supplies, healthcare, temporary shelter). Also apparent was the complex set of provincial and federal policies in place, and persistent uncertainties over funding that complicate and frustrate efforts to achieve these service outcomes. This was most evident as everyone awaited news as to whether HPS funding would be continued or terminated after 2014, with little surprise if the latter occurred. Thus, after 15 years, there was still no faith or trust built up in this partnership.

Most important at these meetings are the observations and concerns of front-line workers from community organizations who document the true dimensions of the local challenges. Observations range from the recognition of a surge in new "homeless faces," a visible increase in homeless youth, out-of-town individuals awaiting postponed medical procedures using the shelters for weeks, to single-parent post-secondary students being referred to a local community agency as their students loans did not allow enough for food and rent after tuition was paid. Meal programs offered by different community and religious organizations—serving some 150–170 people per week—were working well and coordinating efforts to prevent overlap and to meet varied health needs, and a new organizer—Jubilee Urban Movement & Partners (JUMP)—was building support to fill some of the "gaps per week" in meals for the visibly homeless. Shelter programs had effectively addressed all those in need over the winter, but provincial funding, which only covers supplies, was only claimable when the temperature dropped below −10°C (later increased to −7°C for 2013/14, and −3°C by 2016–17). Nevertheless, the Out of the Cold program was considered a "success"—no cold weather deaths—with discussions as to facilities for "out of the heat" for the summer.[6]

On a more positive note, the new Rent Bank was operational through the Elizabeth Fry Society.[7] The bank was initially supported by a contribution from a local credit union to provide short-term loans and prevent at-risk families from being evicted, and there was the prospect that the city might contribute on a yearly basis to the fund (which has since been confirmed). On the downside, there was a significant demand by single individuals that could not yet be accommodated until more funding was in place—but as the director noted—"we're used to having to say 'no'" (however, by the fall of 2013, funding allowed for single individuals to access support). Cumulative efforts continue to demonstrate a commitment to *equality of quality of life* outcomes and reducing hardship, by filling gaps and ensuring improved services for marginalized or vulnerable residents. The formation of a CFP Sub-Committee on Anti-Poverty Strategies (see Figure 1.2) to research and advance local policy options for creating affordable childcare spaces, advancing a "living wage," increasing employment opportunities, and improving service and access to public transit, has resulted in a more flexible scheduling model to accommodate focused contact with local organizations and government institutions in exploring opportunities grounded in the experiences from other communities. These deeper horizontal linkages within and outside the community (via direct contact with other planners and community organizations) have provided important insights and initiatives, but also revealed the extent of the frustration in other small cities.

By June 2013, there was confirmation that the Government of Canada would renew the Homelessness Partnering Strategy for another five years, but with a reduced yearly financial commitment—thus reinforcing the local uncertainty over future funding. Then, in early 2014 it was reported that new conditions in HPS funding (colloquially referred to as "HPS-Version 2.0") had placed a priority on the Housing First model as the most effective method in terms of cost and outcomes in addressing the needs of the most visibly street-entrenched homeless.[8] This would gear the majority of (reduced) funding toward services and infrastructure to support this model—suggesting that the Government of Canada was moving from just managing homelessness to actually solving homelessness (CFP). This was to be supported at the provincial level by the monies committed for affordable housing in 2009, in which it had taken five years to reach separate agreements with each province (Scoffield 2011), finally leading to provincial announcements regarding increased opportunities for community organizations to access funds for affordable housing initiatives. This combination of factors led to a local effort to reconfigure the Kamloops Working Group on Homelessness as a more dynamic and "action focused" entity to end homelessness—called the HomeFree Collective. Comprising very broad representation and featuring consultation to determine local needs and priorities (including an Aboriginal and non-Aboriginal co-chairs),[9] with overlapping representation from the council on various subcommittees to advance policy proposals directed at all three levels of government, the collective has gradually been pared down in structure to accommodate an onerous meeting schedule, unclear lines of communication and authority, and an absence of focus. There is now a primary emphasis on advocating for local and provincial support for the affordable housing component needed if any headway at all is to be achieved in advancing a Housing First strategy as directed by the Government of Canada (see Chapter 7: Conclusion).

There is little doubt that in the case of Kamloops the Government of Canada homelessness initiatives—NHI and HPS—have fuelled an unprecedented level of collaboration among community organizations, and between the local government and community organizations. In this respect, a government-led, *coercive collaboration* was initially very effective in creating a local network and leadership structure in an effort to maximize the amounts of funding available to address the immediate needs of homeless residents. From this has arisen a vast output of research, reports, and planning documents that not only provide a compendium of information on the range of issues but also demonstrate the more sophisticated forms of data collection and analysis that have been employed to determine specific local needs and priorities. However, it is also evident that within this type of transactional collaboration there was only the potential to maintain efforts at managing the local homelessness challenge—as prescribed by the terms and focus of the NHI and HPS. The emergence of the Changing the Face of Poverty (CFP) network, a local *mimetic collaboration*, was necessary in order to expand the participation of community groups and local organizations, foment the level of local planning and

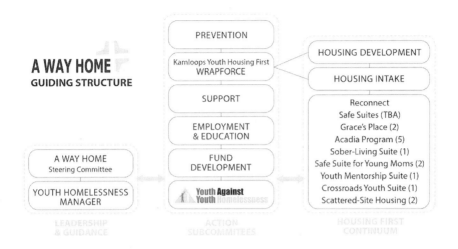

A WAY HOME
GUIDING STRUCTURE

PREVENTION

Kamloops Youth Housing First
WRAPFORCE

SUPPORT

EMPLOYMENT
& EDUCATION

FUND
DEVELOPMENT

Youth Against
Youth Homelessness

A WAY HOME
Steering Committee

YOUTH HOMELESSNESS
MANAGER

HOUSING DEVELOPMENT

HOUSING INTAKE

Reconnect
Safe Suites (TBA)
Grace's Place (2)
Acadia Program (5)
Sober-Living Suite (1)
Safe Suite for Young Moms (2)
Youth Mentorship Suite (1)
Crossroads Youth Suite (1)
Scattered-Site Housing (2)

LEADERSHIP
& GUIDANCE

ACTION
SUBCOMMITTEES

HOUSING FIRST
CONTINUUM

FIGURE 1.3. A Way Home Committee Structure. Courtesy of Katherine McParland, Youth Homelessness Manager for A Way Home Committee.

coordination of services, develop new initiatives, and advance the agenda to end homelessness.

Together, these two types of collaborations have generated an impressive level of community understanding and local knowledge, and, due to the CFP, a leadership initiative with transformational goals, the community appears well-placed to respond to the new Housing First model being adopted by the Homelessness Partnering Strategy should the adequate financial resources ever arrive from provincial and federal sources. Most notable has been the high level of ongoing collaboration despite each organization being ensconced in a competitive environment for federal (HPS), provincial, and local / private sector (e.g., United Way) grants, in which there is a shared conviction that it is most important to just get the money to the local level for services and programs. This has been most evident with the initiative to end youth homelessness, which resulted in a nationally recognized report in 2014 entitled *A Way Home—A Plan to End Youth Homelessness in Kamloops* (City of Kamloops 2014). More impressive, though, is that the Youth Against Youth Homelessness group (YAYH) that drove the planning report process (with support from the City of Kamloops, United Way, the Kamloops Indigenous Friendship

A WAY HOME

Kamloops Youth Housing First

WRAPFORCE

GUIDING STRUCTURE

HOUSING DEVELOPMENT TEAM	HOUSING INTAKE TEAM	FUND DEVELOPMENT TEAM
Research & Partnerships Creating Housing & Programs	*Community Referrals to Housing Continuum*	*Funds to Support Housing & Programs*

Reconnect

Safe Suites

Grace's Place

Acadia Program

Sober Living Suite

Youth Mentorship Suite

Safe Suite for Young Moms

Scattered-Site Housing

FIGURE 1.4. WrapForce – Guiding Structure. Scaled Space Studios. Courtesy of Katherine McParland, Youth Homelessness Manager for A Way Home Committee.

Society, and the Homelessness Action Plan Coordinator) has persisted as a vibrant body since the release of the report, to become the A Way Home Committee. Initiating aggressive outreach to a largely hidden homeless population, and adopting a Housing First model (entitled the *WrapForce*) for those homeless youth between 13 and 24 year of age (many who have "aged out" out of the provincial foster care system and been left with inadequate education and life skills), the A Way Home Committee has developed a strong working relationship with organizations from both the CFP and the HomeFree Collective, and with new partners.[10] The ability of the A Way Home Committee to quickly gain traction, create unique services, and secure local housing space is testament to the flexible leadership within established organizations and the supportive social capital that has developed over many years in Kamloops, with increasing capacity to engage, incorporate, and challenge provincial government agencies and practices. However, local resource limitations for appropriate housing and support services, as in other cities across Canada, have hampered the early momentum in addressing the extent of local needs for youth (see Chapter 7: Conclusion).

Conclusion

The collaboration and leadership initiative generated at the local level by the Government of Canada through the National Homelessness Initiative (NHI) and subsequent Homelessness Partnering Strategy (HPS) exemplifies the strengths and limitations of a *coercive collaboration*. With the purpose of incentivizing a leadership structure at the local level to address the immediate needs of the homeless, the criteria established to determine local needs and priorities were very effective in generating a local collaboration, detailed research findings, and specific services. However, once this leadership was in place, and particular learning outcomes had been achieved as prescribed by the Government of Canada, the collaboration remained limited to the objectives set from above in addressing homelessness at the local level. With a focus on the terms and conditions of membership, "conflict of interest" guidelines, procedural oversight on funding initiatives proposed from within the community, and program compliance, the Kamloops Working Group on Homelessness (KWGH)—while performing a critically important purpose—became bureaucratized and constrained by the limited goals and parameters set by the Government of Canada. Thus, this *coercive collaboration* became an effective mechanism for "managing homelessness" at the local level but not for utilizing the research findings on issues of poverty and affordable housing in advancing a more transformational agenda.

In marked contrast, the *mimetic collaboration* that arose in response to these limitations—the Changing the Face of Poverty network—used the research and local knowledge to focus on the direct link between poverty and homelessness, attempting to fill gaps in services through coordinating initiatives, increasing local awareness on homelessness, and advancing the goal of affordable housing and strategies to prevent homelessness. The strengths of this leadership initiative have been the flexibility in membership, the fostering of smaller collaborations to respond to immediate needs, and the advancement of targeted initiatives to fill service gaps. Most importantly, monthly meetings serve as a critical venue to keep organizations and engaged citizens updated on events, on initiatives from within particular agencies or organizations that provide opportunities for other community groups and their clientele, and on new local challenges, funding opportunities, and the shifting terrain at the provincial and federal levels as to regulations, criteria, and spending commitments. Thus, while the KWGH could create a snapshot of local homelessness needs, the CFP is the main repository of the most current collective understanding on services and gaps in addressing and preventing homelessness. The challenges (and the frustrations) are evident, particularly because the larger federal and provincial partnership that generated these initiatives is divided over goals and responsibilities. There is a sense of critical resignation and lack of trust toward the partners as the collective knowledge on local homelessness has not translated into the necessary financial support to meet these needs and support goals—an aspect of this partnership that still remains elusive after over 15 years. Still, the CFP continues to explore options and opportunities, undaunted by these limitations, by fostering opportunities for community engagement and flexibility in promoting initiatives. As an increasingly young and dynamic core of leaders emerges to continue advancing the goals of the CFP, this collaboration expresses the diverse representation, flexibility, and adaptability that is necessary in addressing such substantial and long-term goals.

In understanding the leadership that has led to this level of social-creative capital, small to mid-size city scale and proximity only provides a context for this ease of engagement—as it is not hard to envision small and mid-sized cities where the more limited goals and transactional leadership set by the Government of Canada have prevailed over a broader agenda and initiatives being taken up by a separate leadership initiative. Community advocates and visiting speakers from other centres have often remarked on the very strong collaborative dynamic in Kamloops, and formerly homeless residents have mentioned the significant availability of services and support compared to other cities. Local advantages in having established organizations and provincial entities are evident, as is the resolve within these organizations to engage with the transformational goals of the CFP. Such continuous multi-sectoral representation and "adaptability" to challenges and initiatives suggest that bureaucratic silos are not as rigid as in higher levels or government, or in large urban centres with more specialized and complex administrative structures. Although local resources are tight and limited and participants confront a demanding meeting and grant application schedule, new initiatives (e.g., A Way Home Committee) are actively taken on out of a larger commitment to ending poverty. The regular participation by city councillors and staff from provincial agencies and the city reveals the high levels of engagement and advocacy in place connecting community groups with various branches of government, but the inability of these connections to translate into resources to match local learning reveals the highly centralized nature of our federal system. Still, with this broad and diverse representation, substantial research and understanding, action plans and ongoing initiatives, there is a firm "community will" to "end poverty and homelessness," supporting multiple goals, including minimizing hardship, fostering cooperation and empathy, and increasing fairness in this city (see Chapter 7: Conclusion).

In contrast, the larger partnership model—comprising the Government of Canada, the provincial government, the local government, and community groups—is more problematic. This stems from the fact that these partners do not share the same goals. While the local level is committed to "ending homelessness" through an increase in affordable housing (but lacks the resources to achieve this), the federal and provincial "partners" are not willing to establish the same outcome at this time. At the provincial level, funding for affordable housing and services is prioritized and targeted based on highest need, which may vary from housing for seniors to mental health to shelter services, without the goal of or commitment to ending homelessness (Personal communication with executive director of community organization). While there is ample evidence of the cost advantages of housing the homeless over just managing homelessness, the provincial government is not alone in reserving a commitment to this goal. Only the governments of Alberta and Ontario have made a commitment and endorsed plans to end homelessness, and it remains to be seen if their financial resolve will endure long enough to achieve this goal (Alberta Secretariat for Action on Homelessness 2008; Schwan 2016). More elusive has been the position of the Government of Canada, which, despite wanting "measurable outcomes" for HPS-funded initiatives at the local level, *does not measure the impact of its funding on homelessness* (Graham 2011, 175). Rather, HPS as a leveraging device is seen as successful for raising matching funds—calculated at approximately $2.61 for every $1.00 dollar invested through HPS. Thus, the Government of Canada does not have a sense of the how many homeless there are in Canada or if cumulative funding over the years has actually reduced homelessness, a fault recognized at the local level. "I'm realizing that if you look across the country, at these Homelessness Action Plans, in cities that have them, [do] they have declines in the number of homeless people in the communities? No. So as an outcome, as to say that we are eradicating homelessness, is a total fallacy. So it becomes something where I support community collaboration to a certain extent, but what interferes with its authenticity is it has to meet the expectations of the funding source, which is Service Canada [Government of Canada]" (Personal communication with executive director of community organization). Having devolved leadership on this issue to the local level, the federal government has adopted a facilitator role, yet retains all the powers to determine the amount of funds available, timelines for renewal, and the criteria and requirements for accessing support (with a confirmed willingness to abruptly end the HPS with little notice—see note 8). This leadership initiative, then, is not a meaningful partnership given the lack of shared goals and unpredictable commitments among the participants and the inability of the local leadership to influence or access the necessary resources to fulfill the goals they have set (let alone the Housing First criteria adopted by the Government of Canada). Rather, as understood locally, the federal government is "just basically off-loading responsibility, under the auspices that we are empowering the community" (Personal communication with executive director of community organization). This confirms that our centralized forms of government "impede and undermine" local initiatives (even when initially funded by the Government of Canada and the provincial government), and inhibit the creation of highly effective horizontal and vertical forms of governance and the strong leadership needed for long-term transformational outcomes (Sotarauta and Beer 2017, 213; Bentley, Pugalis, and Shutt 2017, 196).[11]

Despite the severe limitations within the partnership model, from a local *equality of quality of life* perspective the brief examples of programs and new initiatives reveal the significant contributions of numerous community and religious organizations, concerned citizens, local businesses and employees, and public officials in addressing a major social challenge and supporting thousands of local residents. While occasional grievances are expressed in the local media regarding issues of panhandling, public intoxication, and visible homelessness in various areas of the city, only a cumulative retrospective provides insights into the considerable time, efforts, and local resources that have prevented these issues from becoming a major local crisis generating highly negative impressions of particular areas of the city (for more details and analysis, see Chapter 7: Conclusion). In this respect, the goal of reducing poverty and ending homelessness is a collective effort not just to address the needs of less fortunate residents but also to ensure that the livability, accessibility, and integrity of the whole city is preserved for all residents (as per Montgomery 2013). To this end, the following chapters by Lisa Cooke—on the Shower Project, and Dawn Farough—on the Homeless Theatre Project—exemplify the further unique initiatives that have emerged from these earlier leadership and learning initiatives in minimizing hardship, fostering empathy and cooperation, and building lasting bonds among community members and former strangers.

My research on federal-local homelessness initiatives has its origins in an earlier research project focused on the emergence of social planning by local governments in small and mid-sized cities in BC. Finding that the main incentive for local governments to take up this task had its origins in the funding opportunities from the Government of Canada led me to evaluate the challenges for this local leadership model. Through interviews and ongoing attendance and connections at CFP meetings, other research opportunities emerged from within the community for our undergraduate students. To date, these have included a "needs assessment" report and a study of *best practices in transitional housing for women with children* to support a funding application for a transitional housing facility for women in Kamloops, two policy-options reports for the City of Kamloops, on utilizing the Affordable Housing Reserve Fund and new regulations to preserve affordable rental properties, and three research reports to support initiatives in the local Homelessness Action Plan— one on the range of programs in other cities to increase the availability of affordable housing, a second on the different "housing first" models utilized by community groups in other urban centres, and the latest on anti-poverty initiatives adopted by the other cities (e.g., transportation, affordable childcare). Through the active participation of undergraduate researchers (researching themes, developing survey questions, leading on ethics approval, conducting surveys, editing final reports), new opportunities have emerged on investigating employment opportunities for formerly homeless residents, transportation services for disabled residents, and evaluation tools for the A Way Home Committee's *WrapForce*. These types of focused research projects have been quite effective for developing connections, integrating undergraduate students, and serving particular needs of local community organizations and the City of Kamloops. TRU administration has been increasingly supportive of these projects in recognizing their value in time commitments and as professional outcomes, with flexibility in the use of financial resources and/or course credit recognition for interested students (see Chapter 7: Conclusion for more details). In addition, student understanding of homelessness and local affordable housing challenges has increased, with more events to raise awareness promoted by students groups and faculty in collaboration with community organizations.[12] However, my experience with a large, multi-year community partnership research grant application was revealing as to the local limitations. Over a three-month period of consultation to meet the Fall deadline it was evident that the overlap with other grant application deadlines, board approvals for research participation by community partners (not always forthcoming), prior ethics and workload approvals for provincial government partners, and frequent changes in positions and responsibilities within community organizations prevented the engaged and detailed preparation needed to create a competitive grant application. Overcoming such barriers would not be without major challenges and changes in local financial resources and capacities, and would support the benefits of community-engaged research and efforts within our university to be a more effective knowledge-support structure (see Chapter 7: Conclusion, on developments).

NOTES

I would like to thank Tim Norman, Whitney Mahar, Steve O'Reilly, Brayden Wilson, Theresa Thoms, and Daniela Corno—TRU undergraduate researchers who have made a significant contribution to my understanding of the city. A special thanks to Keely McKibben for all her support and insights in completing this project.

1   An idea taken from large urban centres in Canada, where anti-poverty collaborations were becoming more evident by the 1990s.

2   Only British Columbia and Quebec continued, but with substantially reduced funding (Kelowna Committee to End Homelessness 2009).

3   Kamloops received funding in July 2001, leaving less than two years to meet objectives.

4   The "Task Force convenes local and provincial governments to develop new resources to address issues related to homelessness" (Patterson et al. 2008, 26), and the cities involved were Vancouver, Victoria, Kelowna, Nanaimo, Prince George, Fort St. John, Terrace, New Westminster, and Surrey.

5   The specific funding stream for Youth Homelessness was ended with the renewal of the NHI in 2003 (see Gaetz and Redman 2016, 3).

6   Collaboration between St. Paul's Cathedral, New Life Mission, and Emerald Centre (CMHA) to ensure food and shelter throughout the winter (with space at ASK Wellness facilities if needed). See Sperling (2016).

7   Rent Bank provides low-interest emergency loans for low-income working families threatened with eviction or an inability to pay utilities—providing an alternative to the high-interest loans available through fringe financial institutions. See http://www.kamloopsefry.com/programs-services/housing/kamloops-rent-bank/

8   It was later reported that the Government of Canada had intended to terminate the HPS, confirming local suspicions as to federal resolve, and that the program was only preserved after last-minute lobbying efforts by important figures in Ottawa familiar with the issue and the latest research on the potential cost-saving benefits of a Housing First approach (Macnaughton et al. 2016).

9   "The HomeFree Collective is a community-wide approach to ending homelessness in our community. Members include non-profit housing providers and social service agencies, landlords and property management companies, developers and builders, realtors and mortgage brokers, persons with a lived experience of homelessness, urban Aboriginal community representatives, foundations and individual funders, university professors and student researchers, government agencies, community leaders and concerned citizens, and political representatives from all four levels of government" (City of Kamloops 2015).

10   Support and stable representation from the local business community have been more evident on the A Way Home Committee—perhaps because of the focus on youth and the sense that this early intervention can be most effective in altering life outcomes for this demographic.

11   "However, the scope for strong leadership will also be dependent on the *acceptability* of the degree of the restrictions on decision-making on strategy and action. If the controls or conditions are not *acceptable* to the sub-national body, this will weaken the power of the leadership to shape strategy and action at the sub-national level that address local needs and priorities (i.e. hindering place-based modes of leadership)" (Bentley, Pugalis, and Shutt 2017, 196).

12   Examples of ongoing and expanding university-community engagement in this area include the TRU promotion of local events to raise awareness (see Figure 1.1) and campus forums, such as the well-attended Kamloops Affordable Housing Panel Discussion (October 17, 2017)—hosted by the TRU Student Union Equity Committee and consisting of Jen Casorso (City of Kamloops), Kim Galloway (ASK Wellness), Kelly Fawcett (Kelson Group), Audrey Shaw (Kamloops Real Estate Association), and Terry Kading (TRU).

References

Alberta Secretariat for Action on Homelessness. 2008. *A Plan for Alberta: Ending Homelessness in 10 Years.* Edmonton: Government of Alberta.

Bentley, G., L. Pugalis, and J. Shutt. 2017. "Leadership and Systems of Governance: The Constraints on the Scope Of Leadership of Place-Based Development in Sub-National Territories." *Regional Studies* 51 (2): 194–209.

CFP (Changing the Face of Poverty). http://www.changingthefaceofpoverty.com/.

City of Kamloops. 2009. *Kamloops Social Plan.* Kamloops: City of Kamloops. http://www.kamloops.ca/socialdevelopment/socialplan/index.shtml#.WZGj4FGQzX4.

City of Kamloops. 2014. *Mobilizing Local Capacity to End Youth Homelessness Program.* http://www.kamloops.ca/socialdevelopment/MLCproject.shtml.

City of Kamloops. 2015. *HomeFree Collective.* http://www.kamloops.ca/socialdevelopment/ homefree/#.WXS6DlFGnX4.

Gaetz, S., and M. Redman. 2016. "Federal Investment in Youth Homelessness: Comparing Canada and the United States and a Proposal for Reinvestment." *Canadian Observatory on Homelessness / Homeless Hub.* http://homelesshub.ca/ reinvestinyouth.

Government of Canada. 2008. *The Homeless Partnering Strategy: Partnerships that Work.* Ottawa: Government of Canada.

Graham, A. 2011. "Vision, Collaboration, Persistence and Hard Work: The Canadian Federal Government's Homeless Partnering Strategy." In *A New Synthesis of Public Administration: Serving in the 21st Century,* edited by J. Bourgon, 167–81. Kingston: McGill-Queen's University Press.

Haddow, R. 2002. "Municipal Social Security in Canada." In *Urban Policy Issues: Canadian Perspectives,* 2nd ed., edited by E. Fowler and D. Siegel, 90–107. Don Mills: Oxford University Press.

HAP (Homelessness Action Plan). 2010. *Kamloops Homeless Action Plan.* Kamloops: City of Kamloops. http://www.kamloops.ca/socialdevelopment/HAP.shtml#. Wf3LhHZrzX5.

HAP (Homelessness Action Plan). 2012. *Kamloops Homelessness Action Plan: Life Skills Development Project Report.*

HAP (Homelessness Action Plan). 2013. *Kamloops Affordable Housing Needs Assessment.*

HRSDC (Human Resources and Skills Development Canada). 2008. Strategic Policy and Research Branch. *Summative Evaluation of the National Homelessness Initiative— Final Report.* Ottawa: Government of Canada.

HRSDC (Human Resources and Skills Development Canada). 2011. *National Homelessness Initiative—Background.* Ottawa: Government of Canada. Accessed May 15, 2011. www.hrsdc.gc.ca/eng/homelessness/index.shtmal.

Kading, T. 2012. *The Politics of Social Planning in the Small City.* http://www.cpsa-acsp.ca/ papers-2012/Kading.pdf.

KCC (Kamloops Community Committee). 2001–2007. Meeting Minutes.

Kelly, K., and T. Caputo. 2011. *Community: A Contemporary Analysis of Policies, Programs, and Practices.* Toronto: University of Toronto Press.

Kelowna Committee to End Homelessness. 2009. *Home for Good: Kelowna's Ten Year Plan to End Homelessness.* www.castanet.net/content/1243913711AFT.pdf.

Layton, J. 2008. *Homelessness: How to End the National Crisis.* 2nd ed.. Toronto: Penguin Group.

Macnaughton, E., G. Nelson, P. Goering, and M. Piat. 2016. *The At Home / Chez Soi Project: Moving Evidence into Policy. The Story of the At Home Chez Soi Initiative's*

Impact on Federal Homelessness Policy in Canada. Ottawa: Mental Health Commission of Canada. mentalhealthcommission.ca.

Montgomery, C. 2013. *Happy City: Transforming our Lives through Urban Design*. Toronto: Doubleday Canada.

Murphy, B. 2000. *On the Street: How We Created the Homeless*. Winnipeg: J. Gordon Shillingford.

NHI (National Homelessness Initiative). n.d.. *A Guide to the Supporting Communities Partnerships Initiative (SCPI)*. Ottawa: Government of Canada.

Patterson, M., J. Somers, K. McIntosh, A. Shiell, and C. J. Frankish. 2008. *Housing and Support for Adults with Severe Addictions and/or Mental Illness in B.C.* Burnaby: Centre for Applied Research in Mental Illness and Addiction, Simon Fraser University.

Schwan, K. 2016. "Why Don't We Do Something? The Societal Problematization of "Homelessness" and the Relationship between Discursive Framing and Social Change." PhD thesis, University of Toronto.

Scoffield, H. 2011. "Ottawa and Provinces Reach $1.4 Billion Deal on Affordable Housing." Accessed June 12, 2017. http://homelesshub.ca/resource/ottawa-and-provinces-reach-14-billion-deal-affordable-housing?_ga=2.37303328.1695655720.1509806208-886663890.1509806208.

Smith, R. 2004. "Lessons from the National Homelessness Initiative." In *Special Studies: Policy Development and Implementation in Complex Files*, edited by R. Smith and S. Torjman, 1–32. Ottawa: Canada School of Public Policy.

Sotarauta, M., and A. Beer. 2017. "Governance, Agency, and Place Leadership: Lessons from a Cross-National Analysis." *Regional Studies* 51 (2): 210–23.

Sperling, J. 2016. "Kamloops' Homeless Seeking Shelter from Cold and Mild Weather." *CFJC Today*. December 20. http://cfjctoday.com/article/552964/kamloops-homeless-seeking-shelter-cold-and-mild-weather.

SPARC BC (Social Planning and Research Council of British Columbia). 2011. *Knowledge for Action: Hidden Homelessness in Prince George, Kamloops, Kelowna, Nelson and Nanaimo*. www.sparc.bc.ca.

TRUE Consulting Ltd. 2003. *The Kamloops Community Plan on Homelessness: Interim Evaluation*.

TRUE Consulting Ltd. 2005. *Kamloops Homeless Count 2005*.

TRUE Consulting Ltd. 2007. *Inventory of Service Assets and Gaps For the Homeless – Kamloops, B.C. – 2007*.

UBCM (Union of British Columbia Municipalities). 2008. *Policy Paper: Affordable Housing and Homelessness Strategy*. www.ubcm.ca.

Walmsley, C., and T. Kading. 2018. *Small Cities, Big Issues: Community in a Neoliberal Era*. Edmonton: Athabasca University Press.

2

"What a Difference a Shower Can Make"[1]

Lisa Cooke

The Story

This is the story of a shower, the people who built it, and those who now use it. I am telling this story for several reasons. The first is that it is an incredible example of gift giving, volunteer involvement, and commitment. Upon learning that street-involved people in Kamloops did not have access to a safe, accessible, and free shower facility, a group from the United Steelworkers Local 7619 came together and built one. This tale offers a case study of the capacity of a group of tenacious and socially conscious individuals who identified a need in the community and did something about it. There are lessons to be learned on this matter alone about mobilizing sustained volunteer efforts to see a large-scale project through to completion, the local politics of getting it approved, and the poetic articulations of why those involved did what they did.

There is more to it than that, though. Throughout this collection we are reflecting on the role of researchers as embedded in the processes that we seek to examine and the kinds of collaborations that emerge around social issues to mobilize efforts aimed at addressing them. As we do, we are exploring the relationships between leadership, learning, and quality of life

the Politics &
Poetics
of GIVING
& RECEIVING
in the Small City

A CURA RESEARCH
CABARET PRESENTED
BY DRS. LISA COOKE &
WILL GARRETT-PETTS

march 21
11:30 *am*

SMALL CITIES CURA
CAMPUS ACTIVITY CENTRE RM 314
THOMPSON RIVERS UNIVERSITY
900 MCGILL RD, KAMLOOPS, BC

Please join the researchers for a discussion on giving and receiving in Kamloops. The story starts with one local union (United Steelworkers Local 7619 from Highland Valley Copper) that built a shower for ASK Wellness in Kamloops' North Shore area. What started as a good idea, one coming from a place of great intension, became, according to newspaper accounts, "a fulcrum for this whole basket of social issues." The business community initially opposed the project, citing the prospect of escalating insurance premiums and possible loss of local business, while social workers and street nurses saw in the shower project an opportunity for the marginalized to access a facility important for maintaining self-respect and basic hygiene. The project, which eventually received the North Shore Business Association's blessing, is now completed and open for public use.

This presentation invites you to explore a significant case study of small city gift-giving, one replete with expressions of positive and negative reciprocity: charitable donations of money and labour, good intentions, misunderstandings, media representations and misrepresentations, studies of perceived benefits and losses, and the political implications of giving and receiving—the politics and poetics of it all.

Please RSVP to Sherry Bennett shbennett@tru.ca to reserve your place

FIGURE 2.1. "The Politics & Poetics of Giving & Receiving in the Small City."
Courtesy of TRU Office of Research and Graduate Studies.

LISA COOKE

in small city settings *and* the value and contribution of our academic skill sets to this process. As an ethnographer observing the building, opening, and operation of this project, I was of no use to the steelworkers in the actual building of the showers. I have no plumbing or tile-laying skills, and if anything was in the way with my tape recorder and notepad more than I was helpful. Rather, the skills that I bring to this collaborative effort are academic. I can tell the story of the "Shower Project," as it has come to be called by those involved, for the lessons to be learned about what it takes to pull a gift like this off. By examining how a group of steelworkers from a local mine joined forces with a non-profit social services agency to form what Dubinsky (2006) would call organic and self-interested collaborations, we can see that it is precisely because of these collaborations that the Shower Project was possible at all. By situating this effort in the specifics of this small city, Kamloops, we can see that proximity, existing relationships, and tight social networks created the space to nurture this project from conception to completion as an example of transformational leadership. Not only has this project changed the ecosystem of street life in Kamloops by providing a much-needed facility that previously did not exist, but the entire ecology upon which such efforts can occur is impacted by the collaborations and relationships that made it possible. This alone is worthy of investigation.

Additionally, and something that I can bring to this discussion as an academic, is a critical examination of the flip side of this beautiful gesture of social consciousness and awareness. What I lack in tile-laying skills I can (at least in part) make up for in critical engagement with the political contexts that left this public amenities gap in the first place. There is a lack of government support for street-involved and vulnerable populations not just in this city but all over the province and country (Gaetz et al. 2013). It was the shock that people in their own community did not have access to safe, dignified shower facilities that inspired this group of steelworkers to pick up the cause. They saw a gap and did something to fill it. While there is no way to be anything but impressed by the commitment of the steelworkers to do something about this glaring hole in social services, that they did let government institutions off the hook. Street-involved and vulnerable people in Kamloops now have a safe place to take a shower and wash their clothes. This matter never needed to hit the political radar of the government institutions that should have been ensuring that there never was this gap in the first place. Thus we should take note of these showers, the people who built them, and those who now use them for what we can learn from the process of how they came to be, the kinds of collaborations and alliances needed to get this project started and finished, *and* for what researchers can contribute to the conversation aimed at ensuring that vulnerable populations in small-city settings like Kamloops are not left out of conversations about "quality of life."

The Scene—Opening Day

It was early morning on September 9, 2011. A large trailer was unloaded in the back alley behind the ASK Wellness Centre in Kamloops. The sun was already warm as the crew started setting up grills and tables. Before long people were chopping onions and brewing coffee. More and more people arrived and got to work. There was a lot of talking and laughing, but not a lot of directions being given. People just seemed to know what to do. This crew had clearly done this before.

Before long the alley was filled with the smell of pancakes and bacon. By 8:00 a.m. people were emerging from the neighbourhood to check things out. By mid-morning word (and smell) had spread and a crowd was gathering. Plates of fresh fruit and hot food were being served up. There was no end to the number of pancakes or cups of coffee on offer. As long as people were there, food was served. The chatter and laughing among the cooking crew never dulled as people worked around each other all morning long.

Just as the breakfast crowd started to thin, new coolers and boxes emerged from the trailer. As quickly as the breakfast spread was packed up, a lunch meal was laid out. Pancakes were replaced by burgers and the prep carried on. Before long another round of people started to turn up and the flurry of activity continued. There was so much food that when people had eaten enough they were offered "to go" containers to take some with them for later. Even dogs were not denied a burger or a hot dog. Off to the side of the action there was a large box of unopened new toys. Every child who passed by that day got one. No one was left out of this event. Everyone was greeted with a smile and warmth that was contagious.

Several people spent the entire day socializing, eating, and hanging out. The spirit of generosity was matched only by the sounds of laughter and the smells of delicious food.

Hanging on the building behind the grill station was a banner with the words "United Steelworkers Local 7619." This was a big day for members of the USW Local 7619. It marked the official opening of what has come to be called "The Shower Project." For three years leading up to this event, members of the steelworkers local had been coming and going from the basement of the ASK Wellness Centre. They came on their days off from the local mine site where they work. They gathered materials, skilled trades workers, and labourers in a coordinated effort to transform the basement of the centre into a "first-rate shower and laundry facility for the less fortunate."[2] The total estimated cost for material and labour for this project was upward of $70,000.[3] These funds were paid in cash and donated time by the United Steelworkers Local 7619.[4] The result is the conversion of an unfinished garage space without a foundation into a high-quality, wheelchair-accessible laundry and shower facility, with a finished doctor's office space as a bonus.

The first time I stood in the basement of the ASK Wellness Centre the construction of the project was nearing the final stretch. It was a cold late-fall morning and I was meeting one of the volunteers who was laying tile. The concrete room was chilly on this Saturday morning, the tile layers' day off from the mine. That is how this project came to completion—on cold (or hot), early (or late) days off. People gave their time and expertise to transform a raw, unfinished space into this incredibly appointed facility. One of the volunteers recalls, "In the beginning someone had an idea of trying to return a little dignity to the homeless in the sense of proposing what they called a plastic corner shower. That's all they said. We are going to build a plastic corner shower for the homeless so they can come and clean up and get some of that dignity returned to them. We sort of ran with it . . ." Indeed, they did. The facility that officially opened for business on September 9, 2011, is far more elaborate than a "corner shower stall."

Reflecting back on the journey, Bob Hughes, the Executive Director at ASK Wellness says, "I think that everyone expected it would be done in six weeks. Little did they know that the building was totally incapable of withstanding this level of heating and water supply." And yet somehow, three years later, a fully accessible tile shower, full toilet and vanity, on-demand hot water system, and top of the line washer and gas dryer were installed, operational, and open for business. We will return to the question of "how" in a moment, but first let's contemplate why. Why did this group of steelworkers from a local mine site decide to build a shower in Kamloops?

Showers and Food

As people gathered on this September day, very few knew what all the fuss was about. It was the smell of food, not the sound of running water that brought people to the back alley that day. As people learned what we were celebrating they wandered inside to take a look. Listening to people chat about the new facility, I heard comments like "Oh, awesome" and "Really? For us? We can just use this?" One gentleman stood in the shower room for a long time looking around before he said anything. He was paying careful attention to the details of the workmanship and the specifics of the facility. Finally he said, "Those guys out there built this for people like me to use? Incredible. I worked construction a long time and I know good work when I see it. This is good work." Pride in the workmanship of this facility is evident throughout the room. It is clearly stated on one wall of the shower where the USW logo has been carefully tiled onto the wall. This was important to the tile layer, who told me of how he designed the way that he cut and set the tiles so that people using the showers would know who the gift came from "long after we're gone from here."

As I toured the facility with a young woman she checked to see how the locks on the doors worked. After she was finished looking around she said, "So we can just go in there and lock the door? Alone?" Yes, you can. That was the whole point—dignity, privacy, safety, and quality. In the words of Bob Hughes:

> It has the highest end washer and dryer that you could buy. It has hot water on demand. These guys did not skimp and they I think did that not to be grandiose, but to say, "These people deserve that type of quality."

The matter of quality is a point of great pride for this group of steelworkers.

Members of the United Steelworkers Local 7619 have been actively putting on "cooks" since 2006. Around the time when copper prices were rising and profits were high at the mine, union members started looking for ways of "giving back" to the community.[5] A group started putting together cook events at various organizations throughout the community. Before long they had purchased a trailer and some equipment, and these events became regular fixtures in the area. Laura Drennan, an active participant in the ongoing regular cook events that the group puts on, says, "We only serve good food. If I wouldn't serve it to my family, we wouldn't serve it to anyone. Everyone deserves the best quality food. That's the point. Not just to feed people, but to offer quality food." This same sense of pride in quality is upheld in the shower facility. It is by way of these cooks that the Steelworkers and Bob Hughes and the ASK Wellness Centre first connected. Of these events Bob recalls:

> You would not believe the spread of food these cats put together. . . .
>
> As much bacon as you could possibly eat. Sausage after sausage and fruit and pancakes. They literally will make a meal that—it will be shocking what they put together. We knew them in that capacity where they just show up, sometimes as part of the United Way and sometimes just independently and say, "We can contribute," and they will show up with thirty guys and they will start cooking and they will do everything. They will bring coffee. They will bring tea. They will bring the juice and the water. Everything. They do this incredible meal. So we knew them in that capacity and we were always incredibly grateful.

There is something beautifully poetic about the relationship between this Shower Project and food. That it was the smell of bacon and burgers wafting through the neighbourhood that drew people to the shower facility brings this project fully back to where it started. Not only did this group first connect with ASK Wellness by way of cook events, but this shower started off with a meal. I will let Jim McCarthy explain:

How it got started was many years ago we were out cooking for the less fortunate. That's how we started the program.[6] . . . We did one at St. Vincent De Paul. We actually
did it for women and children. Most of the time when you
go to a lot of homeless events, a lot of women don't show
up so we made it special. The day before Mother's Day in
2008. . . . Some women said that some women wouldn't
show up because they believed they'd have to wash before
they came here.

It had never occurred to Jim, despite his years of working with homeless people and organizations that serve them, that people in Kamloops
would not have access to showers. More than that, he had no idea that
this would be such a barrier for some to access the kinds of things that he
and his colleagues were doing. In his words, "It never entered my head. So
we thought, nowhere to wash in Kamloops? So I approached the union.
Could we do a project to build showers and a washroom where people
could have dignity?"

And so what began as an effort to provide good food and a special
event for women and children turned into a three-year project to build
a free, accessible shower facility in a community. In essence, the Shower
Project started off as a "failed gift." Many of those for whom the Mother's
Day brunch was intended did not attend because they felt self-conscious
about not being able to get cleaned up before they came. The scare quotes
around the word "failed" reflect the caution (and hesitation) with which
I use the word here. I in no way mean to suggest that the efforts of the
steelworkers to present the Mother's Day event failed. Great care was given
to every detail. Laura Drennan recalls the special care packages that were
prepared for the women. Others speak with pride about the flowers and
tablecloths. Every effort was made to ensure that this event was a success,
and for those who attended, it likely was. I have chosen the word "failed"
to describe this gift not to suggest that the Mother's Day brunch was unwanted or unappreciated, as is sometimes the way the term is deployed in
the literature on gifting.[7] Instead I am following Venkatesan's (2011) lead
of tracking the social life and transformative quality of a gift that started
out not having the intended outcome that it was hoped it would achieve.

LISA COOKE

In the case of the Mother's Day Brunch, not everyone for whom the event was intended felt comfortable attending. From this perspective, by tracking the transformation of this gift, from "failed" to successful (for lack of better words) we are able to trace just how complex the impact of this act of giving is. What is transformed is not just the gift itself, from a meal to a shower, but the very terrain upon which such a gift can be given, and received, in this community.

The Ecosystem of Street-Life and the Ecology of Compassion

It is one thing to have an idea to build a shower facility for street-involved and vulnerable populations in a community. It is quite another to find a place to put it. You need an agency or facility willing to receive the gift, and its ongoing maintenance, cost, and logistical operations. You also need community support.

From the start, the steelworkers had the former. Executive Director Bob Hughes welcomed the idea and worked hard to ensure that ASK Wellness would be a willing partner in this project. From the inception of the idea to the completion of the project, Bob and his team welcomed the gift of the showers. Bob recalls some of the conversations he had at the time that the idea was proposed and some of the questions that were raised:

> Do you realize what that entails? Do you have a contract? What is it going to cost to operate this? Who is going to manage it? These questions were quite frankly irrelevant to me because it was an idea that you couldn't say no to. Not only because it was valuable to our clients, but when you have that kind of level of interest in committing to a non-profit organization or charitable organization, heaven forbid that you would put obstacles up over things that I would argue are manageable.

Members of the broader community, however, were less enthusiastic. The local business community in particular was resistant to the idea. Since their arrival in the neighbourhood in 2005, ASK Wellness had worked hard to nurture a working relationship with the North Shore Business Improvement Association. There had been some initial concern when ASK purchased the storefront facility in the heart of the neighbourhood. As they worked to change the demographic and economic composition of the area, the North Shore Business Improvement Association felt that ASK's mandate to provide harm reduction programming and services for street-involved and vulnerable populations was at odds with their goals of economic development and urban renewal. The reality was that ASK arrived in that particular neighbourhood when they did because there was an immediate need in that very spot. Bob Hughes describes the area in 2005 when they moved in:

> This corridor was a kind of epicentre for social discord in Kamloops. Eighteen women working in the sex trade in one morning driving to work. Count them—boom, boom, boom. Our outreach worker walking down Tranquille Road, picking up over 50 discarded intravenous needles and turning around and picking up 30 more on the same path. People openly trafficking in drugs on the street. It was a social disaster in this corridor.

ASK Wellness moved into the neighbourhood because those who needed them most were already there. The political challenge for Bob Hughes and the team at ASK was to nurture working relationships with their new neighbours that were mutually beneficial.

ASK stands for the Aids Society of Kamloops, and their focus has always been on harm reduction programming for vulnerable populations, in particular intravenous drug users and sex trade workers. As the organization has grown since its inception in 1992, so too has the range of services they provide. Bob Hughes describes their philosophy as follows: "We work with whatever walks through the door. Not whoever, but whatever. That includes anybody and anyone." As a result they now have a network of low-barrier housing units that they own or manage. They have street outreach workers connecting with bylaw officers around homeless camps and providing needle exchanges. They offer free condoms and needle exchange facilities at the office. There is a computer in the lobby that people can come in and use. They have a program specifically for women in the sex trade called the SHOP program. They offer transition skills and employment training programs. And now, thanks to the steelworkers from Local 7619, they have a free, accessible, safe shower and laundry facility.

Housing the showers, as Bob suggests, just made sense for ASK Wellness. As an organization committed to broadening the resources available in the ecosystem of street-involved life in Kamloops, the showers and laundry offer one more node in a network of services aimed at meeting people where they are and having them "walk away with more hope than they came in with."[8]

Local businesses did not all see it the same way. Despite the great strides made in collaborative relationship building between ASK and the North Shore Business Improvement Association, the Shower Project raised suspicion and concern. Interestingly, it was fears of sexual impropriety that were the initial concern. ASK's roots as an outreach service provider for the prevention of HIV and AIDS, and a hazy link drawn between these showers and gay bathhouses, sounded homophobic alarms among some. Not only would the shower potentially attract undesirable people to the area, the fear was that it would also attract morally questionable sexual practices.

At the time, then general manager of the North Shore Business Improvement Association Peter Mutrie stated that the building and installing of showers at ASK Wellness was "a fulcrum for this whole basket of social issues."[9] Much of the anthropological literature on gift giving and gift societies focuses on the holistic systems within which acts of giving and receiving are situated (Mauss 1967; Weinbren 2006).[10] Marcel Mauss (1967, 1) sums it up best when he writes:

> Each phenomenon contains all the threads of which the social fabric is composed. In these total social phenomena, as we propose to call them, all kinds of institutions find simultaneous expression: religions, legal, moral and economic.

While his focus was on what he called "archaic" societies and the moral and social economies through which acts of giving and receiving were used to negotiate social contracts, what is interesting about Mauss' conclusions for our purposes is this foundational notion that acts of giving and receiving offer incredible insights into the whole social complexes from which they emerge. The Shower Project is one such instance. As Peter Mutrie notes above, the shower exposed a host of social issues, relations, and tensions.

Urban gentrification, economic diversification and renewal, and community rebranding efforts shape the ways that energy, resources, and compassion flow in a neighbourhood (Wasserman and Clair 2011, 73). They attempt to alter the social and material ecosystems of urban spaces. In the case of Kamloops' North Shore, much effort has been invested in economic and aesthetic revival of the area. Concerns about the Shower Project flowed largely from these efforts. Just as some were trying to "clean up" the area, others wanted to build something that would attract those less desirable elements that gentrification efforts were attempting to displace. (And by "elements," I mean people, street-involved individuals living in various states of precarious vulnerabilities.) Through hard work and mutually respectful dialogue, Bob Hughes had negotiated a good working relationship with the business community in the area. The idea of the showers, however, struck a nerve.

Once again, Bob and the team at ASK had to navigate these frictions. In addition to their seemingly limitless commitment to advocating for the needs to their clients while maintaining healthy community relations, what Bob Hughes also knew was that just below the surface of this tension was a fundamental compatibility. Once homophobic worries about bathhouse escapades were quelled, Bob was able to secure an incredible amount of community support for the Shower Project.

Bob did what Wasserman and Clair (2011, 73) suggest by paying attention to the nuanced patterns of community making of everyone in an area. In so doing, what becomes apparent is that everyone has a lot more in common than they might first think. Wasserman and Clair (2011) suggest that street-involved communities often have attitudes and practices similar to those of people engaged directly in gentrification and renewal projects. So as tensions manifest on the surface between those advocating for services for low-income and street-involved people and those interested in growing local economic development opportunities, at their core, both groups often want the same things—safe communities where people can thrive. To his credit, Bob Hughes navigated complicated political waters, did not give up, and was able to reveal to the business community that everyone was on the same team, and that a free shower and laundry facility would serve everyone's collective goals.

By peeling each layer back, what becomes apparent is that the friction initially created by the Shower Project sparked only at the surface. Local business associations and owners were busy trying to "clean up" the area, and the idea of a facility that would attract homeless and street-involved people appeared to contradict this effort. This was the first point of contact. Goals hit, friction, spark.

The great thing about friction is that it is energy. Of this, anthropologist Anna Tsing (2005, 5) writes, "A wheel turns because of its encounter with the surface of the road; spinning in the air it goes nowhere. Rubbing two sticks together produces heat and light; one stick alone is just a stick." When things rub up against each other they produce heat, light, energy, friction, and out of this energy created, new configurations become possible. Tsing (2005, 4) continues, "Cultures are continually co-produced in the interactions I call 'friction': The awkward, unstable, and creative qualities of interconnection across difference." These moments of encounter, unequal and heterogeneous as they may be, can lead to new arrangements of culture and power, new flows of energy and resources, new collaborations. This is what happened with the Shower Project. Not only did the ecosystem of street life change with the addition of this resource, but the ecology of compassion shifted in a way that opened up new terrain for new kinds of relationships between ASK Wellness and those they serve and their neighbours in the business community.[11]

With the surface tensions burned off, what were left were compatible goals. A shower facility would actually offer street-involved individuals a chance to get cleaned up, literally. From there, perhaps meeting prospective landlords or employers would be possible. The ASK Wellness Centre was already firmly established in the neighbourhood. Combined, these arguments not only made quick work of oppositional pushback but also revealed that everyone had the same goals. As Wasserman and Clair (2011) suggest, in the nuanced spaces in between these arguments, everyone wants the same thing, and building a shower facility in a space that is already there and already serving the community does not contradict the efforts of those interested in neighbourhood gentrification and economic development.

The steelworker from Local 7619 did not intend to cause conflict. In Jim McCarthy's words, "We just build stuff. That's what we do." As Bob was negotiating the political terrain for the project, the steelworkers drew up plans and got to work building. Combined, these efforts were the momentum that kept the wheels turning. Each time the wheels came around, they hit the surface and sparked something. When they did, Bob Hughes was there to tend to the sparks. Eventually the surface tensions burned off, and what started to spark was community support and involvement. Momentum for the project grew and more people became involved. Word spread and local business donated materials. As the need for specific tradespeople came up, they were recruited from the mine site.[12] A new configuration emerged out of the friction.

When the Shower Project opened on September 9, 2011, it did so with unified support from the North Shore Business Improvement Association and the community. The transformative quality of the gift of the Showers Project is tremendous. The steelworkers did not give up. They just built it. Bob Hughes and the team at ASK were able to pave the way for that. The material change to the space in the basement of ASK, stripping the structure to its raw core and then building it up again, is a fitting metaphor for the way this project was able to pull back the surface layers of privilege and prejudices to reveal a common desire. It turns out that both sides were never that far apart, and it took a group of steelworkers building a shower to unravel and ease existing tensions.

Marcel Mauss (1967) suggests that we could look at acts of giving for what they reveal about an entire social complex, for each act holds in and through it every thread of social fabric. This means that they can, at times, also change that fabric. The showers are that kind of gift. Bob Hughes writes in a letter of thanks to the United Steelworkers, "The impact of these facilities has been profound. . . . On behalf of the ASK Wellness Centre and the community as a whole, thank you for being part of the transformation of the entire social fabric of Kamloops."

There is a safe place to shower and do laundry. There is a place where men and women can have privacy and dignity. The value of this alone cannot be overstated. Bob Hughes continues:

The impact of these facilities has been profound. Women and men who haven't bathed in several days and who are wearing dirty clothes enter our facility having heard from agencies and businesses throughout the community that this service exists, leave in clean clothes, freshly shaven and groomed, and for once in a long period of time, a sense of dignity that only clean clothes and shower can provide.

Carman, the coordinator of the SHOP Program at ASK that offers support for sex-trade workers in the community recalls:

> During the winter season I had a young lady who came in every few days; I know she was living in someone's basement with no running water. It was cold and she would take these long showers, so long that we would be knocking on the door to make sure she was ok. All she wanted was to sit down under the warmth of the water and be out of the cold for a while . . . The donation and time given by the steelworkers is more than just a washer and drying or a shower. It's about restoring dignity in a person's life . . . The shower built by the steelworkers has been an incredible blessing to our SHOP program participants.

One of the users of the showers states:

> I am homeless and looking for a place to rent. I have been using the shower and laundry at the ASK Wellness in the North Shore until I find shelter and it has been totally awesome.

Another says:

> I think that it is very nice of people to help the homeless so they can be clean and have clean clothes too. I have used the laundry facility and I was so grateful they had everything I needed. I again I would like to say thank you.

Everyone involved in the Shower Project should be very proud of the contribution that this gift makes to peoples' lives. The showers and laundry provide a much-needed resource in the ecosystem of urban street life in Kamloops. But the transformative power of the Shower Project is more than that. As Bob Hughes suggests above, it has changed the social fabric, the ecology, of giving and compassion in Kamloops. This project came up against community pushback and logistical complications that could have ended it. Instead, together ASK Wellness and the steelworkers persistently moved forward, and in so doing changed the terrain upon which giving and compassion can occur in this community. This is the difference a shower can make.

How Did They Do It?

It is one thing to have a great idea. It is another still to find a host organization willing to accept a gift of this magnitude. It is quite another to actually get the job done, especially by volunteers. So how does a group pull something like this off? I have asked this question many times. "What does it take to get a culture of giving like this going and then keep it going?" I have asked people flipping burgers at cooks, members of the Union Executive, those involved in the construction of the showers, and union members at other events. Without fail, every one of them has said "leadership." It takes strong, committed leadership. Given this resounding response, and that leadership is one the focus points of this collection, it is worth fleshing this out a bit. To that end, I'll change my question: "What does strong leadership in this context look like?" The Shower Project offers a fascinating glimpse at the complexity of the question of leadership, and the levels of leadership and networks of relations needed to inspire, sustain, and manage large-scale giving practices.

As mentioned earlier, the Shower Project was not the first act of giving that the steelworkers from Local 7619 had engaged in. Rather, it flowed out of an existing culture of giving within the local. They had already been engaging in the cooks for a few years and were well known in the non-profit organization world for these impressive spreads. They were also well known within the United Steelworkers as a local setting with an impressive standard for collective giving. Members of the local tell with pride the story of when they took their trailer and grills to a district meeting in Saskatoon and put on a cook event at the Métis Friendship Centre there. They served 500 meals that day and demonstrated through the practice of giving what other locals could do in their own communities. It is reported that as a result of this cook in Saskatoon, several locals returned home and purchased the needed equipment to start their own cook programs. As a tribute to their reputation as leaders-by-example of community-based generosity, several district managers in the United Steelworkers turned up to applaud Local 7619's efforts at Shower Project's opening event.

Getting and keeping this kind of culture of giving within any group or organization requires internal leadership that inspires active participation from members. When asked, "What does it take to start and keep doing this?" one of the research participants responded, "It helps when you have someone that's really hard to say no to." A core group of individuals has congealed around these cook events to create a kind of central hub for giving activities, and the energy around the practices of giving is so contagious that it really is hard to say no to participating. This core group that attends to the logistics and organizes the events welcomes participation from anyone wanting to chip in.

The energy and commitment of this group cannot be overstated. Having spoken with each of them on several occasions I can say that their dedication is uncompromised. One member of group, Laura Drennan, recalls that when she walks down the street in Kamloops now people do not ask her for spare change but rather ask when the next cook will be. Just like the showers, these meals are part of the ecosystem of street life in Kamloops.

The other thing people who participate in these events talk about eloquently and without hesitation is the sense of personal satisfaction that comes from active giving practices. Of what she gets out of her involvement in the cooks, Laura Drennan says:

> For me it's a recharge of my battery. Recharge. I'm a much better mother, parent, friend after I've experienced doing the cook . . . When we don't have a cook for a month or two, I'm calling the Jims and saying "where are we going next."

I really need to get out there and do it again. I need to re-charge the battery, it's getting low.

One of the "Jims" Laura is referring to is Jim McCarthy, whom we have heard from throughout this story. The other is Jim McLean. McLean's involvement in the cooks is key. He has experience working as a caterer and is often the architect behind coordinating the volumes of quality food that the crew produces. Of why he does this on his time off, McLean says:

> I feel compelled to. I've recognized how fortunate I've been and I also know how close I've been to being where these people are . . . It would be a shame if we didn't do something to give back. And do it in a way that lets people know that they are respected. To give them a little bit of dignity. When we feed people we don't just feed them, we treat them with respect and that's every bit as important as the food as far as I'm concerned.

As momentum around the cook events grows, the group has an eye on succession planning. They realize that it is important to get and keep younger members of the local involved in these events if the culture of giving is to continue over the long term. To this end they are sure to advertise events and openly share tales from the front lines of cooks. One of the members is always present with his camera documenting the events and creating beautiful slideshows to share with members at the job site. In Laura's words at the Shower Project opening, "We are just collecting people along the way as well, to give. As can see behind me, there's about 20 individuals here we've exponentially collected. Started out with I think six of us and every time it gets bigger."

But a core of individuals willing to continuously beat the drums of giving projects is not enough to sustain large-scale giving practices from an organization the size of an entire union local. Local 7619 of the United Steelworkers represents approximately 1,100 members. Not all participate in every event, but everyone's dues go to paying for them. That means that there is a key need for bureaucratic leadership from within the local to ensure that there is collective support for the projects. This requires a delicate negotiation between the needs of the entire membership as a formal social network, the energy and enthusiasm of those wanting to participate in giving projects, and the management of community requests for help.

On the matter of the responsibility of the local to represent the needs of all members, Local 7619 President Richard Boyce says that with every proposed giving project the group asks, "Will this grow the union, make it stronger?" Projects cannot distract from the needs of the membership or the executive's responsibility for those needs, and they need to be in keeping with the ideological value base of the union itself. Boyce also suggests that the leadership style needed from a bureaucratic end needs to be informal and open. When you are asking people to give their own time and money, it cannot come as a directive. Instead, the leadership role is to nurture a culture of giving whereby people feel included and inspired to give.

Jim McCarthy, a member of both the core group of active givers and the local executive, says of the spirit behind the culture of giving in the local:

> It was a real group effort, but the big one is the funding from our local 7619. This is our money. This is our money that we spend on dues. That we have now spent on a project in the community. Sometimes you get bad press for being a union member . . . but all we do is if you are on a mine site or a job site, your goal is to make sure people are looked after. That's our goal and it goes right back down to the base. That's what you are trying to do. That's no different than what we are doing here. Our goal is to extend caring for people within the job site as well as off the job site within our communities.

Jim is hitting on a very important aspect of leadership here. It is by way of the careful negotiation between the needs and responsibilities to members and those of the broader community that the specific culture of giving, nurtured and thriving among the steelworkers, works. I would also argue that this fundamental ideological compatibility gives this delicate relationship a solid foundation upon which to stand. By growing a culture of giving out of the same principles of the labour movement that insist that the collective needs to look out for each individual, a climate of support is nurtured.[13] Without this support, this vibrant culture of giving would dissolve. At the opening of the Shower Project, Jim McCarthy suggested as he pointed toward the crews serving food and laughing, "This is an actual union meeting you know, whichever way you want to look at it."

The steelworkers from Local 7619 have the well-earned reputation now for being a crew that gets thing done. As a result, they field requests from organizations for contributions. Managing this aspect of the culture of giving within the local requires another level of leadership. Each request needs to be vetted through the membership and the executive. Questions need to be asked of it. Can the group commit to it? Will it grow the union? Is it compatible with the ideological principles that guide that practice of giving? And is there a group willing to take the lead on it? Once the group decides on a project, as we have seen with the Shower Project, there is little that can stop them. The following diagram attempts to capture the reciprocal relationships between formal, informal, and hybrid networks of relations required to usher a project such as this one from idea to completion. There is a need for formalized structural networks. At the same time, these showers would never have been built were it not for the sustained efforts of individuals within the steelworkers and ASK Wellness who kept the project going. I have included municipal, provincial, and federal levels of government as formal networks not because of any direct contribution made in the building of the shower facility but rather because of how the efforts of the United Steelworkers and ASK Wellness to address the need in the community serve, in many ways, to let these formal structures off the hook. The Formal/Informal Hybrid networks identified here reflect the ways that participants in the project offer their time, resources, and effort as both members of formal groups/networks and as individual community members. Informal networks circulate throughout this project—from those who happen into ASK Wellness and use the shower to members of the broader community of Kamloops.

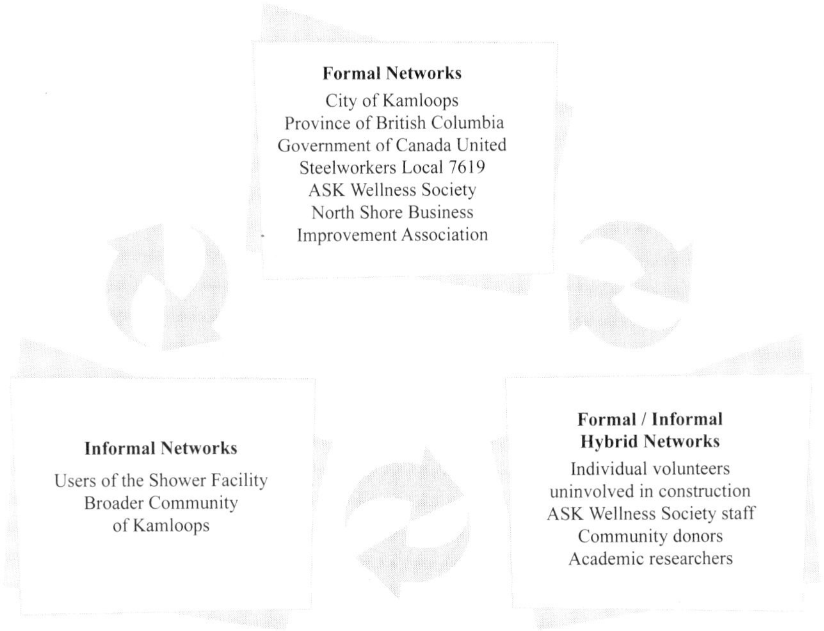

Formal Networks
City of Kamloops
Province of British Columbia
Government of Canada United
Steelworkers Local 7619
ASK Wellness Society
North Shore Business
Improvement Association

Informal Networks
Users of the Shower Facility
Broader Community
of Kamloops

**Formal / Informal
Hybrid Networks**
Individual volunteers
uninvolved in construction
ASK Wellness Society staff
Community donors
Academic researchers

FIGURE 2.2. Shower Project Network by Lisa Cooke. Design by Moneca Jantzen, Daily Designz.

On to the Next Project . . .

A colleague and I hosted a "research cabaret" event at our university in honour of the Shower Project. We invited all those involved in the project to attend. After an inspiring conversation about this project, the crew started talking about their next appointment. They were heading down to another non-profit organization in Kamloops to take some measurements and make a work plan. When asked what they were talking about, one replied, "We thought that we'd take advantage of this opportunity that we're all together in town to go check out our next project. We're installing an industrial dishwasher at a non-profit downtown." And just like that, they were off. They did not bask too long in the successes of the Shower Project (even as my colleague and I were trying hard to honour them) before they were off and at it again with the next one. Jim McCarthy had foreshadowed this at the opening of the Showers when he said:

> Now for me and the Steelworkers all I see is to look for the next project. How can we enhance people's lives? I don't know what that will be but I know we will be looking for one. As well as doing the monthly meals that we do. We will be doing other things and I don't know where that's going to go from here.

What is unique about this kind of giving practice is that there is a notable distance between the giving and the receiving. Once the project is completed, the steelworkers move on. The gift is given. That leaves the receiver of the gift to accept, manage, operate, and maintain it. This requires another level of leadership—one open to taking on the front-line operational end of things once the gift has been given.

It also requires an openness to the organic ebbs and flows that come from having a project like this constructed by volunteers on volunteer time. Coordinating the efforts of specific tradespeople with work schedules at the mine site meant that there were stretches of time when little was happening in the basement at ASK. Bob knew that the door needed to be open to having people come and go when they could and that patience was key. So in addition to the political prowess needed to negotiate complicated political terrains and convince reluctant stakeholders that this project was both a good idea and feasible, Bob and the team at ASK Wellness needed gracious patience. Of this Bob says:

> You never put the squeeze on volunteers. You can't. It's unethical and it's not fair. You really don't have a level of accountability on volunteers where you can say, "Where were you? You didn't show up?" I said to Jim, "Finish it whenever you can. No pressure on our end."

Just as the steelworkers are guided by an ideological mooring that grounds the culture of giving within the local, the leadership at ASK Wellness demonstrates the same philosophical consistency that allows for a culture of giving to occur organically. This philosophical anchor in his style of leadership meant that Bob Hughes was never preoccupied with measurable outcomes. As a researcher, I've found this project so ethnographically rich and full of promise that I must confess to a persistent wish to glean glowing success stories from it. I have been looking for the magical story of an individual who as a result of being able to wash his or her clothes and take a shower was able to secure permanent housing and get a job. The reality is that these outcomes are not measurable. This kind of outcome is impossible to track in real (or ethnographic) time. There is no direct cause-and-effect line between any two points on the spectrum of street-involved life. Bob Hughes knows this much better than I and reminds me of it when he says (in response to my pressing for "the magical story"):

> In my experience, and my opinion—is to never look for an outcome. In the same way that we can't take responsibility for people's mistakes and failures, we don't get to take credit for their successes.

Just as the steelworkers did not stick around to bask in the glow of their success and praise for their efforts, Bob reminds me that some things are not measurable, nor are they ours to measure. What matters is that anyone who needs or wants one can take a hot shower in a safe space. They can wash their clothes if they want. What they do with that is neither ours to own nor to claim. This is such a well-placed caution and reminder, particularly for those of us concerned with conclusions and tidy "findings." It is also a powerful ideological current that shapes the very leadership style that made this project possible at all. Had Bob been overly focused on outcomes and measurable deliverables, the showers would likely never have been built. There were too many sound arguments made against it. By shifting the focus away from the impacts of the showers and instead placing his faith in the spirit of the thing, Bob nurtured a space (political, logistical, and physical) that allowed for the steelworkers to create and give this beautiful gift.

Research, Leadership, and Learning

While Bob Hughes may have reminded me that my ethnographic gaze intent on finding clear outcomes was misplaced, there is an important role for research in this story. Each of the chapters in this collection reflects on how our specific research projects and processes are embedded in unique ways to the very things that we seek to examine. Taking this question further, we need to ask what academic research specifically contributes to the initiatives we are examining. My tape recorder and notepad did little to help the steelworker build the showers. But if we as researchers are to explore and write about the kinds of things that we are examining here—theatre productions with street-involved populations, volunteer-run adult learning programs, community gardens and free produce, student engagement and service learning, community action against homelessness, and building showers—our doing so needs to accomplish something more than bolstering individual academic careers. The research process needs to be part of a collaborative dialogue that seeks to do something about the things that we write about. Dubinsky (2006) notes that several factors come together in Kamloops as a small city to create the social and geographical proximities needed to nurture a strong culture of participation (see Chapter 7: Conclusion for a cumulative assessment of these features). Based on Dubinsky's (2006) framework for types of collaborations, the central relationship in this story is the one between the steelworkers and ASK Wellness. This collaboration is at once organic and self-interested. Emergent conditions around the steelworkers cook events forged a relationship with ASK that evolved to one that allowed them to work together toward a specific self-interested goal. But what kind of collaborative relationship does research have with this project? It is self-interested in that my career will be served by this study and any presentations or publications that emerge from it. That does little for anyone else. In the spirit of the very thing I examine, the culture of giving out of which these showers were build, there needs to be more to my contribution than my making tenure and promotion.

This goes for all of us presenting our work in this collection. As representatives of the university working to nurture productive and mutually beneficial relationships between our institution and the community in which we live and work, we need to be accountable for what we do. The kinds of questions we ask, the ways we seek out answers, and what we do with what we find needs to contribute something to the wider conversation about life in our city. Montgomery's (2013) assertion that what is needed in "city life" is attention to "systems of building, planning, and thinking" (62) that work either against or toward nurturing urban experiences of joy and belonging offers good counsel here. We cannot just study hardship and misery. Rather, we need to pay attention to experiences and relationships, in all of their complexities, for what they say about the lived realities of "quality of life" in our cities.

To that end, what I lack in tile laying skills I can make up for in critically engaged scholarship that takes up the matter of why there was no accessible, free, safe shower facility in Kamloops until the steelworkers built one. I can also insist that the gift of this facility by the steelworkers should not let government institutions off the hook for not identifying or doing anything about this gap. The flip side of the incredible efforts of the steelworkers is that governments and public sector institutions are granted a pass on this particular issue. Not only did they never need to identify the gap in the first place, but now that it is filled, they can continue to ignore the conditions that created it. The steelworkers did not take on this project as a political stance. They "just build stuff," as McCartney says. I don't build stuff, and I can make this political. The steelworkers had the social capital to pull this project off. I have the cultural capital to ensure that their efforts are acknowledged while still shedding light on the magnitude of the neglect on the part of government institutions such that people in this city did not have access to a safe, clean, free, accessible shower facility; and so I must. If we strive for a "happy city" and take Montgomery's (2013) goals to heart, the baseline needs to be that every citizen's basic needs for safety and well-being are met. The steelworkers saw this and did something about it. ASK Wellness works at this every day. Both offer examples of leadership through which I have learned much about my role and responsibility as a researcher to this conversation.

NOTES

I would like to thank all those who shared their time with me over the past four years that I have been involved in this project. I have learned much from each of you. I would also like to thank Dr. Will Garrett-Petts for first telling me the story of the showers and for his continued support of this research. This work has been financially supported in part through a SSHRC CURA grant and by Thompson Rivers University research funds.

1   Credit for this title belongs to Laura Drennan, a member of United Steelworkers Local 7619.

2   Interview with the author, November 2010.

3   General consensus among those interviewed have the total cost of the project around $70,000.

4   In addition to the investment made by steelworkers, ASK Wellness Centre invested approximately $15,000 in the construction costs of the project (Personal communication, Bob Hughes, Executive Director of ASK Wellness Centre).

5   Interview with the author, September 9, 2011.

6   The "program" that Jim is referring to here is the same one described above.

7   Margaret Rucker et al. (1992) use the term "failed gift" when discussing unwanted gifts given and how people dispose of them. While in the context of their study this use of the term is fitting, I am not using the term the same way here.

8   Bob Hughes, personal communication.

9   Peter Mutrie is cited in Bass (2008).

10   Others have critiqued Mauss' theory of the gift as being fundamentally reciprocal. Jacques Derrida (1992), for example, suggests that once a social contract of reciprocity is engaged by way of a gift it is no longer a gift at all. Rather, a gift must be free of all social obligations. In the case of the Shower Project, as will be explored throughout this chapter, I argue with Mauss that in this case there is a degree of reciprocity involved, as the steelworkers all talk about how much they get out of participating in these giving events. So while they think of them as "gifts" they also appreciate what they receive in return. Erica Bornstein (2009) offers a lovely reflection on the notion of Derrida's "free gift" in India for those looking for an ethnographic example of the opposite of what I am saying here.

11   Borrowing from several sources, I am conceptualizing ecosystems here as networks of relations that form communities that interact in the same environment. Ecology encompasses the systems and dynamics of the relationships between and within these networks (Snyder 1995; Salen 2008; Wasserman and Clair 2011).

12   The only trades work that the steelworkers needed to contract out in this project was the electrical work. Everyone else, from gas fitters, tile layers, plumbers, and labourers, were recruited from the mine site.

LISA COOKE

13   Weinbren (2006) offers an interesting social history of the relationship between friendly societies, the Good Samaritan, and the labour movement in the UK. Many of the narratives of giving collecting throughout this research reflect many of the same kinds of ideological threads as Weinbren explores, namely an acute awareness of the importance of the rights of the collective and the responsibilities of the individual to that collective.

References

Bass, D. 2008. "ASK and Showers Are OK's." *Kamloops This Week*. April 28. http://www.kamloopsthisweek.com/ask-and-showers-are-okd/.

Bornstein, E. 2009. "The Impulse of Philanthropy." *Cultural Anthropology* 24 (4): 622–51.

Derrida, J. 1992. *Given Time: I. Counterfeit Money*. Chicago: University of Chicago Press.

Dubinsky, L. 2006. "In Praise of Small Cities: Cultural Life in Kamloops, BC." *Canadian Journal of Communication* 21:85–106.

Gaetz, S., J. Donaldson, T. Richter, and T. Gulliver. 2013. The State of Homelessness in Canada: The Homeless Hub Research Paper. http://www.wellesleyinstitute.com/wp-content/uploads/2013/06/SOHC2103.pdf.

Mauss, M. 1967. *The Gift: Forms and Functions of Exchange in Archaic Societies*. Translated by I. Gunnison. New York: Norton.

Montgomery, C. 2013. *Happy City: Transforming our Lives through Urban Design*. New York: Penguin Random House.

Rucker, M., T. Balch, F. Higham, and K. Schenter. 1992. "Thanks But No Thanks: Rejection, Possession and Disposition of the Failed Gift (Abstract)." *NA—Advances in Consumer Research* 19:488. http://acrwebsite.org/volumes/7346/volumes/v19/NA-19.

Salen, K. 2008. "The Ecology of Gaming." In *The Ecology of Games: Connecting Youth, Games, and Learning*, edited by K. Salen, 1–20. The John D. and Catherine T. MacArthur Foundation Series on Digital Media and Learning. Cambridge, MA: MIT Press.

Snyder, G. 1995. *A Place in Space*. Berkeley, CA: Counterpoint.

Tsing, A. 2005. *Friction: An Ethnography of Global Connection*. Princeton, NJ: Princeton University Press.

Venkatesan, S. 2011. "The Social Life of a 'Free' Gift." *American Ethnologist* 38 (1): 47–57. doi:10.1111/j.1548-1425.2010.01291.x.

Wasserman, J. A., and J. M. Clair. 2011. "Housing Patterns of Homeless People: The Ecology of the Street in the Era of Urban Renewal." *Journal of Contemporary Ethnography* 40 (1): 71–101. doi:10.1177/0891241610388417.

Weinbren, D. 2006. "The Good Samaritan, Friendly Societies and the Gift Economy." *Social History* 31 (3): 319–36.

No Straight Lines: Using Creativity as a Method to Fight Homelessness

Dawn Farough

Prologue

The following chapter was written in the summer of 2013. It is based on interviews with a local group of academics, community workers, and artist/activists called No Straight Lines (NSL) and theatre companies dedicated to working with and telling the stories of disadvantaged and marginalized people. The chapter focuses on the initial planning stages of a community-engaged theatre and research project involving NSL in collaboration with homeless and marginally housed individuals. This planning stage was prior to the recruitment of the homeless actors and writers; rehearsals had not yet commenced. Figure 3.2 (The Planning Stage) represents the memberships and social networks involved in this stage of the project. During the peer-review process for this chapter, the NSL project took shape and social networks expanded as individuals and groups entered the succeeding phases of the project. Figure 3.3 (Reflections from the Field: Inside the Rehearsal Room) and Figure 3.4 (Outside the Rehearsal Hall), illustrate the numerous individuals and groups who, at various times, contributed

FIGURE 3.1. "Home/Less/Mess," Bonnie McLean, illustrator, *No Straight Lines Presents: Home/Less/Mess bringing stories of homelessness out of the dark.* Production announcement courtesy of Bonnie McLean.

to this local initiative. I have attached an Epilogue in order to update the reader on the rehearsal and performance phases of the project.

Introduction

Despite public stereotypes about the homeless, those who find themselves without an address and often without any shelter come from many different backgrounds and have taken a variety of paths to homelessness. Solutions to homelessness are also varied. The belief that many paths "with very different corners and turns to navigate" (Genshorek 2013) lead out of homelessness has inspired the name for a group of community workers, academics, and activists—No Straight Lines (NSL). NSL is currently designing a very ambitious and somewhat unconventional method of tackling homelessness in the small city of Kamloops, British Columbia. Using participatory research, the group plans to work with a group of homeless and marginally housed individuals who will create and then perform a play about their lives and their experiences of homelessness. This chapter focuses on the nature of and possibilities for collaboration between academics (representing the disciplines of theatre, literature, and sociology), community workers, and artist/activists. Three of Dubinsky's (2006) frameworks for collaboration (self-interested, mimetic, and normative) are discussed. Interviews with members of NSL highlight the diverse views of group members regarding the strengths, weaknesses, and challenges of their project. How will group members handle the process of collaborative research, differing opinions regarding personal and group goals for the project, possible power struggles, and varying definitions of social justice? Since one of the frameworks of collaboration is mimetic in nature, I will also draw upon existing literature in theatrical studies and the social sciences in order to ask what this group can learn from previous theatrical projects involving marginalized community members.

Background

NSL is one of several initiatives on homelessness resulting from a partnership between the United Way, Thompson Rivers University (TRU), and the Kamloops Homelessness Action Plan (HAP). This rather eclectic group, which began to meet on a regular basis in December 2012, consists of representatives from the Elizabeth Fry Society, the City of Kamloops, ASK Wellness Centre, the United Way, HAP, TRU faculty from Theatre, English, and Sociology; the Canadian Mental Health Association, White Buffalo Aboriginal Health Centre, Jubilee Urban Ministry Partners, and the Kamloops Arts Council. The group is very open and welcomes any interested individual from the community. Therefore, new individuals are constantly joining the project. My relationship to this project is as a member of NSL and a sociologist at TRU.

The ultimate goal for the group, a collaborative approach culminating in a live performance of a play written by and starring individuals who have experienced homelessness, was on the table right from the beginning. NSL has met on a regular basis to determine how to make that

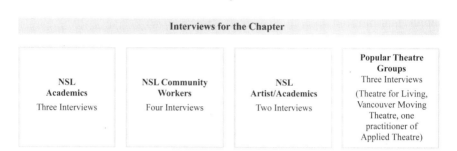

The Planning Stage (prior to recruitment of the homeless writer/actors)

The *No Straight Lines* Development Team (NSL)

The United Way, Thompson Rivers University (TRU), City of Kamloops

Kamloops Homeless Action Plan (HAP), Elizabeth Fry, ASK Wellness Society

Kamloops Art Council, JUMP, Interior Community Services

White Buffalo Metis & Aboriginal Health Society, Community Volunteer

Interviews for the Chapter

NSL Academics	NSL Community Workers	NSL Artist/Academics	Popular Theatre Groups
Three Interviews	Four Interviews	Two Interviews	Three Interviews (Theatre for Living, Vancouver Moving Theatre, one practitioner of Applied Theatre)

FIGURE 3.2. Theatre Project Network 1 by Dawn Farough. Design by Moneca Jantzen, Daily Designz.

goal happen. As one might imagine, the group has a never-ending list of practicalities and logistics to sort out: appropriate spaces for workshop, rehearsal, and performance spaces; gaining support from local agencies in order to recruit from the homeless population; preparing for mental health contingencies and access to food, transportation, and daycare; budgeting for art supplies, props, costumes, and musical instruments; and addressing funding, media, and marketing. However, we have also tried to work out the academic, artistic, and "stakeholder" kinds of questions as to why we are involved and what we hope to accomplish.

Many of our discussions have considered power imbalances. We know that we have various agendas, that most of us have very different (and more privileged) backgrounds from those we expect to "carry" this project, and that the homeless will need (and should expect) to get a great deal out of this endeavour. And so, we have asked some difficult questions: "How can we balance our own agendas with the needs of the participants?" "How can we show leadership without being overbearing, and what does leadership mean in a collaborative process?" "How can we remove intimidation every step of the way and work together in a trusting environment?" "How can we be sensitive to individuals who come from very different backgrounds from our own?" "How can we empower homeless individuals?" Some members of the group have worked on collaborative projects before and know the difficulties of "getting along" and working toward consensus on shared goals and projects. Others know the "literature" on collaborative projects from theatre studies or the social sciences. Within this literature, there are some helpful techniques that will be discussed later in this paper.

Self-Interested and Normative Collaboration

For the academics in the group, the necessity of asking "What is unique about this project?" is not just academic. Our participation does include elements of self-interest. We require grant money and we have scholarly activity and research elements of our jobs that need to be satisfied. Therefore, we need to prove that we will be conducting research that is in some way "unique" and contributes to the knowledge creation of our various disciplines of theatre, literature, and sociology. Academic collaboration is not easy, and it can take one of three forms: multidisciplinary, interdisciplinary, and transdisciplinary.[1] During this planning stage, it is not clear which form our collaboration will take.[2] Disciplines have their own built-in vocabularies, concepts, theories, and methods. Each field has an "epistemological style"—a distinctive approach to producing and evaluating knowledge (Lamont 2009). In addition, "epistemic or disciplinary cultures" (Cetina in Lunde, Heggen, and Strand 2012), referring to ways of interacting based on education, training, and work environment, develop in conjunction with epistemological styles. Power relations are an important component of disciplinary cultures where hierarchies of academic prestige determine allocation of important economic resources. In their examination of a large research project involving academics from a range of disciplines and faculties (natural sciences, social sciences, and humanities) as well as clinicians, Lunde, Heggen, and Strand (2012) analyze conflicts and misunderstandings that led to profound weaknesses in the academic collaboration. These included: research questions not agreed upon and therefore defined differently by various groups; qualitative researchers felt disempowered by quantitative researchers and often tried to "mobilize 'moral power'" (207); clinicians favoured applied knowledge and therefore were unable or refused to communicate with academics who valued theory and methods, while those in natural sciences dedicated to the relationship between hypothesis and method had little in common with humanities folks who emphasized the importance of "verbal clarity, openness, and level of verbal reflection" (202). Perhaps most importantly, no obvious leaders emerged since no one felt that they could or should lead the project.

University ethics boards have become an institutional reality for most academic researchers, and they have the power to redirect social research. Van Den Hoonaard (2011) argues that ethics boards have a positivist bias built into their expectations and judgments because they were originally structured for biomedical research. Therefore, disciplines with epistemic styles which do not fit neatly into the positivist research model often move toward methods of data collection promoted by the ethics boards. In sociology and anthropology, for example, the methodologies of participant observation and fieldwork are in decline while proposals using interviews and focus groups are rapidly increasing. Van Den Hoonaard (2011) notes that these methods are favoured because they have "a clear beginning and an end, the interview can be encapsulated by an interview guide or protocol" (267, 268). One of the surprises awaiting the NSL academics was the extent to which the normative requirements for research as ascertained by the TRU Ethics Committee would create a kind of artificial separation within the overall project. The sociological research was subject to much more rigorous standards than the theatre component. To clarify, the homeless / recently housed participants do not need to formally consent in order to participate in theatre rehearsals or the play itself, but they do need to fill out consent forms and be warned about issues of anonymity and confidentiality when formally interviewed by the research team about their experiences in the collaborative rehearsal process. The ethics committee is not concerned with how the homeless / recently housed are recruited for the purposes of the "artistic" side of the research, but it is concerned about recruitment for the purposes of ethnographic observation

DAWN FAROUGH

and formal interviewing. Since the same participants are involved, this has left members of the research team scratching their heads as to how to comply. A letter of instruction from the ethics committee states: "This application would be far easier for the PI [Principal investigator] and for the REB [Research Ethics Board] to manage if it was focused only on the research component instead of being interwoven with the theatre section." Apparently, "art" is not research and "artists" are not researchers. Therefore the theatre faculty can decide for themselves how to proceed "ethically," without bureaucratic guidance or interference.

One of the questions asked of the NSL members was "Do you consider yourself a volunteer?" "Why or why not?" Because so much of the collaboration is based at least partially on self-interest, most NSL members answered "no" to this question. For example, one of the community workers stated: "Not myself, no. Luckily we do have that piece where I'm paid to follow through, carved out. Several hours a month out of my paid position to keep with this project." In a similar vein, an academic member told me: "I look better on paper when I've done this and I feel like projects like this are expected of me from my institution because they pay me for those three months that I don't have to come in every day. So I feel like it's a lovely way to pay back to keep working for my professional activities." The artists/activists were divided on this question. One said: "Well I'm not interested in getting paid. I am doing this. As I understand, volunteerism is a service that comes with some personal sacrifice. So yes, service and sacrifice are two activities that human beings should have in their lives." However, another felt that the concept of volunteerism reeked of "charity" and a "one-way street" and therefore didn't capture her reasons for participating in the project: "But from my own personal side of it, it's like I'm glad that I get to see something in action and see how it works because I will learn from it. So for me personally, it's an educational experience. It's something that I'm going to get something out of, no matter what happens."

It would be incorrect, however, to view self-interested collaboration as always connected to job requirements. When asked about their personal goals for the project, some members of NSL linked their self-interest with giving back to the community or a sense of the need for social justice or social change. As one member declared:

Number one, I think that theatre has the potential to change lives. I think that we always have the potential to do good, and I don't think that there's enough of that. . . . As a society, our society of theatre can change lives for the better and I wanted to be involved in a process like that. Also, and quite intimately, two years before I got this job I was receiving Christmas hampers from our local good will agency because I was in school and we were very poor. I got handouts from our community and it was shaming. It felt horrible at the moment, but I believe in paying it forward so I'm in a position now, where I can pay it forward.

Mimetic Collaboration

Dubinsky (2006) defines mimetic collaboration as that based on emulation: the "guiding maxim 'if it worked there, it will work here'" (9). Canada has a history of collective and alternative theatre. The work of theatres such as Headlines Theatre in Vancouver, as well as Passe Muraille, Mixed Theatre, and Theatrefront in Toronto, was known to many of the original members of NSL. For over 35 years, David Diamond and his company, Headlines Theatre in Vancouver (now called Theatre for Living), have produced plays with various community groups on issues such as gang violence, substance abuse, residential schools, refugees, prison life, and homelessness. Diamond's work has been cited as a model for the NSL project. Ironically, the very first play by Headlines Theatre (in 1981) dealt with the shortage of affordable housing in Vancouver.

When discussing the uniqueness of the project, NSL members agree that this project is unusual as an approach to homelessness because, typically, academic research on poverty and the homeless, as well as public policy approaches to rectify the social issue or "problem" of homelessness, have very little to do with creativity. Quantitative methodologies and policy papers rule the day. The project is also unusual in that it will take place in a small city, whereas similar theatre productions have been located in large cities such as Vancouver or Toronto. What NSL proposes to copy or emulate is the use of theatre and collaborative techniques to empower members of disadvantaged community groups and draw public attention to their situation and experiences.

In looking at relevant literature, in both theatrical studies and the social sciences, I found Filewod's categorizations of "popular theatre"[3] to be helpful. Filewod (2011) comments that popular theatre consists of two broad yet overlapping sectors: "One sector is the continued use of theatre as a form of community mobilization, political dissent, and radical challenge in movements for social justice. The other is what is known as 'applied theatre,' which works within institutional frameworks (schools, prisons, health care, and development agencies) to produce collaborative knowledge and analysis. Often these applied theatre applications work in concert with government programs" (257).

The NSL project plans to combine elements of both of these sectors. As is the case with the first sector, the NSL project will take place in a community rather than an institutional setting; the notion of social justice may be interpreted in different ways by NSL members, but individual empowerment as well as community mobilization and awareness are key objectives. However, the project will also use the social science methods more commonly found in applied theatre to produce and analyze collaborative knowledge.

Both sectors of popular theatre as defined by Filewod tend to use a method of collective creation. Whereas most plays are authored by a single person, collective creation simply refers to a process wherein a group develops and writes a play (or a series of scenes or episodes) with the intention of performing in front of an audience (Wallewein 1994). In popular theatre, collective creation typically takes two forms. Members of a community group (often disadvantaged) write and perform a play in a collaborative effort that also involves at least one theatre professional (see, e.g., Diamond and the work of Headlines Theatre/Theatre for Living) or academic (see, e.g., Conrad 2009 and Valentine 2006). Or, alternatively, actors are hired to perform the script developed collaboratively by the researcher and/or theatre professional and community members (see, e.g., Kazubowski-Houston 2010). The NSL project will use the first form of collective creation.

In addition, because audience reaction and mobilization is as important for NSL as participant empowerment, NSL members have been considering the use of audience discussions after the play, focus groups, and audience surveys. These techniques are often used in applied health research studies such as those by Cox, Kazubowski-Houston, and Nisker (2009), which hope to engage the public/audience with respect to health-related issues and policies. Finally, the NSL project will be ethnographic[4] in nature and will therefore involve extensive fieldwork and participant observation of rehearsals as well as the final play or plays. In this way, the project will mirror the work of Kazubowski-Houston (2010).

NSL has determined that a series of "non-threatening" workshops designed to "break the ice" and awaken the creative and artistic talents of the homeless must precede the writing and rehearsals leading to the final show. The art activities within the workshops may be led by TRU faculty, Kamloops Arts Council contacts, musicians in the group, and friends (Genshorek 2013). It is hoped that the workshops will deliver a core group of homeless individuals who will then work together with theatre faculty from TRU to write and perform a play about their experiences with homelessness. The play will then be performed before a live audience in Kamloops. The entire process will be documented.

The Process of Collaborative Research and "Empowerment"

Many of the NSL members have had experience with a collaborative process—whether in the form of a collective creation in theatre or other art fields, collaborative research in an academic setting, or job-related teamwork. While they all acknowledge that collaboration can be painfully slow and cumbersome, the benefits of collaboration are seen to outweigh any drawbacks. Why is collaborative research important to the members of NSL? The answer is that collaborative research is tied, in the minds of NSL members, to notions of teamwork, community, creative freedom, idealism, trust, confidence building, and most of all, empowerment. Empowerment is seen as especially important when dealing with disenfranchised populations. As one group member explained:

> We need to give them power right from the very beginning and . . . when you are talking about a disenfranchised

　　　　　　　　　　　　　　　　　　　　DAWN FAROUGH

population . . . they understand hierarchy, even in sharper focus than we do. And . . . on the street there is a hierarchy and . . . in a seniors' home, there's a hierarchy. In whatever population we are talking about, we need to lift them up power wise, or they won't have a voice and . . . we are talking about people who are tramped down to the degree where they don't usually feel like they have a voice. I do feel like we do need to empower them. And I do think we need to empower them by feeding them and taking them there and telling them, and letting them know, by our gestures, that they are important. And by sharing and letting them know that we are all there together as one—a lot of the theatre kind of team building we talk about. But, yes, I think empowerment is absolutely essential. But I think we need to empower the group too through ritual. Ritual, I think, is extremely important with the theatre experience like this. That if they get used to the way that things work, and if they are working the same way every time, that we build trust that way. So I think it's empowerment plus trust. I think they are all tied together as one.

There is a long tradition of using theatre to empower disadvantaged and marginalized people. The work of Brazilian director Augusto Boal and his "Theatre of the Oppressed" is central to this tradition. Inspired by the Marxist educator and fellow Brazilian Paulo Freire, as well as theatre practitioner Bertolt Brecht, Boal advocated a community-based model designed to give voice to groups that were marginal within society. Boal, using the Marxist terminology of "oppressor/oppressed," argued that only the dominant groups within society (the oppressors) had a voice. "Monologues" existed to the benefit of a few, but no actual meaningful "dialogue" existed between people. Boal's interactive political theatre techniques were designed to create "counter-narratives" as well as interaction and community between the performers and audiences. The techniques force performers and audience members to become active learners rather than passive entertainers and spectators. Knowledge is created through the interaction of both parties. Further, both participants and audience members develop a much-needed critical social consciousness about their communities and their place within them and therefore become active in promoting social change.

Canadian David Diamond practises his own version of Boal's work in his "Theatre for Living." Diamond has moved away from the more Marxist elements of Boal's work (what Diamond calls the "oppressor/oppressed" model).[5] Instead, Diamond envisions communities as a series of fluid and dynamic networks of communication which can, over time, produce shared systems of beliefs, values, and goals (2007, 16). As our patterns of behaviour change, our societal structures will also change. For Diamond, theatre is "a symbolic and primal language" and therefore the perfect "vehicle for living communities to tell their stories" (2007, 23). The processes involved in interactive theatre allow people from disadvantaged communities to discover that they "are experts on their own lives" and that they can "create art" as well as their own realities. Diamond's work mirrors that of Boal, in that the ideals of individual and community empowerment, the development of a critical social consciousness, and the ability of the ordinary person to create knowledge and become an expert on his/her own reality are as important to Diamond as they were to Boal.

Within the social science literature, the perceived benefit of collaborative research between academics and community members is that the power imbalances between the academics, who are "experts" in their fields, and the research participants, who are "studied," is addressed. In theory, both parties learn from one another as they create knowledge together. In sociology this comes across in the notion of "public sociology,"[6] and in anthropology "collaborative ethnography" is a good example. In both cases all participants are supposed to be equally involved in planning and decision-making processes. Of course the ideal is often not met; articles abound on the difficulties encountered in these kinds of collaborations.

Many social scientists see the value in performance as a tool for knowledge creation. As in the history of political theatre, self-expression is tied to consciousness raising and subversion. Sociologist Norman Denzin (2003), who uses theatre as a method to challenge racism and produce race awareness in the United States, believes that when performance is used as a sociological method, it allows for the kind of critical self-reflection and consciousness raising that challenges mainstream thinking and common-sense knowledge. Disadvantaged people become less submissive and start to envision a different kind of democracy. For anthropologist Dwight Conquergood, academic research connected to performance should contain a "triangulation of three perspectives—accomplishment (the making of art and culture); analysis (the interpretation of art and culture); and application (activism, the connection to the community)" (in Roberts 2008). However, as Roberts (2008) cautions, advocacy is not an easy issue for social scientists dedicated to performance studies and social change. Social scientists are well aware that mainstream society teaches the value of common-sense knowledge to individuals. The concept of "false consciousness" is foreign to most people. Therefore the challenge becomes how to be respectful of community members and allow their experiences to guide the research while, at the same time, being faithful to the theories, critiques of society, and methodologies of one's academic discipline (Roberts 2008).

The literature shows mixed results when analyzing projects similar to that proposed by NSL. On the positive side, academic and activist Kristin Bervig Valentine is confident that her performance classes (and resulting plays) for women in prison were beneficial both on a personal and a broader societal level. She states: "My hypothesis is that mind-liberating activities generated by performance and creative writing programs . . . increase effective communication skills that help women avoid actions harmful to themselves and others. By acquiring these skills they increase their abilities to avoid reincarceration when they are released from prison, thereby benefiting themselves, their families, and their communities" (2006, 321). Diane Conrad produced a play with "at-risk" high school students in order to better grasp their perceptions of their behaviour. Like Valentine, Conrad is very positive about what she was able to accomplish using participatory performance ethnography with the high school students. She felt that she was able to cultivate their awareness of their risky behaviours and help them look for solutions or responses to their issues, and that the process gave them agency in and responsibility for their behaviour (2009).

Power Struggles

However, not all academics and artists are positive about their collaborative projects. One of the most compelling tales of power struggles in this area of research comes from the work of Magdalena Kazubowski-Houston (2010). Kazubowski-Houston is from both a theatrical and a social science background (she is a performer, director, and anthropologist). In her book *Staging Strife: Lessons from Performing Ethnography with Polish Roma Women*, Kazubowski-Houston reflects upon the process of writing and staging a play with the Roma women of Elblag, Poland. Initially Kazubowski-Houston's goal was to draw public attention to the ethnic, class-based, and gendered violence and discrimination encountered by the Roma women, and she hoped that "her project would constitute consciousness-raising of both participants and audience" (2010, 15). Kazubowski-Houston wanted to do serious political theatre that would speak out against racism and sexism and not perpetuate stereotypes; however, she encountered many setbacks and surprises. Although she collaborated with the Roma women during the writing and rehearsal periods, the women refused to act in their own play.[7] Kazubowski-Houston was forced to hire non-Roma Polish actors and thus was faced with three different factions with three different agendas. The Roma women had a vision of theatre that was like a "soap-opera." They wished to show the joyful, positive aspects (as they saw it) of Roma life. They wanted their potential audiences of non-Roma and Roma to think "well of them." The actors were scornful of this, believing the Roma women to be "passive" about their oppression and lacking any understanding of true "art" and critical, realist, political theatre. The Roma women were also critical of the actors; they didn't trust them and they had their own stereotypes of the non-Roma. Kazubowski was stuck in the middle and forced to mediate between two groups, a process she often quite disliked. Dealing with many of the same issues NSL has discussed in our many meetings, Kazubowski-Houston struggles with how to balance the various agendas of her participants, how to conduct collaborative research that will be respectful to her participants but also lead to a PhD dissertation, and how to be sensitive to the different backgrounds of herself, her actors, and the Roma. Many times, the power games threatened to derail the entire production. In the end, the play did go on, but Kazubowski-Houston was left to contemplate whether her project had the desired outcome of social change: "On the one hand, I had accomplished what I had to do. I had produced a play with the Roma women, and everyone seemed reasonably happy with the outcome. On the other hand, it hadn't set Poland ablaze, and the women's lives seemed no better for it" (2010, 177–78). Although it is true that the Roma women did not perform in their own play and this led to many of the power struggles, Kazubowski-Houston notes that she did develop two other ethnographic performances in Poland where the participants performed on the stage and yet power struggles were still very much a part of the rehearsal process (2010, 193).

I asked the NSL members for their views on potential power struggles within our research project. For the most part, NSL members are positive about the group's ability to get along with each other:

> I think that everyone seems to be very respectful of the different lenses that people are viewing the project through. Just in the several meetings that we've had, it's clear that— you know [name of group member] would have a clear theatrical lens. She understands it in terms of performance and the arts and theatre. But she's also very willing to listen to someone who actually works with our clientele and understands that that's not going to work for them or there's no way that that will apply. So I think, in that way, everyone's been very responsive, which is great.

The participants, however, are the "great unknown." One member expressed the following:

> I guess in terms of a power struggle between ourselves and the participants, I guess my only trepidation there would be that we have a clear goal in mind for what we would like to achieve and there might not be a complete buy-in from the participants that are involved. There might be, I don't know if a power struggle maybe is the right term, but there certainly could be a difference of opinion in how we are going

to get there or what it is they would like to achieve. At times, working on a project like this, it can be like herding cats and so trying I guess to be respectful of the participants' circumstances and their knowledge, I suppose. And trying to lead them where we would like to be.

Strengths, Weaknesses, and Challenges

Every project has strengths and weaknesses. In this section, I use interviews with NSL members to highlight the views of the group regarding the strengths, weaknesses, and challenges of the project.

Strengths

> *This is a very exciting project. A part of what is exciting about it is the unknown. I have no idea. With any collective, even with a bunch of seasoned professionals who have all done it before, part of the attraction of doing such a project is you have no idea where it is going to end up.* (NSL member)

Every member of NSL described the "unknown" elements of the project—would we have enough participants, would they show up on a regular basis, what would they want to write about?—as its strengths and, potentially, its ultimate downfall. The unknown is exciting and liberating but also terrifying. Other strengths cited by NSL members included the composition of the group, the size of the city of Kamloops, and the belief that this project was a "leaping-off point" for projects in the future.

As expressed in the section on power struggles, the group itself is viewed as an asset. Members mentioned that "we are respectful of one another in this talking phase of the process" and that there is an "open-mindedness" and "creativity of everybody involved." The composition of the group is seen as providing solid strengths with a great combination of education and experience. One member commented:

Well I think the group we have around the table is tremendous. . . . Partnering with TRU has just been incredibly exciting so we have a lot of strong educational background around the table. It's just thrilling to see that combined with the people, like I said, who work front line with these people who live and breathe what that experience of being on the street is. That mixture of education and experience is great. I think that's going to be a real strength for us.

The size of Kamloops was also seen in a positive light. Group members believe that closer proximity leads to better and closer connections between community members:

I feel like we have the right size of community where it's easier for people to feel connected. We are only a very few degrees from everyone else in the community. You know someone who knows someone who is related to someone. So I think we are in a good position where everyone will feel—no one is too far away here I guess. For me I feel like it's a good sized community for us to be able to launch something like this, because of the proximity.

Furthermore, assistance from the local theatre company will be readily offered: "For example, if we need or want help from Western Canada Theatre, enough of us know people at Western Canada Theatre well that that might happen. It might not happen in Toronto, for example." There is also the belief that culture is not considered to be as elitist in Kamloops as it might be in larger centres:

I don't think culture is particularly scary here. Maybe it is for some level of the population, but I think theatre is not seen here as being elitist. That you have to dress up to go to and only the upper 10,000 get to go. So I think it will have, I hope it will have a bigger impact on the city as a whole, or on the population as a whole, than a similar project would do in Vancouver because it's so hard to reach the entire population in a giant city. And I know we are not going to reach the entire population, but it seems like it's more contained and more controlled.

Lastly, the size of the city seems to mean that Kamloopsians may not be as jaded as those in big cities and may look forward to something new and challenging:

> It's the first time we've done something like this here. So I hope people get really excited and engaged and that we won't have a problem selling tickets, because it's so new and different. People are always looking for stuff to do in Kamloops, and, hopefully, even a few people from around the district might show up, but I'm not going to place any goals there. The size of the city is key, for sure. Because to my knowledge, this is the first time anything like this would have happened here.

Finally, the last strength mentioned was the possibility that this project may lead to many others:

> I think a lot of things are pointing to this development group wanting to do other things and more things. Lots of energy, lots of excitement, lots of ideas. I think the timing is good for a group like this in Kamloops to come together and address these issues in a creative light. And I think that this project is just going to be the beginning. I think there will be more fun projects and more things will build off of this and this will be an awesome first project.

Weaknesses and Challenges

> *What if nothing happens? That's like the worst case scenario.*
> (NSL member)

What if nothing happens? What if, after all the philosophical discussions, planning, and organizing, nothing happens?! We do not know who the participants are going to be and we do not know what they may or may not be willing to do. As one member acknowledged, "We are working in the dark." Any project that focuses on human subjects needs to deal with the fact that "people are changeable and people are fluid and mercurial. So one day they may say A and the next day they may say Z" (NSL member), but this project also deals with a population thought to be challenging. On the one hand, NSL members are trying to be careful with any biases or prejudices they may have about the homeless or recently housed population. On the other hand, they readily admit that it would be foolish not to discuss and worry about the challenges they may face in dealing with this disadvantaged group. The following two quotations illustrate this dilemma:

> I'm nervous that our biggest challenge will be the reliability of the people that we will be working with, based just solely on their circumstance, not on who it is that we are working with. I think there could be challenges there. Like I said, having them adapt to a new type of environment like this and their comfort level and overcoming any barriers that they might have to participating.
>
> The process might be made difficult by their own issues, which might just be maybe they would lose interest. Because they would find out what is expected of them and they might just think that that is too much for me to give or I don't know if I can do this. Or maybe I don't have it in me—maybe I'm not talented enough to give—I'm not that kind of person. The other thing could be that maybe they would just get tired. They just physically get fatigued by it. That they might anticipate something else. They might not understand the depth of what we are doing. Maybe they would think, "Oh we are just going to do a little skit," kind of thing. And so just learn some jokes and sing a few Johnny Cash songs and that will be enough. And then there's the other side of it: that maybe it would bring things out of people; the creative process might bring out disturbing feelings

or just make them feel too raw. That might be a problem too where they would need to have somebody help them through that and maybe it would scare them off. The worst case scenario? I guess "it's too intense. I just don't want to do this."

The level of commitment required when working on a theatre production would be difficult for anyone. As one NSL member commented:

> You need a really high commitment level. Theatre is not brain surgery, but you need kind of an inappropriately high commitment level to make it work because it's a group project and every member of that group has to be there. Has to be contributing. Has to care as much as everybody else . . . which is why people in theatre will work through pneumonia and just crazy things. . . . If there isn't that level of commitment then it just implodes. From the outside it looks kind of crazy, but it's the only way it can work.

Other projects have dealt with the level of commitment in various ways. Theatre for Living, for example, has potential cast members go through a real interview process. They sign a contract and are provided an honorarium. If they do not show up for workshops or rehearsals, they get one warning. If it happens again, they are "fired" (Interview with David Diamond and Liza Lindgren 2013). On the other end of the spectrum, Savannah Walling, who has directed plays in Vancouver's East End, tolerates missing cast members to the extent that typically not everyone shows up until the dress rehearsal. People read their lines on stage if necessary (Interview with Savannah Walling 2013).

Group Goals

I think they are rather lofty and I'm all for lofty because if you shoot for the moon you are going to hit harder, you are going to go further than you thought you would. (NSL member)

Although each member of this group inevitably has his/her own priorities and agendas, NSL has agreed on a preliminary list of goals used to guide the project. These goals address themes of therapeutic creative expression, life skills, public awareness, community involvement, knowledge creation, and documentation.

Therapeutic Creative Expression

No Straight Lines wants to make a difference to the quality of lives of the participants through artistic expression. This is an important goal for the group. According to the Committee Minutes:

> One of the central objectives of this project is to put at risk individuals in touch with themselves and other like-minded individuals, through a variety of creative media and methods of expression. The challenges and emotions associated with homelessness are complex, and they are different for each person who experiences it. Creative expression can help people access and share these complex emotions to begin to come to terms with difficulties, challenges and trauma in their lives. (Genshorek 2013)

Yet this goal is not straightforward for group members. The community workers expressed the strongest enthusiasm for therapeutic creative expression. One said, "I know art is key to your sanity for a lot of people so that's personally why I'm really passionate about this project." Another pointed to the fact that those who experience poverty often do not have access to the kinds of resources that are needed for creative endeavours and therefore were being denied therapeutic outlets available to more affluent individuals. Other group members were more reserved in their enthusiasm and felt the need to qualify their remarks. For example, one NSL member said: "I don't like theatre as therapy, as a rule" and "I don't think theatre has to be 'masturbatory.'" Another, while acknowledging that "the ability to speak your truths is more empowering than you can imagine," said that the first goal had to be "a good show—artistically a good show" and therefore the art form had to be the priority. Placing therapeutic creative expression too high on the list of priorities could result in a "self-indulgent" end result, something that most audience members would not want to see. According to this member, the "reality of theatre is that it's live and therefore there has to be someone on the other side to receive the live things. If it is to have an audience, it has to have value to that audience. And watching somebody else's therapeutic wank is not of interest to an audience."

This member's comments echo David Diamond's assertion that Theatre for Living rehearsals and productions are never allowed to be group or individual therapy sessions. In an interview Diamond stated that his actors are actors first and foremost. They never play themselves on stage. He makes it clear to them that they are playing characters and that their expertise and creativity is in aid of making art and serving the larger community. The notion that actors from disadvantaged groups are "broken" and their involvement in the creative process is because we're "going to fix you somehow" is, in his view, "disrespectful," "presumptuous," and "makes for really bad theatre" (Interview 2013).

Life Skills

> *The life skills required to maintain housing are complex, and they are different for each individual. By utilizing different forms of creative expression people can begin to build skills and confidence that help them with the complexities of maintaining housing and/or employment.* (Genshorek, NSL Minutes 2013)

The community workers in the group use a UNICEF definition of life skills as "psychosocial abilities for adaptive and positive behavior that enable individuals to deal effectively with the demands and challenges of everyday life" (HAP 2012). The Kamloops Homeless Action Plan report on life skills considers the following to be essential life skill considerations for those who need to obtain and maintain housing: "financial management, family management, health and wellness (including substance abuse and mental health), self-management (including employment readiness) and social skills (such as communication and conflict resolution)" (2012). Kamloops has a life skills network that meets monthly "to discuss life skills-related community information, collaborate to improve service and share expertise" (HAP 2012).

NSL community workers speak of "hard" and "soft" life skills. Hard life skills refers to the use of concrete techniques and knowledge that allow an individual to successfully complete an activity such as paying bills or budgeting. Soft skills, on the other hand, refers to "people" skills: skills revolving around interpersonal relationships and communication. The majority of NSL members hope that the project will provide soft life skills. For example, one NSL commented:

> Being able to confidently speak in front of people. Feeling like what you have to say is important. Being able to work in a group. Being able to meet deadlines. Being able to think creatively . . . the hope is that the group together will go, "Ah, this works better this way. Let's try this and find out what we think about this." So they will have this opportunity to creatively problem-solve. And meeting a goal. Just setting a goal and then meeting it. That's a skill that three-quarters of people coming out of high school don't have.

The Kamloops Homeless Action Plan report on life skills does not mention hard life skills in conjunction with the NSL theatre project. Only soft life skills are mentioned: "Some of the skills that are anticipated to be developed in the Theatre project include communication and teamwork, time management, stress management, respect and empathy" (HAP 2012).

Occasionally there have been discussions around possible hard skills, in particular, skills leading to employment. These discussions worry some members of NSL. The following two quotations illustrate this concern:

> This isn't training them to be actors. God help us. We don't need any more actors. That's an awful life. Especially for somebody who has not got their shit together. Acting attracts people who are unstable and then it beats them up. It's awful.

People who have trained for years and years and years in theatre don't get work. It's the dumbest career to think that you think you are going to get into, especially if you think that's going to get you off the streets. That will drive you to the streets probably.

One NSL member quipped: "It would be great if we could give them an over-the-counter prescription of life skills, right? And after ten days of taking them faithfully you are cured." In his mind, life skills is about helping people integrate into the community, but he also questioned the "functionality" of mainstream North American life, asking whether the mainstream was just as "dysfunctional, if not more dysfunctional at a systemic level than the individual lives" of our homeless participants. Still, this member had success in past projects (one dealing with young people who had dropped out of school and were living in shelters and on probation) where hard as well as soft life skills had been improved:

> There wasn't really anybody in this project that had any kind of normalcy or regular life. So what we tried to install in them was life skills. Yes they were getting paid to be in this project. They had to get to work on time. They had certain tasks and responsibilities that they had to carry out. But we said to them, "Okay now that you think you are really hot shit because you know how to paint, act, and work as a group, what are you going to give back to the community?" So that was the main life skill that we wanted to put on the table—before anything else, before how to manage a budget. We basically said okay "are you feeling better about yourselves?" You feel like you've had a voice? You've got something to offer? What are you going to do with that? . . . So in the end, yes, they became more aware of the community at large. They became more aware of other community issues, as well, they learned to pick up the phone. They could cold call, build a set, do a budget—all that kind of stuff. I would say the main thing was, this is about making ties with your community.

Another member argued that integration into the community and the development of soft skills are prerequisites for the hard life skills: "Teaching life skills isn't going to work if you haven't got the feeling of being part of the bigger picture of the community at large, of being part of the society at large" and "you need to have the personal confidence in yourself before the life skills are really going to have any effect. So you can teach people how to balance their finances or whatever life skills you are going to teach them, but . . . until they get a sense of themselves and the confidence that money is not a scary thing, it's not going to work."

Public Awareness and Community Involvement

No Straight Lines wants to increase community awareness and knowledge of homelessness in Kamloops. The homeless play project is seen as an innovative way of engaging the public. The hope is that awareness will lead to participation and active support for local initiatives to end homelessness. The Committee Minutes note that:

> Homelessness can be a difficult topic to approach for the general public who may not have past experiences. It is our hope that by offering the issues of homelessness in a new, and perhaps more approachable way, we will be able to reach a variety of members of the public with meaningful messages that change their perceptions and grow their knowledge. Mechanisms such as surveys will be developed to measure changes in perceptions about the issues of homelessness. (Genshorek 2013)

Furthermore,

> Our goal in documenting the process is to have a physical record of the project that can be shared with participants, project partners, other interested groups, and the general public. Our goals to increase awareness about homelessness, theatre and the arts will connect with this goal in a

survey of the audience at the performance to understand perceptions. (Genshorek 2013)

Both sectors of popular theatre (discussed earlier in the chapter) involve the audience in a manner not found in traditional theatre. However, there is a profound absence of data about the audiences who participate in the interactive productions. Most of the data available on audiences (demographic and opinion based) comes from the applied sector of popular theatre. The applied sector is much more conventional in its use of audiences but is also much more likely to use social scientific methods in its approach to understanding the nature and opinions of the audiences who attend these productions. On the other hand, the *theatre of the oppressed* sector involves the audience in a more creative manner.

The Theatre of the Oppressed, as developed by Boal, and the adaptations by Canadian theatres, such as Headlines Theatre/Theatre for Living in Vancouver and Catalyst Theatre in Edmonton, use techniques that allow audience members to intervene and change the course of a play. In popular theatre, divisions between audience members and actors are deliberately blurred. For Boal, audience members are "spect-actors." They are not just passive spectators watching a finished and polished production over which they have no control or voice. Instead, the audience is invited to act and to help re-create various scenes in the play. In Boal's model of "forum theatre," the show plays through as written the first time around. Then, the actors re-start the play, and at any time an audience member can yell "stop," come up to the stage and re-create the scene with his or her solutions to the problem presented. If the audience disagrees with the spect-actor's solution, a member shouts "magic!" and a general discussion ensues. For Boal, the forum model helps the audience understand that their ideas are important, that interactive dialogue between many people can disrupt or disturb "fixed categories of social power" (Halvorson 2010, 124), and that social change is their responsibility.

The Legislative Model is a version of forum theatre designed "to bring theatre back into the centre of political action—the centre of decisions—by making theatre as politics rather than merely making political theatre" (Boal in Halvorson 2010, 125). A play by Headlines, *Practicing Democracy* (2004), is said to be the first example of legislative theatre in Canada.

DAWN FAROUGH

The writers/actors were people affected by cuts in welfare in the city of Vancouver. The suggestions and comments by audience members were formalized into a legislative report presented to Vancouver City Council after the final performances. The goal of legislative theatre is to change laws and policies.

A more conventional way of involving audiences and promoting awareness can be found in the many health performance studies that seek to engage the public on policy issues and establish empathy so that audience members understand what it feels like to walk in the shoes of someone who has a mental illness, cancer, Alzheimer's, or cystic fibrosis, to name just a few of the issues covered in Canada (Alvarez and Graham 2011). After the play, audiences, in large or small groups, are invited to discuss the issues presented.

Geographers Geraldine Pratt and Caleb Johnston used talkback sessions and audience feedback surveys for their play on immigrant nannies. Based on Pratt's interview transcripts, *Nanay* explores issues around the shortages of childcare in Canada and the experiences and challenges of women who come to Canada from the Philippines as temporary workers under the Live-In Caregiver Program. States Pratt, "Perhaps the most extraordinary aspect of the eventfulness of theatre is the opportunity it creates to stage public conversations between people who would not ordinarily speak to each other on an equal footing: domestic workers with employers, nanny agents with community activists, childcare activists with Philippine community activists, local government officials with domestic workers" (Pratt and Johnston 2010, 177). *Nanay's* audiences reported that they had learned from the play and the audience discussions. As well, the play generated meetings between various advocacy groups (2010, 178). Although Pratt does not mention legislative theatre in her work, it is clear that new policy initiatives could be a possible outcome of *Nanay*.

Cox, Kazubowski-Houston, and Nisker discuss and evaluate their methods of audience engagement in "Genetics on Stage" (2009). The authors used large audience discussions as well as smaller focus groups following their play *Orchids*, which investigates a complex and controversial technique called pre-implantation genetic diagnosis (PGD). PGD is used to decide whether embryos created through in vitro fertilization are viable. Canada currently has no legislation or policy guidelines on this technique. The researchers wished to educate the public on the various scientific, clinical, ethical, and social issues involved with PGD. They wanted the audience to feel empathy for the actors and the difficult decisions involved in various scenarios and to leave the theatre with informed opinions on the issue. They also wanted the audience to understand "that their attendance at the play constituted participation in research and in a real policy exercise" (2009, 1476). Cox, Kazubowski-Houston, and Nisker found that there was a higher degree of interaction in the focus groups than in the large audience discussions. During the general audience discussions, many of those who spoke identified as "experts" of some kind and presented their arguments in such a way that those with less expertise were intimidated and silenced. The authors note that most of the audience members were highly educated and female. Therefore the audience was not as diverse as they would have liked. This was in spite of the fact that the performances were free and the researchers had advertised in community and popular magazines and newspapers as well as on the *Orchids* website and with various professional and advocacy groups. Participants in the focus groups were pleased with their experiences and said that they felt freer to express themselves in the smaller groups. One of the drawbacks of the focus groups was that "in some groups, a lack of self-consciousness and casual use of language led to more overt joking around and, occasionally, the emergence of 'unpopular', racist or other perspectives offensive to the facilitator or participants" (2009, 1478).

While most of the social scientists using performance research were optimistic about audience learning and reactions, Kazubowski-Houston (2010) felt that the compromises she was forced to make during the writing and rehearsals of *Hope*, her play with the Roma women of Poland, undermined her original goal of challenging the audiences on racist and gender-based stereotypes and inequalities. Many of the audience members focused more on the entertaining and theatrical techniques of the play than on the political issues Kazubowski-Houston hoped to illuminate. However, Kazubowski-Houston does note that she was unable to carry out formal post-performance discussions with the audiences because the Roma women objected, fearing that they would be at risk (189).

The NSL project will not use either the Forum Theatre or Legislative models. Our methods for audience engagement and evaluation will be similar to those of the health performance studies and will include observation of audience responses as recorded with field notes during the performance, audiotaped large group audience discussions and smaller focus group discussions following the performance, and a survey that will be handed to the audience as they enter the theatre.

I asked NSL members for their views on audience composition and engagement. NSL members hope for a diverse audience. Ideally NSL would prefer that the audience be mixed in terms of its demographics and experiences. For example, one member commented:

> My ideal audience would be ten percent other homeless people. Ten percent low-income people. Just all the way up to Milobar [the mayor of Kamloops]. So that there were people there who had the full range of experiences, people there who could actually do things financially to effect some change.

There were concerns about "not wanting to preach to the converted" as well as not wanting the entire audience to be the "typical audience for mainstream theatre in Kamloops . . . the fifty year old female teacher." Another NSL member said that we need to talk about these issues very early on in a person's education and so she felt that she would like to see high school kids attend the play.

The various goals for audience reaction and engagement with the play and planned discussions included: changing people's perceptions of the homeless and challenging the status quo; building empathy and connecting with the audience on many different emotional levels; and mobilizing audience members to take action and become involved with the issue of homelessness in their community.

Most NSL members feel that they have a very good idea as to what the average Kamloopsian thinks about members of the homeless population. Some have already had conversations with members of the public:

> I recently had a conversation with a woman who I would consider to be upper-middle class. She was a senior citizen, quite comfortable in her lifestyle . . . and she doesn't

understand why homeless people or poor people need to eat every day. Like eat three meals a day.

Others think that we all have a hard time letting go of the stereotypes:

> I would love it if there were people who came with solid pre-conceived ideas of how those people are all just lazy drug addicts and they should know better and who come away going "Oh."
> . . . people just picture the one type of person, you know, the one person—the street entrenched guy that has got his hat out on the sidewalk and that guy needs help for sure. But we are talking about a much bigger issue than that.

In addition, most NSL members believe that the average member of the public is in denial about the role of luck in a person's life and how easy it often is to slide into poverty:

> I hope that we'll have liberal people that come to it and come away with "I had no idea how easy it was to fall into that situation". . . . Because I think most of us who aren't homeless think that we are pretty safe from that. Nothing that serious is ever going to happen to me. But I also, I think we will discover that most of those people who were homeless felt the same way before they got there.

Changing people's perceptions and their stereotypes about homelessness is not easy, but NSL members believe that the format of the play, which is so different from a media-driven "three minute elevator pitch," will be capable of engaging the public much more deeply emotionally and intellectually. As one member explains:

> This is a complex problem, right? There's no one, single right answer and people need to understand that it is complicated. So this seems like the perfect way to deliver the messages really clearly. It's difficult to deliver it clearly

because there are so many facets to it, right? . . . Hopefully we connect with them at a lot of different levels. I would like to see them laugh and cry and be in shock and be amazed and be comforted at different points. Because that's life and hopefully we can portray what life is like for these people. So when you journey through their life you would see, yes there's some levity, there's some fun. They have a social network. They are hilarious. They tell great jokes, but they have also gone through these things that I've never heard of anyone going through before, right? That kind of shock and then hopefully some relateability where they see that these people are just like their son, their cousin, and their aunt. It touches them in a deep way that makes them cry hopefully. Something like that.

If the play can manage to build empathy and educate the audience, will it also be able to mobilize audience members into advocating for social change? One member felt that the audience experience could result in certain individuals taking "incremental steps":

Yes, that would be ideal, for there to be a motivation for them to advocate for what they see as being necessary for change. Even if we don't get to the stage where they feel motivated to really be involved. Provided they are moved from being indifferent to being open to learning more. I think that is huge. Once they've had the experience of seeing sort of first hand, what these participants have lived through, whatever they chose to express. From there, if they are open to learning more about what the issues are and what the challenges are, then from there I feel like we are in a good position to be able to—people can guide themselves into an area where they feel it's appropriate for them to make a change. If they do want to start volunteering more or if they want to advocate more or if they want to donate more. Whatever the case may be.

Other NSL members admitted that since our own group had no idea what the "call to action" would look like, it wasn't realistic to expect mobilization on top of awareness:

> I guess I'm a bit of a control freak in that I feel you have to have a plan. So I feel like if we expected mobilization then we should have a clear and concise idea of what that mobilization should look like. I don't feel like we do, or maybe can, or should.

Lastly, one NSL member argued that the size of Kamloops may be helpful in both audience or public awareness and mobilization:

> I see the same people on the street over and over again. On the North Shore and Downtown. The audience members will see some of the performers in their daily lives after the performance is over. This may have an impact. This wouldn't happen in a big city. If you saw the play in Vancouver and lived in, say, Shaughnessy, would you ever see any of the performers again?

Social Justice and Social Change

Linked to the goal of mobilizing audience members is the ideal of social justice and/or social change. When I asked the question "How important is the issue of social justice or social/societal change to you," I did not define the terms. I let each member in the group elaborate on what this meant to them and, then, how important this was as an expression of their efforts in the project. Every single member told me that this was "majorly important," "absolutely pivotal," or "very central to my life." Homelessness is a huge issue, and quite rightly one member stated that "there's no changing this issue without complete re-evaluation throughout society." However, every NSL member acknowledged that there were limitations to what we could expect to accomplish with the project: "How much social justice can you put on the table at one sitting?" Most members felt that "individual change" was more realistic and that it was possible on three levels: the project would change us (the NSL members),[8] the homeless or recently housed participants, and some of the audience members. Beyond that, it was thought possible that the project could be an important first step to further grassroots community projects of a collaborative and activist nature. We're on the "right track," said one NSL member.

Conclusion

The No Straight Lines initiative on homelessness in the city of Kamloops is a collaborative work in process—one that has emerged through the discussions and planning efforts of academics, community workers, and artist/activists and will continue with the added participation of unknown members of the homeless or recently housed population. This is a project that takes group members well out of their comfort levels and into the "unknown" on a number of levels. Interviews with NSL members highlight personal and group goals as well as their excitement and concerns for their project. Three of Dubinsky's frameworks for collaboration (self-interested, normative, and mimetic) help explain why certain individuals came together to work on this project and why the project has been designed in a particular manner. The NSL project is in very early stages and the group has much to learn from previous research involving similar methodologies. Both sectors of popular theatre, as identified by Filewod, are important for this fledgling project. Collective collaborations, in terms of creativity, knowledge creation, and analysis, are viewed as crucial to the group. Individual empowerment and public/community empathy and engagement are key objectives. The literature from theatrical studies and the social sciences reveals that projects similar to the one proposed by NSL have strengths and weaknesses. On the positive side, the performances (and the processes involved in collaboration) do seem to lead to a greater awareness for many participants and audience members. From an awareness and empowerment perspective, many researchers believe that their projects enabled both the participants and audiences to examine their issues as well as their beliefs and to re-evaluate aspects of their life experiences. Some researchers also believed that participants and/or audiences showed signs of mobilizing for concrete changes. On the negative side, power struggles between participants in the collective process may lead to serious problems, the researchers may find themselves more "politically motivated" than their disadvantaged participants, audiences may not be as diverse as anticipated, they might not "catch" intended messages, and they may not express the empathy or the learning hoped for in large group discussions and smaller focus groups.

Epilogue

Reflections from the Field: Inside the Rehearsal Room

Rehearsals commenced in the spring of 2014. A small theatre in a poor area of Kamloops was chosen as the venue. Our "getting to know you" stage of the project took place in a rather tiny front room of the building, which shared its space with a Sushi restaurant. Prior to the first rehearsal, an important issue needed to be negotiated between me and one of the theatre professors as well as one of the front-line workers. There was a serious hiccup in our self-interested collaboration. Concerns were raised about the possibility of the "non-homeless" (i.e., academics and support workers) outnumbering the homeless participants during the rehearsal process. From the point of view of the theatre professor and front-line worker, the number of people within the rehearsal room should be as small and intimate as possible. However, I had already specified on grant applications and in the ethics paperwork that I would be at most, if not all, of the rehearsals and that two "service learning" students would accompany me. We would be participant observers—participating in all disclosures and activities and documenting the process through a sociological lens. One of the English Literature professors also had a service learning student who would act as a scribe to the group. I wondered about the lack of communication between this colleague and me. However, I was also reminded of Lunde, Heggen, and Strand's (2012) research on conflicts between disciplinary and epistemic styles and cultures. In addition, although this particular theatre professor was part of the NSL from the beginning and had been to all the meetings, she was not involved in the lengthy ethics board process and probably had no idea as to what had been signed off on or the design of the complete project. In the end, I agreed to rotate the

FIGURE 3.3. Theatre Project Network 2 by Dawn Farough. Design by Moneca Jantzen, Daily Designz.

students so that one less person would be in the room at all times. The English Literature professor said that she would not come to rehearsals. I knew from my previous interviews that the artist/activists had planned on attending rehearsals as well, but this was no longer to be the case. They were forced to volunteer in other areas of the project. In the end, we began with approximately ten homeless or recently housed participants and six academics/students/service workers in the rehearsal room. From my perspective, the homeless participants were enjoying the attention from the rest of us and expressed considerable curiosity about our lives and the project. When I explained that I would be taking notes (as would the students), none of the participants complained or showed any discomfort.

The academics and support people arrived early for each rehearsal and then the participants started to roll in. Some were always on time while others were chronically late. NSL had rules about attendance and arriving on time for the participants, who are being paid for their efforts, and the theatre faculty patiently reviewed the rules in every session. We always began with the telling of our "stories," and this took several of our four-hour sessions to complete. I was amazed at the length of some of the stories. I expected the participants to be somewhat shy or reticent. This is the case for only a small minority; most of our participants loved to talk and had no trouble taking centre stage for as long as possible. The stories varied, but there were the expected similarities: dysfunctional childhoods involving foster care, abuse, and neglect; addictions to drugs and alcohol; and few support systems outside of the homeless community and subculture. Some participants were temporarily housed but feeling nervous that they would be back on the street eventually. Others were "camping." The men outnumbered the women. One of the women worried that the men would judge her and consider her story "not good enough." The men countered her fears, declaring that they could not imagine being pregnant or having to look after children while living on the street. However, at least two of the men declared that the social service system favoured women and children over men. Everyone in the room was required to disclose their personal history, and the participants asked questions if they felt that something might be missing. Some of the academics and students apologized about their privileged lives, and the participants called them on that—they wanted details, not apologies.

I reflected on the arguments in political theatre and the social sciences about using theatre as a method to allow for a critical self-reflection and consciousness raising that challenges mainstream thinking and common-sense knowledge. Through theatre, disadvantaged people become less submissive; they start to advocate and envision a different kind of democracy. I quickly discovered the paternalism behind Boal-inspired theatre methodology. The homeless were neither submissive nor lacking in a critical social consciousness. I noted in my reflective journal:

> Three of the homeless men are already very critical of mainstream society; they discuss the divisions between the poor, the middle-class and the wealthy, analyze racism and the lack of spirituality in mainstream society, and comment on the average Canadian's total disregard for the environment. They seem more politically aware than the majority of my sociology students. They are also very critical of their own families. Ironically, their family backgrounds, to my way of thinking, seem to be less abusive than that of the average participant in the group. Rather than tales of foster care, physical abuse and rape; they talk about family members judging them or not being able to understand their lifestyles. All three have battled addictions. Their identities are very strongly tied to a certain way of life which they see as superior to that of the mainstream. They are devoted champions of the homeless and "would never want to become like the rich people they know."

I wonder if this process will simply confirm their already firm ideas about mainstream society and their place within it, or will further self-reflection ensue? Certainly there is leadership in the homeless community and subculture. The homeless population in Kamloops have their own leaders and champions—those like "Mike," who made his rounds daily, talking to all his homeless friends, giving them advice, and telling the social service workers about the individuals he thinks may be in jeopardy. Another individual I will call "Ian" proudly informed us that he was the mayor of the tent city in Edmonton, that his personal hero was Jack Layton, and that his goal in Kamloops was to develop another tent city. The NSL collaboration is supposed to support social change, and I am reminded that all the NSL members told me that the issue of social justice or societal change was majorly important to them. However, it is becoming apparent to me that social change may look very different to Mike and Ian than it does to the majority of NSL members.

Conceptualizing power and analyzing inequalities is a core issue for sociologists. The macro-level or grand theories of Marx, Weber, and feminist theorists present a "power-over" viewpoint wherein power comes from a capitalist class, elites, or patriarchy. The homeless are typically understood as individuals at the bottom of the class hierarchy in any capitalist economy. On the other hand, sociological research derived from the symbolic interactionist tradition, or from the work of Foucault, views power as interactive, relational, and situational. My fieldwork presented different types of power struggles between my research subjects, and in all of these, the homeless actors utilized power. In examining the power struggles between the actors as well as between the theatre faculty and the actors, it was obvious that I needed to think about how the homeless actors wielded and performed power on an interactional and micro-level. One of the earliest sociologists stressing the interdependence and relational aspects of power is Norman Elias. Elias argues:

> In so far as we are more dependent on others than they are on us, they have power over us, whether we have become dependent on them by their use of naked force or by our need to be loved, our need for money, healing, status, a career, or simply excitement. (cited in Dunning and Hughes 2013, 66)

NSL was extremely dependent on the homeless actors. There would be no play or research project without them. We had spent a lot of time and effort in planning the project, but we were asking a lot from people who were either currently homeless or recently (and marginally) housed. Individuals dropped out of the process for various reasons and we never really knew whether the play would become a reality. The collaborative efforts to generate a script took months, and during that time there were numerous power struggles—most of them between the actors themselves. Initially, the power struggles were based on who might have the most deserving story and who really shouldn't be there. For example, one actor had a problem with another actor because this individual was recently housed. Later, a major issue emerged around race. An Aboriginal actor told another that as far as he/she was concerned, she/he wasn't a real Indian. The animosity between the two of them threatened the collective creation process to the extent that a social service agency was called in to perform a healing and conflict resolution circle. Their efforts were appreciated but the conflict was not resolved. Discussion followed as to whether one of the actors should be voted out of the group. In the end, this did not happen.

Other conflicts were caused by differences in social and cultural capital. One of the actors had increased her/his social capital. By hanging around with social service providers, increasing her/his level of education, and applying for work positions within the social service sector, she/he had greatly increased networking capacities. Unfortunately, all of this individual's positions to date were temporary and lacking in long-term job security. She/he was often homeless between jobs and forced to "couch surf." She/he also had to deal with the fact that fellow actors often made fun of those in the group they thought were trying too hard to get ahead. I witnessed a conversation between this individual and another actor where her/his social work ambitions were gently mocked: Actor 1: "I'm trying to be in social work, why should I work at 7 Eleven?" Actor 2: "I can get you a job at A&W. I got compliments on my fries."

If we understand cultural capital more from the perspective of Bourdieu (1979), the emphasis is on how body language, linguistic styles, social skills, and tastes in food, fashion, entertainment, hobbies, etc., are associated with social class and embodied by all of us. We display our class positions with our bodies and in our interactions with others. We perform "class." In interactions where class positions are similar, people feel comfortable because the cultural capital is familiar and understandable. In interactions where class positions are different, people with lower cultural capital will feel uncomfortable and will likely not participate or will gain little from the interaction. All of the homeless actors were aware of how their "subculture" of homeless individuals differed from the mainstream and of how often people judged them for lacking the correct cultural capital. For example, an actor stated: "I always wear my best clothes and make-up when I'm in the welfare office so people will think I'm an advocate or something." Another actor referred to the Value Village as the "V&V Boutique" and humorously informed me that "it's where we dress for success." Finally, a conversation among three of the actors is very revealing of how aware the homeless are of cultural capital differences but also of how changes in cultural capital can cause conflict within the homeless community: Actor 1: "The manners in the culture we're in is definitely different from when you are higher upper." Actor 2: "Yeah. But I'm still going to judge some guy who eats like a dog." Actor 3: "If someone tells me to get educated, I'd be mad and tell them to F Off!" Actor 1: "I've been taking flak from outside this door. The people I'm with think—if you're in theatre, you're queer."

What occurred on the interactional level always needs to be seen within the context of macro-level societal realities of homelessness. Lacking adequate shelter is exhausting. Individuals were not always able to choose their roommates and sometimes they really disliked them. One actor was kicked out of his/her facility due to a "hot piss test" (personal communication, June 25, 2014). Our actors often had health issues: problems with their teeth and problems with their medications. One of the actors was hospitalized just before the performances were to begin and we didn't know whether she/he would be able to participate. There were mental health issues. Friends died and there was always talk of funerals. At the societal level, these were vulnerable and relatively powerless people compared to the majority of people in the community. On the micro-stage however, our actors were incredibly strong people who understood the interdependency of the play and research project. Furthermore, since the play was about homelessness, the actors felt that they were the experts and as a result were very invested in their stories and what the play should be communicating to the public.

How was the local university (TRU) viewed by the homeless actors and the community partners? For many Kamloopsians, the university has an elitist image, and I've heard community members throughout the years refer to their university as a somewhat inaccessible place up the hill with inadequate and expensive parking. Upon returning home from one day in the "field," I received an e-mail from the research office at TRU inviting me to a champagne and cheese party. The academics in NSL are part of a successful cohort of TRU academics who have been awarded a large grant. The e-mail asks me to extend the invitation to the community partners involved in our research project. I wonder how the NSL front-line workers will perceive this invitation—homelessness in Kamloops and champagne and cheese at the university—and I am slightly embarrassed about the university's elitist image. One of the service workers, in telling her story at rehearsal, made a point of saying that she enjoyed her Sociology classes at TRU but decided to become a social worker since she couldn't stand the idea of being out of touch with people and "ivory tower" in her thinking and behaviour. On the other hand, one of the homeless actors had a very positive experience with a TRU program called Cope-Meca.[9] Cope-Meca's mission was to help alternative students with personal development, networking, and academic work. This homeless actor passionately believed that Cope-Meca was one of three institutional programs and services that had dramatically changed his life for the better. Unfortunately, TRU has now cut the Cope-Meca program.

The Performance

The play, *Home/Less/Mess*, opened to sold out audiences for five successful performances. The process leading up to the play was as messy as anticipated. After approximately one month, a core group of committed actors formed; however, some of the actors later left the group for various reasons. It seemed to take forever to complete the script, and there were power struggles—obvious "in your face" struggles between the actors and sometimes between the actors and social service workers, as well as more sophisticated and subtle ones between research partners. All of the actors dealt with anxiety due to the time commitments demanded from them, the emotional toll of telling and retelling their stories, conflicts with families and roommates, mourning lost friends and attending funerals, ongoing health issues, losing and gaining "homes" over the summer, and performing onstage. Many of us thought the play would never see the light of day. In the end, however, six actors managed their anxieties and completed the project and play. The script came together and audiences streamed into the less-than-posh Stage House Theatre located in a run-down area of the city. The vast majority of audience members remained for the question and answer period after the play and over 300 completed the surveys.

Support for the Actors and the Play

BC Interior Community Foundation, United Way,
Kamloops Art Council, Thompson Rivers University,
TRU Actors Workshop Theatre, Project X, Western Canada Theatre

Food Donors

24 restaurants, Two churches, Kamloops Food Bank,
Daybreak Rotary Club, New Life Mission, Ask Wellness Society,
Royal Inland Hospital Foundation, Individual Volunteers

Art Auction and Fundraiser

26 individuals from the community,1 grocery store, 1 meat store,
3 restaurants, 2 pharmacies, 1 art gallery, 1 dance company,
1 sports team, 1 design company, 1 catering company, 2 theatre
companies, TRU Culinary Arts, Kamloops Symphony Orchestra,
Walmart, The Royal Inland Hospital

FIGURE 3.4. Outside the Rehearsal Hall: Sponsors, Donors, and Supporters.

What kind of learning experience was this for the actors and the audience? Were the actors "empowered" and did audience members experience empathy, education, and the necessary motivation for engagement? Early interviews with the actors reveal that all gained something from the experience, whether it was in the creative process and the joy of performing; a therapeutic and cathartic release in telling their stories; an educational and leadership capacity from sharing ideas and insights about homelessness; interactional skills gained from socializing with others and learning tolerance; or the development of better communication skills, more self-awareness, or self-confidence. As for the audience, in some ways, it was not as diverse as we had hoped—there were more women than men and university-educated folks were over-represented in comparison to the general population—but on the other hand, there was more diversity in age and income levels than that commonly found in theatre audiences. Typically, gender, income, level of education, and age are important variables in predicting audience attendance in theatre and other performing arts. In Canada, women, and those with higher incomes and educational credentials, are more likely to attend than other groups (Hill Strategies Research Inc. 2003). The audience for *Home/Less/Mess* differed in that the largest category of attendees reported an annual household income before taxes of less than $25,000. However, the second largest category of attendees reported an annual household income of $100,000+. While some members of the audience were well aware of the issues of homelessness before seeing the play, it turned out that we were not just preaching to the converted. Many audience members reported that the play made them more aware of the issues, provided insight into the lives of the homeless, and helped them respect and feel connected to homeless individuals.[10] They admired the actors and used adjectives such as "amazing," "open," "honest," "brave," and "passionate" to describe them. They felt that the play was important for the community, and for the first time, many understood the difficulties homeless people have in negotiating impersonal, rigid, and complex government bureaucracies. As well, although most respondents cited affordable housing, increased funding, and a restructuring of the "system" as the primary solutions to the problem of homelessness, a significant number argued that the community needed to "get involved." Some promised to be personally involved in the fight to end homelessness. We need, argued one audience member, to work on "developing a sense of responsibility for each other." Many audience members ended the survey with a "thank-you" to the participants and organizers of the project and play, along with a plea "to do it again" (see Chapter 7: Conclusion on the broader significance of production and performances).

NOTES

1   A transdisciplinary approach is the only form that clearly breaks down and transcends disciplinary boundaries. Academic collaboration becomes a process that generates research questions, theoretical, and methodological frameworks unique to the research project. In a multidisciplinary collaboration, researchers work together periodically, but they maintain their own disciplinary boundaries and often publish in their own journals. Finally, interdisciplinary research projects are those where knowledge is shared and links are made between the various disciplines in order to understand the topic under investigation (Brock University 2015; Harvard University 2015; Stember in Jensenius 2012, Washington University School of Medicine 2015).

2   For an analysis of the multidisciplinary collaboration during the rehearsal process, see Farough (2016).

3   Definitions of popular theatre vary. Filewod defines popular theatre as theatre which uses methods that are participatory in nature and directed toward community activism (2011). Errington (in Conrad 2009) sees popular theatre as "issues-based, socially critical, or critically reflective drama" (174).

4   The project will be documented with the use of ethnography. Ethnography, in the classical sense, involves extensive fieldwork using participant observation. The researcher participates with the group she/he is researching and "observes," supplementing written field notes with methods such as formal and informal interviewing, document collecting, surveying, filming, etc. (Madden 2010). The project will involve an ethnography of the process of collective creation with the homeless in the workshops and rehearsals, the actual performances, audience reaction to the performances, and possibly a follow-up with the homeless participants.

5   Diamond (2007) explains that as the oppressors come from the same living community as the oppressed and their behaviour (like that of the oppressed) needs to be challenged and changed, his work also "makes space to investigate the fears, desires and motivations of the oppressor" (38).

6   Public sociology is defined as "sociology done as a partnership where sociologists and public organizations and interest groups each bring their own agenda and then negotiate the actual direction that research will take. . . . Sociology which reaches beyond its own disciplinary boundaries to involve the larger community in public discussions about the nature of society, its values, and any gap between what society promises its members and what it delivers" (Burawoy 2004, 7).

7   The women changed their minds several times, but in the end their concern about what the other Roma in their community would think of them was the deciding factor. They "did not want to make a laughingstock out of themselves in front of other Roma" (Kazubowski-Houston 2010, 72–73).

8   Many of us realize that we are "pretty ignorant about the homeless population and their experiences and why they are where they are and that they are not all the same" (NSL member).

9   The Cope (Career Orientation and Personal Empowerment) Program, developed for women, merged with the Meca (Men's Education and Career Alternatives) Program at TRU in 1998 (Schmiedl 2015).

10   For a full analysis of the audience survey results, see Farough (2016).

References

Alvarez, N., and C. Graham. 2011. "Performance and Health." *Canadian Theatre Review* 146:3–5.

Bourdieu, P. 1979. *Distinction: A Social Critique of the Judgment of Taste*. London: Routledge.

Brock University. 2015. *Transdisciplinary Research: Beyond Boundaries*. http://www.brocku.ca/trans-disciplinary-research.

Burawoy, M. 2004. "The Critical Turn to Public Sociology." In *Enriching the Sociological Imagination: How Radical Sociology Changed the Discipline*, edited by R. Levine, 309–22. Boulder, CO: Paradigm.

Conrad, D. 2009. "Exploring Risky Youth Experiences: Popular Theatre as a Participatory, Performative Research Method." In *Method Meets Art: Arts-Based Research Practice*, edited by P. Leavy, 162–78. New York: Guilford Press.

Cox, S. M., M. Kazubowski-Houston, and J. Nisker. 2009. "Genetics on Stage: Public Engagement in Health Policy Development on Preimplantation Genetic Diagnosis." *Social Science and Medicine* 68:1472–80.

Denzin, N. 2003. *Performance Ethnography: Critical Pedagogy and the Politics of Culture*. Thousand Oaks, CA: Sage.

Diamond, D. 2007. *Theatre for Living: The Art and Science of Community-Based Dialogue*. Victoria, BC: Trafford.

Dubinsky, L. 2006. "In Praise of Small Cities: Cultural Life in Kamloops, BC." *Canadian Journal of Communication* 31 (1): 85–106.

Dunning, E., and J. Hughes. 2013. *Norbert Elias and Modern Sociology*. London: Bloomsbury.

Farough, D. 2016. "The Messy Business of Art, Research, and Collaboration: Audience Engagement in *Home/Less/Mess*." *Journal of Contemporary Drama in English* 4 (2): 320–38. doi:10.1515/jcde-2016-0022.

Filewod, A. 2011. *Committing Theatre: Theatre Radicalism and Political Intervention in Canada*. Toronto: Between the Lines.

Genshorek, T. 2013. *No Straight Lines*. Meeting Minutes. Kamloops, BC.

Halvorson, B. 2010. "Theatre for the Living and Practicing Democracy: Negotiating the Monologic Beast." In *Popular Political Theatre and Performance: Critical Perspectives on Canadian Theatre in English, Vol. 17*, edited by J. Salverson, 124–29. Toronto: Playwrights Canada Press.

HAP (Homelessness Action Plan). 2012. *Kamloops Homelessness Action Plan: Life Skills Development Project Report*.

Harvard University. 2015. *Harvard Transdisciplinary Research in Energetics and Cancer Center*. https://www.hsph.harvard.edu/trec/about-us/definitions/.

Hill Strategies Research Inc. 2003. *Performing Arts Attendance in Canada and the Provinces.* http://www.hillstrategies.com.

Jensenius, A. R. 2012. *Disciplinarities: Intra, Cross, Multi, Inter, Trans.* http://www.arj.no/2012/03/12/disciplinarities-2/.

Kazubowski-Houston, M. 2010. *Staging Strife: Lessons from Performing Ethnography with Polish Roma Women.* Montreal: McGill-Queen's University Press.

Lamont, M. 2009. *How Professors Think: Inside the Curious World of Academic Judgment.* Cambridge, MA: Harvard University Press.

Lunde, A., K. Heggen, and R. Strand. 2012. "Knowledge and Power: Exploring Unproductive Interplay between Quantitative and Qualitative Researchers." *Journal of Mixed Methods Research* 7 (2): 197–210.

Madden, R. 2010. *Being Ethnographic: A Guide to the Theory and Practice of Ethnography.* Thousand Oaks, CA: Sage.

Pratt, G., and C. Johnston. 2010. "Translating Research into Theatre: Nanay, A Testimonial Play." In *Popular Political Theatre and Performance: Critical Perspectives on Canadian Theatre in English, Vol. 17,* edited by J. Salverson, 173–79. Toronto: Playwrights Canada Press.

Roberts, B. 2008. "Performative Social Science: A Consideration of Skills, Purpose and Context." *Forum Qualitative Social Research* 9 (2): Art. 58. http://www.qualitative-research.net.

Schmiedl, L. 2015. "A Remarkable Richness of Heart." *Bridges* 13:7.

Valentine, K. B. 2006. "Unlocking the Doors for Incarcerated Women through Performance and Creative Writing." In *The Sage Handbook of Performative Studies,* edited by D. Soyini Madison and J. Hamera, 309–24. Thousand Oaks, CA: Sage.

Van Den Hoonaard, W. 2011. *The Seduction of Ethics: Transforming the Social Sciences.* Toronto: University of Toronto Press.

Wallewein, D. 1994. "'Collective Creation': A Multidisciplinary Drama Program." *The Clearing House* 67 (6): 345–47.

Washington University School of Medicine. 2015. *What Is Interdisciplinary Research?* St. Louis: TREC Center. http://www.obesity-cancer.wustl.edu/en/About/What-Is-Transdisciplinary.

The Kamloops Public Produce Project: A Story of Place, Partnerships, and Proximity in an Edible Garden Setting

Robin Reid and Kendra Besanger

Introduction

In this chapter we describe a grassroots-initiated urban agriculture project introduced in Kamloops, British Columbia, in 2011. As one of the first urban agriculture projects of its kind in Canada, the "Public Produce Project" interrupted the prescribed logic of a downtown urban space by creating an innovative response to issues of sustainability and food production at the local level. It was Kamloops' first fully public garden project, and it transformed a derelict urban lot into a fertile garden oasis. Its public success demonstrated the capacity of the community to produce free food in an urban setting, and it prompted residents and the municipal government to rethink the potential of edibles in urban spaces. The garden lasted two full growing seasons in its initial location and was moved to an alternative location after those two years. It also catalyzed the creation of a permanent, municipally funded public produce garden in the city's McDonald Park in 2012, a development that offers a cautionary note about

FIGURE
4.1."Public
Produce,"
drawing and
digital design by
E. Hope, 2011.
Poster courtesy of
Bonnie Klohn.

the potential gains from vertical linkages (as per Dale and Newman; see Introduction), particularly in a small city where financial limitations may open avenues for powerful global corporations to manipulate local spaces to their own advantage.

While acknowledging that one garden in a small city cannot address the multiple dynamics of food production at the global or local levels, the Public Produce Project successfully demonstrated that edible gardens and urban agriculture initiatives are able to challenge our perception of where food production can take place and to prompt conversations about the potential for municipalities to grow food in urban settings. If we imagine cities as "strategic terrains," as Duxbury (2014) suggests, we can conceptualize localized, creative, and innovative projects within cities as strategic, local responses to global conditions (1). Kamloops' first public produce garden became a "strategic terrain" for initiating conversations about innovative urban agriculture initiatives in the city and, consequently, about the larger, globalized food system. Its physical location in the downtown core, combined with its open access concept, meant that people from all walks of life could access the garden and participate in these conversations. Open access and participation are important aspects of building equality and improving quality of life in cities in general. As the author of *Public Produce*, Darrin Nordahl (2009), points out, "the best place[s] to realize the environmental, economic, and equitable benefits of a more local system of agriculture may not be in some rural or exurban location, but in and among the places we pass by daily on our way to work, home, school, commerce, and recreation" (8). The physical location of the Public Produce Project was exactly this: half a block from City Hall, adjacent to a well-travelled sidewalk, on a main street. It sat across the street from a locally owned restaurant that prides itself in serving local food. It shared a wall with the Kamloops Immigrant Services office, a community organization that "deliver[s] programs and activities designed to facilitate immigrants, visible minorities, first-generation Canadians and their families in becoming full and equal members of Canadian society." A locally owned café, a volunteer-run thrift store, and the city's main Royal Bank branch were the garden's other nearby neighbours. It is significant to note that the garden was located on a route that employees from City Hall, the BC Lottery Corporation (BCLC), and the Cornerstone, a large office building containing approximately 20 businesses, walked every day to get coffee or go for lunch. This means that dozens of people passed by the garden on a daily basis for two full growing seasons.

To assist in our discussion of the Kamloops Public Produce Project and to frame the concepts of *leadership, learning,* and *collaboration* as fundamental concepts in building *equality of quality of life* in a small city, we draw on a range of authors offering theoretical and practical insights into transforming urban spaces and ultimately changing our relationships with each other and our cities. Charles Montgomery (2013) reminds us that the power to change the way we live, work, and play in our urban spaces often is in our own hands and, fundamentally, rests in thoughtful, playful design. The Kamloops Public Produce Project exemplified the potential for playful, welcoming design to engage residents and influence policy by leading through example. Within the context of empowerment and the re-visioning of urban spaces, we also recognize the work of Duxbury (2014), which draws attention to the importance of localized, collaborative social processes and networks as being significant to building sustainable cities. We draw on the work of Dale and Newman (2010) to explore the role of government and the network structure that supports bridging, bonding, and vertical forms of social capital. Through a Community Capitals Framework (CCF), Emery and Flora (2006) illustrate how increases in social capital can create a spiraling-up process that mutually reinforces other community capitals—a necessary condition of sustainable community development. If the flow of assets increases across community capitals (natural, cultural, human, social, political, financial, and built), then the assets gained in one capital are likely to increase assets in another capital, resulting in an upward spiral (2006). Consequently, the "best entry point to spiraling up is social capital" (23), as it draws on connections among people and organizations and provides the social "glue" to make things happen (21).

In the context of the garden, the interaction among the natural, cultural, human, social, political, and financial capitals stimulated an increase in assets across all of these community capitals. The location of the garden (natural), the initial startup grant (financial), and the abilities and skills people used to build the garden site and access further resources (human) resulted in an increased flow of assets across the capitals. Social capital is perhaps the most important in mobilizing resources, bringing people and organizations together, and creating an integrated strategy to make things happen. In the context of a grassroots approach, the increase in social capital also builds political capital as people find their own voice and through alternative actions contribute to the well-being of the community. Emery and Flora (2006) suggest the entry point for community change begins with critical investments in social capital. Additionally, Lon Dubinsky (2006) provides a foundation for exploring the theoretical implications of the geographical and social proximity of people, organizations, and neighbourhoods. Dubinsky suggests, "Proximities within a

ROBIN REID AND KENDRA BESANGER

city equally give meaning, shape, and effect to cultural production and participation" (96). Dubinsky expands on this, explaining that "proximity in its many forms is a key factor in the cultural life of the small city. It has symbolic significance and determines to some degree the location and flow of social and cultural capital" (97). The concept of *proximity* is useful in understanding the impact and influence of the Public Produce Project because it helps to frame the garden project through the factors of *access, public interaction,* and *political visibility. Proximity* also works to connect the physical garden space with discourses of place, community collaboration, and leadership.

In addition to framing the Public Produce Project through the concept of proximity, we suggest that the project successfully transformed a space into a place. As such, we draw from social geographers and place theorists such as Doreen Massey, Yi-Fu Tuan (1974), and Lucy Lippard (1997), who, among many others, suggest that spaces become places when people spend time in them, care for them, tell stories about them, and, connect with them. Doreen Massey's work (1994) provides a vocabulary to discuss the "need to conceptualize space as constructed out of interrelations, as the simultaneous coexistence of social interrelations and interactions at all spatial scales, from the most local level to the most global" (264). Massey's seminal text *Space, Place, and Gender* laid the groundwork for an understanding of space as socially constructed. In an interview from 2013, Massey reminds us that spatial relations are material but never void of social interactions or exchanges; in fact, social relations themselves produce geographies (Warburton, 2013). Tuan (1974) considers the ways in which people interact with and form attachments to space, suggesting that "what begins as undifferentiated space becomes place as we get to know it better and endow it with value" (6). Lippard (2013) points out that it is easier to identify a place than it is to create one and, most importantly, that understanding a place requires spending time in that place to understand its social complexities and details: "It's hard to make a place. It's easier to recognize a place, but that means you have to learn to read it, see what it's used for, who goes there and why, where, when" (3).

We framed our study of the Public Produce Project as a space transformed into a place through citizen-led engagement, and we narrowed our focus to the intersection of geographical space and place theory and the discourse of alternative food politics (Harris 2010; DuPuis and Goodman 2005; Hinrichs 2007; Massey 2007; Amin 2002). How we construct our social and political relationships with place is of considerable significance to how alternative food initiatives are perceived in the context of urban spaces.

Our Approach

As researchers, our own proximity to the project was integral to our research approach. We were both involved as participants in the Kamloops Public Produce Project from its outset. In 2011, we participated in the project's conceptualization and construction, and the planting and maintenance of the garden. We also contributed to the *Strategic Plan (2012)* and the *Public Produce Start-up Guide (2012)*. In addition, we contributed to several municipal and community grant proposals between 2012 and 2013. While we were not the primary grant holders, we did contribute to the grant applications. Grassroots-level initiatives often lack the kind of research that is so critical to the success and longevity of citizen-led projects. As researchers, we were able to use our research results to highlight the value of community-university research partnerships through letters of support for KFPC's grant applications, progress reports, and presentations to City Council. In the capacity of participant observers, we were able to witness, document, and participate in the complex issues of leadership, networking, community collaboration, and funding—all the realities that need to be considered when reflecting on what it means to *act locally*.

The Kamloops Public Produce Project has been an ideal project to engage with, not only as an object of academic inquiry but also as a place of lived experience and praxis: "lived experience is central [. . .] to the subject of place" (Lippard 1997, 5). Thus, the purpose of this chapter is not to engage in an objective case study of the garden or to draw broad generalizations about gardens or garden projects. Instead, we use this chapter as an opportunity to provide a critical, pragmatic discussion about the complexities of the Public Produce Project, with the hopes of illuminating what it means to work collaboratively to transform a space into a public place, with a desired outcome of improving both quality of place and equality of quality of life.

Formal Network Linkages

Kamloops Public Produce Project
Thompson- Shuswap Master
Gardeners
Kamloops Food Policy Council
Interior Health Authority (funding)
Tri-City Contracting (land)
Urban Systems
Kamloops Community Gardens
City of Kamloops
Thompson Rivers University
(Small Cities CURA)

Media
Our blog, Facebook,
email, posters
Local Media Outlets:
TV, radio, newspaper

Donors
Royal Bank of Canada, Artizan
Horticulture, Home Hardware,
Painless Underground Irrigation,
Everyone's Eden, Greenhouse
Design and Construction

Informal Network Linkages

Community Groups
School District #73
Interior Community Services Interior
Indigenous
Friendship Society
Kamloops Food Bank
Open Door Group's Garden Gate The
United Way
Kamloops Farmers Market

**Individual Community Members
with similar interests:
food security, urban spaces,
healthy city**

Cooks, Gardeners, Wanderers, Artists,
Municipal Government Staff, Farmers,
Teachers, Students, Nurses, Carpenters,
the Elderly, Restaurant Owners,
Downtown Business Owners,
Kamloops Immigration Society

FIGURE 4.2. Public Produce Project Network by Robin Reid and Kendra Besanger.
Design by Moneca Jantzen, Daily Designz.

The Story of the Garden

Early Spring

In January 2011, a building was razed at the east end of Victoria Street, the main street in downtown Kamloops. In the wake of the demolition, a space taking up half a city block was left vacant.

Curious about the newly vacant space, a few Kamloops residents who had previously connected through a local not-for-profit agency called the Kamloops Food Policy Council (KFPC)[1] met to discuss ideas for the future of the site. At the time, the group members imagined a garden oasis in the middle of downtown: a space filled with benches, raised garden beds, and edible plants. A few weeks later, the residents set up a meeting with Casey VanDongen, the person they thought was the sole owner of the land, and the group pitched the idea of installing a temporary, edible demonstration garden on his site. During that meeting, the group learned that the space actually consisted of three lots, not one. At that point, VanDongen was unable to develop anything on the site because his lots were split in two by the second owner.[2] VanDongen expressed an interest in purchasing the middle lot, so he could own the entire space, but had been unable to do so up until that point. So, when the group proposed setting up a temporary garden, he offered up one of his two lots: the narrow lot, adjacent to the Cornerstone Building, on the west end of the space (see Figure 4.3).

After gaining permission to use the lot, the group needed to secure funding in order to move the project ahead. One of the group members, a co-chair of the Kamloops Food Policy Council and, by profession, a dietitian with the regional health authority, Interior Health, alerted the group to a grant opportunity with Interior Health. In March 2011, the group successfully applied for $4,500 in funding through Interior Health's Community Food Action Initiative Grant. The funding provided the group with essential resources to go forward and leverage other sources of funding, both in cash and in kind. The process of writing the grant also helped the group establish the primary objectives of the garden as well as a project timeline.

SOUTH	SOUTH	SOUTH	SOUTH
Lot A Vacant (owned by VanDongen)	**Lot B** Vacant Owner/developer began erecting a building in 2013	**Lot C** Vacant (owned by VanDongen) Site of produce garden	**Cornerstone** **Building** Kamloops Immigrant Society Office and 20+ other businesses
NORTH	*NORTH*	*NORTH*	*NORTH*

FIGURE 4.3. Division of Vacant Space on Victoria Street in Kamloops.

The group stated that the garden would do the following:

- Act as a demonstration project for public produce
- Increase awareness about local food security and healthy food
- Act as a tool to educate residents about growing edibles
- Encourage the creation of municipal policy that would support urban agricultural initiatives on public and private land

The group partnered with two local Kamloops organizations to submit the grant to Interior Health: the already nationally successful Kamloops Food Policy Council (KFPC) and the well-established Thompson-Shuswap Master Gardeners Association. The application was successful, which was a fundamental to the success of the project. *Without the $4,500 in funding, it would not have been possible for the group to leverage the human and financial resources necessary to build the garden.* The grant money funded the levelling of the lot and the purchasing of the wood and soil for the raised beds. But, perhaps more importantly, it also allowed critical communications and community outreach work to be done. The group was tasked with asking for community and business support for a project that the community had never seen before. Knowing this would be one of the biggest challenges, the group hired a local artist very early on to create a poster and a visual identity for the project. From there, they had the capacity to go out into the community and explain the project's purpose and ask for support.

In addition to the grant funding, the connections and proximity of the group to the local community made outreach possible. The core working group of the Public Produce Project came to consist of the co-chair of KFPC (also a dietitian at the Interior Health Authority); the Kamloops Community Gardens coordinator (also a landscape designer by trade); the president of the Thompson-Shuswap Master Gardeners Association; an assistant professor at Thompson Rivers University (TRU); students in Visual Arts and Interdisciplinary Studies programs at TRU; a resident who had grown up in Kamloops and had been attending KFPC meetings for a few months, prior to the initiation of the project, and became the project's coordinator; and, more peripherally, other members of the KFPC.

The individuals who formed the Public Produce Project working group had relevant and diverse strengths, insights, and skill sets, as well as important local connections and networks to contribute to the project. They differed in background, age, and experience; some had never gardened, while others had made careers of it. Each group member also had specific ties to the local business community that made in-kind donations possible. For example, the irrigation was installed by a local company who provided in-kind labour and supplies in exchange for having their name on the welcome sign. The actual construction and daily maintenance of the garden relied heavily on the collaborative efforts of volunteers, community organizations, and local networks. These varied types of networks are what Dale and Newman (2010) pronounce as crucial to "accessing more diverse kinds of capital, particularly social linking ties" (8). Collaborative strategies are fundamental to Emery and Flora's (2006) "spiraling up process," whereby the flow of assets increases across community capitals (natural, cultural, human, social, political, financial, and built), resulting in a mutually reinforcing increase in all assets. The group members' previous investments and connections to their local community meant they could effectively utilize and mobilize their networks and resources to the benefit of the garden.

In addition to the materials and expert labour donated by local companies, contributions from local not-for-profit organizations were essential to the garden's progress and success. The combined and collective labour, time, and resources of the group and all of the community contributors successfully leveraged an astounding $35,000 from the initial $4,500 grant. A "Day of Caring" was organized through the United Way. Through this initiative, Royal Bank of Canada (RBC) employees spent a day in the garden moving soil into the raised beds. On that same day, a smaller not-for-profit organization called Garden Gate also provided labour and donated seedlings. Garden Gate is a local horticulture project and training centre that promotes healthy eating and active living for persons with mental health challenges. Students from the nearby Stuart Wood Elementary School helped with the planting of the garden, which also engaged them in conversations about edible gardening and food security, and brought a younger generation from the community into the garden. In one day, three otherwise unrelated groups spent time in the space together, contributing to a local place-making initiative that would not have been possible without their participation. One way to understand the strength built through these community partnerships is through Dubinsky's (2005) notion of "culture of participation; a type of social capital stretching across sectors, age groups and neighbourhoods" (81).

The garden also engaged university students and professors. Students from TRU were given an opportunity to apply innovative and creative methods to engage with the space. For example, one student in the Visual Arts program at TRU documented the development of the garden though a series of photographs. Another Visual Arts student constructed a biodegradable mural on the back wall of the Cornerstone building, directly adjacent to the garden. Additionally, a Bachelor of Interdisciplinary Studies student at TRU used qualitative research methods to investigate public responses to the garden. These three students came into contact with the garden through Community University Research Alliance (CURA). In essence, the garden provided an ideal space for work study projects and research collaborations with community partners. All of these engagements built community awareness and connections, while simultaneously sharing knowledge and resources fundamental to community collaborations (Garrett-Petts 2005).

Early Summer

At the beginning of May 2011, the garden beds had been built, soil had been delivered, but edibles had not been planted yet.[3] Residents were starting to hear about the project, but many were still unaware. The KFPC hosted a two-day public produce event, consisting of a local stakeholders' workshop and a public talk given by Darrin Nordahl, author of *Public Produce* (2009). Nordahl is a landscape architect and community planner who has used public produce policies and practices to transform the urban landscape of Davenport, Iowa. The KFPC hosted Nordahl at Thompson Rivers University for a public presentation about the potential of public produce to transform cities. Additionally, a stakeholders' workshop called "Designing Healthy Cities" was hosted by the City of Kamloops and facilitated by Nordahl and two employees from Urban Systems, a local urban design firm. The goals of the workshop were to:

- inform key stakeholders of the progressive, community-minded initiatives taking place in urban settings—specifically to discuss development, design, and policy as they relate to the production of local food.

- begin creating a strategy that would move Kamloops forward in both policy and practice.

The workshop attracted approximately 45 people and successfully created a space for discussing practical ways through which we might collectively address urban food production initiatives. Workshop attendees (stakeholders) included private business owners, municipal staff, Thompson-Nicola Regional District (TNRD) staff, Interior Health Authority (IHA) staff, members of not-for-profit / community organizations, School District 73 staff, developers, and city councillors. Duxbury (2014) has highlighted the importance of "collaborative social processes, diverse knowledge and perspectives, and citizen participation" (1) as being significant to city planning and citizen responses to issues of sustainability at the global and local levels, and the workshop exemplified the power of citizen participation and perspectives. The goals of the workshop and the initiation of the garden on Victoria Street were complementary because they empowered people to imagine alternatives to traditional urban landscaping. Nordahl's concept of *public produce* invites people to consider municipal land as ideal for growing food. He argues that municipalities have land, staff, irrigation, and all of the resources required to maintain parks and gardens; thus edibles can be grown assuming a redirection of resources. As a result of this collective visioning process and the citizen participation, the City of Kamloops gathered key citizen input for future public produce initiatives in Kamloops.

A few weeks after the workshop, the garden was planted by way of the "Big Public Plant-In." City councillors, business owners, community organizations, students, and friends and family of the core public produce group participated by planting seedlings that had been donated by community organizations. Local master gardeners led the plant-in and incorporated important educational gardening tips throughout the day. For Charles Montgomery (2013), the pursuit of urban happiness relies on strong positive relationships that build community across private and public spaces. Thus, the "Big Public Plant-In" exemplified the kind of space and event where such relationships are formed, and the garden site, thereafter, became a nexus for these kinds of relationships.

Summer

Throughout the summer, the garden thrived. It was well utilized and very well respected. Beans disappeared quickly, squash blossoms were harvested, tomatoes ripened beautifully and then vanished, and the space became a tiny, fertile oasis in the middle of the city's downtown core. "Lunch and Learn" workshops were held in the garden; edibles were donated to downtown businesses (to extend the garden's reach along Victoria Street); and information about the garden was distributed during public events and street carnivals.

By mid-August, the garden was in full bloom and the team organized a grand opening—another chance for site-specific community engagement. Citizens, community organizations, the mayor, downtown business

FIGURE 4.4. Educational signs in the garden. Photo by Bonnie Klohn, 2011.

FIGURE 4.5. Onsite photo—Kamloops Public Produce Project. Photo by Bonnie Klohn, 2011.

ROBIN REID AND KENDRA BESANGER

owners, and the media were invited to share a midday potluck feast to celebrate the grand opening and marvel at the success of this tiny, temporary, and delicious garden. The grand opening, aptly named the "Gala in the Garden," brought even more publicity to the Public Produce Project. Through the workshops, volunteer sessions, and celebrations, the garden came to exemplify the power that vibrant public spaces hold, and the persuasive political potential they can create when successful.

Putting the Garden into Context: Community Collaboration

How we collaborate, and with whom, is important to the overall success of any project that relies on community support. Dubinsky (2006) acknowledges that collaboration, through multiple organizational structures, relies on a lexicon of "strategic alliances, shared resources, co-productions, co-sponsorships, and cross-sectoral partnerships." He also suggests that these collaborations "govern, if not determine, the organization of many activities, including cultural production and participation" (99). In the beginning, the Public Produce Project was faced with three large challenges: raising adequate funds for the project; putting forth a new, unusual, and untested idea in the community; and acquiring credibility as a new community initiative. In order to meet these challenges, the Kamloops Public Produce Project—as a new, unknown group—needed to partner with an organization that had already established itself in the community. As mentioned, this partnership was beneficial during the grant-writing process and helped them to secure adequate funds for the project, but it was also beneficial to the project's continued success in the community. The KFPC, being a well-established, grassroots organization, had already experienced significant success in the community. When the Public Produce Project reached out to the community for support and in order to grow awareness of the garden project, they were able to reference the KFPC, which already had name recognition throughout the community. The Public Produce Project's connection to the KFPC was also particularly helpful in dealing with the municipality. The KFPC had been working with the City of Kamloops for many years, so the fact that the Public Produce Project operated beneath the umbrella of the KFPC added to the validity of the project. It also made connecting with the right city staff much easier. Establishing connections with decision makers and authority figures such as government helps build "vertical ties" and enhances the network structure described by Dale and Newman (2010). They argue that "the network structure that is necessary for sustainable community development is one that is open, diverse, and involves social capital ties at the bridging and vertical levels" (9).

The Public Produce Project's connection to the KFPC also made connecting with volunteers much easier and, not surprisingly, these volunteers became an essential part of getting the idea of the garden out into the community. Not only could these volunteers tend to the garden on a daily basis, they were able to connect with local businesses in the downtown and spread the word. Through the "Adopt an Edible" initiative, the volunteers provided one small planter full of edible plants to each of the businesses to place outside their storefronts. The planter pots served to initiate a discussion with customers about the garden initiative down the street. Eleven businesses participated in the initiative and maintained their edibles throughout the growing season. A few of the businesses continued to grow edibles in pots the next year. Although Adopt an Edible did not last as a community-driven initiative, several downtown restaurants continued to grow herbs on their patio, even after the Public Produce Project was moved to its second location (on the North Shore of the city). In April 2013 the garden was moved to Elm Street on the North Shore. Through a partnership with a private landowner and a community organization called ASK Wellness, the garden found a new home. The actual location of the garden is described by the garden coordinator as an "in between site," one that is between a shopping area and a main street on the North Shore that sees more vehicle traffic than pedestrians. In the first season the garden was well received by residents in the area, as indicated by one resident who described it as "a miracle in her neighbourhood." She also recalled two seniors from the nearby Renaissance seniors low-income apartment building walking by and stopping to share their stories of their own gardens they had tended before moving into assisted living (see Chapter 7: Conclusion for more insights into the South Shore and North Shore landscapes, and the new public produce leadership).

ROBIN REID AND KENDRA BESANGER

The motivation for establishing collaborative networks in the context of the garden were closely aligned with what Dubinsky (2006) identifies as an *organic* collaboration—and *self-interested* collaboration. While the Public Produce Project's initial collaboration with the KFPC happened organically, through various serendipitous meetings and conversations and brainstorming between community members, the formal partnership was created knowing that the KFPC would provide legitimacy and mentorship for a young project, still in the early stages of conceptualization. This purposeful alignment is what Dubinsky (2006) refers to as *self-interest,* collaboration whereby "one or more parties will be specifically self-interested from the outset—on the lookout, as it were, for possible partnerships and alliances" (100). Dubinsky (2005) has pointed out that long-standing pools of social and cultural capital are instrumental in providing a continuity of engagement and participation in cultural activities in Kamloops, and the same can be said for the success of the Public Produce Project. According to Dubinsky, social capital in Kamloops is built on leadership and citizen participation, social ties, alliances, and other supportive voluntary activities (82). The Public Produce Project is an enactment of the culture of participation to which Dubinsky refers. The goal from the outset was to demonstrate, through practice, the capacity that community groups and municipalities have to make their cities more food-secure. The outcomes that were achieved by the end of the 2011 summer growing season well surpassed the initial expectations set out by the group, and good news arrived in 2012 when the project was granted access to the lot for a second year in a row.

Putting the Garden into Context: The Transformative Power of Engaging Spaces

One of the goals for *equality of quality of life* set forth by Montgomery is the notion that cities "should enable us to build and strengthen the bonds between friends, families and strangers that give life meaning, bonds that represent the city's greatest achievement and opportunity" (43). In support of this goal, Montgomery (2013) draws from a number of examples around the world where people have taken slices of urban land and transformed them into spaces that are interactive and engaging. The 120 x

15–foot parcel of land the garden project occupied was a long and narrow shape, and we hypothesize that the size and shape of this garden played an important role in encouraging interaction among strangers. The narrow width brought people into close proximity, which encouraged conversation and engagement. Montgomery (2013) proposes that "with the right triangulation, even the ugliest of places can be infused with the warmth that turns strangers into familiars by giving us enough reason to slow down" (167). Architect William Lim (2002) shares this perspective when he suggests that "the unexpected can sometimes be realized in the transformation of cracks and gaps from dead zones to extraordinary vibrant sites" (2). Perhaps the garden was a "hinge between an ordered and disordered space" that encouraged people to slow down and take a look (Jones 2007, 72); or perhaps it was the aesthetic and welcoming design that came forward and punctuated the neglected awkward spaces. Drawing on Dutch architect Jan Gel's studies of street edges, Montgomery has focused on the emotional responses people have to antisocial spaces versus spaces of conviviality. In his own study in New York, Montgomery found people were more likely to feel despondent and walk quickly through urban spaces of blank walls, sharp edges, uniform facades, or those fallen into disrepair. On the other hand, people are more likely to walk more slowly and pause in urban spaces that contain varied forms and functions, openings, and inviting features (Montgomery 2013, 161).

The Public Produce Project garden was a peculiar space in that it interrupted the normal flow of the downtown core. Its presence was unexpected and surprising. Additionally, its public, non-gated design also challenged pre-established notions of gated community gardens. Unlike most community gardens, public produce gardens are not gated, and individually leased plots do not exist. The food belongs to no one specifically and is accessible to everyone. Furthermore, anyone can contribute to the space through watering, weeding, and general maintenance; and no one is restricted from entering the space. In a public park, you can enjoy the space freely but you cannot pick the flowers or plant something in the garden beds. In community gardens, you most often have a key, a designated lock, and a sense that whatever you plant will be yours to eat when it is ready. In a public produce garden, there are no guarantees that what you planted will be there when you want it. At the same time, you can take anything you want and contribute however you please. The space itself invites public engagement and challenges the sense of ownership that so frequently dictates public behaviour in urban spaces.

The potential benefits of public produce are many, but it is also important that the language used to describe the garden does not create a perception of inclusion and exclusion. For example, when the Victoria Street garden was first relocated to Elm Street in 2013, the term "poverty reduction garden" was being used. The KFPC engaged in a discussion about the implications of this terminology, and it was decided that any reference to poverty reduction was inappropriate. One garden that subsists on such a small amount of funding cannot take on the burden of such a task as poverty reduction. Such language also reinforces the perception that public produce and urban agriculture initiatives are for the poor. The signage used for the entrance of the garden is equally important in ensuring the public perception is consistent with the notion of free, accessible food for everyone. The signage used at the entrance of the Victoria Street garden, "Kamloops Public Produce Project," was moved to the entrance of the garden on Elm Street to maintain consistency in the messaging and encourage access and participation in the garden from all members of the community.

Putting the Garden into Context: What Does *Public* Mean, Anyway?

The *public* garden concept was not immediately clear to people. Some were confused as to the purpose of the garden: Was it public or private? Who was the produce intended for? According to Reid, Besanger, and Klohn (2013), "The concept of *public* produce is new to most people, the concept of *free* is foreign to many and the concept of *communal* is not something that our society practices very often" (219). Comments collected from people visiting the garden and through a comment/suggestion box at the entrance to the garden indicated that many appreciated the garden but had not taken any food because they wanted to leave the produce for those in need. The assumption that public produce gardens are only for times of necessity or for those in need may belong to a history of people coming together in the production, harvest, and preservation of food during times of economic hardship, such as the Victory gardens during World War II. In her book *City Farmer*, Johnson (2011) acknowledges that public food gardens (in North America) are often assumed to be for those in the lower socio-economic classes for which the need to grow food reflects an individual's circumstances and reduced status (Reid, Besanger, and Klohn 2013).

In addition to the perception that the garden was created for "those in need," numerous comments from the public expressed surprise that the ungated garden had not been vandalized. Through interviews and informal conversations with the general public passing through the garden, there was a general concern that the garden would eventually be vandalized—because of the downtown location and the fact that it was not gated. One patron stated, "People will ruin it. What's the point? Everything gets vandalized anyway." Another patron voiced a concern that was heard frequently: "people will contaminate it," and hence they would "never eat from the garden." Before the project commenced, a city councillor suggested that people might "inject the tomatoes with heroin." These assumptions are particularly noteworthy in that they speak to a perception that places without supervision or gates will be vandalized. The garden was never vandalized or contaminated, and garbage was never found in the produce planters, which suggests that a certain respect was given to the plants. In its two-year existence in the downtown core, the garden was never mistreated. On the contrary, the garden promoted community interaction and respect. Business owners nearby suggested that the garden improved that part of the street and even made the area more inviting for patrons.

Interesting questions emerged from interviews with the Public Produce Project coordinators regarding the social construction of place. For example, do we know whether the space was respected because it was public or because it was a garden? Would the treatment of the garden change if the garden were to be situated in a different place in the city? Do we respond differently to community-generated spaces than we do to public parks? Does bottom-up, participatory design elicit a different kind of respect or engagement than top-down design supported by corporate sponsorships? The intent of the garden was to create a place where everyone would feel welcome and could enjoy both as a place of reprieve and as a source of healthy food. The diversity of people who used the garden for various purposes is worth noting—business people, pedestrians, homeless people, students, city staff, commuters, and patrons of the downtown all spent time in the garden. Each visitor to the garden had their own personal stories to tell.

A woman visiting Kamloops Immigrant Services[4] was thrilled to see Asian greens such as mizuna and kohlrabi in the garden, since she had not encountered these vegetables in Canada (Reid, Besanger, and Klohn 2013). The brightly coloured garden bench provided a peaceful place for a young business owner to take a break and think about her grandmother who had recently passed away. Around this same bench, cigarette butts and empty bottles were found by a volunteer during a scheduled early morning watering. Interestingly, this small amount of garbage was placed directly under the bench, not in the garden beds themselves. We hypothesized that people had spent some evening time in the garden, enjoying one another's company and a few drinks. The garden transformed an awkward and unusable space into an open access community space: a place of refuge and conviviality that challenged public perceptions of how we engage with urban spaces.

Putting the Garden into Context: Place, Proximity, and Politics

By now, the problematic characteristics inherent in the conventional food system have been well documented, including the physical and psychological disconnection that occurs when our food comes from places we don't know and is distributed through complex systems we don't recognize (Tracey 2011). Within alternative food networks (AFN), some activists view food systems embedded in the "local" as the counter to the unsustainable structure of the "global" domination of the conventional food system (Harris 2010). However, employing a defensive perspective of localism in response to globalism is criticized by number of authors as reactionary and regressive (Hinrichs 2007; DuPuis and Goodman 2005). According to Harris:

The message from critical commentaries of AFN activism, and indeed from critical human geography, is that in order to explore the politics of such place-based activism, concepts like "place" and "the local" cannot be taken as ontologically given: they must be recognized as social constructions (366).

With respect to the literature, Harris is in agreement with a number of authors (Agnew 2005; Creswell 2004; Massey 1999; Hinrichs 2007) who point out "that space and place are defined with reference to each other; and that the terms are co-constitutive" (359). Within this perspective of space and place as relational, the global and local nexuses inform each other as opposed to being binary opponents. For Harris, this assertion of place as open, collaborative, and constituted through social relations is viewed as vital to maintaining the possibility of generating political change from "grassroots" organizations (359).

In the case of the Public Produce Project, the garden was a grassroots pilot project intended to engage the community in new approaches to food security issues and urban agriculture. Although the City of Kamloops' Sustainable Kamloops Plan (2010) acknowledged the potential for edible landscaping practices and food security, and urban agriculture was becoming part of the public lexicon, it takes time for city administrators, elected officials, and urban planning departments to embrace the ideology of edible landscapes at the municipal level. For example, during the early months of developing the public produce garden, a group of anonymous food activists engaged in "guerrilla"-style planting of edibles in planter boxes in the public square outside of the main public library and Thompson Nicola Regional District (TNRD) administrative building. The location of the square and administrative offices is five blocks east of the public produce garden, at the opposite end of Victoria Street. Although members of the public voiced their support for the "guerrilla" edibles by writing letters to the editors of local newspapers, the produce was eventually uprooted by the TNRD administration, who was not very happy about the surreptitiously planted vegetables. The TNRD "had a liability concern and had intended to planters for floral beautification of the square" (Youds 2011, June 17). The response from the TNRD reveals how traditional decorative landscaping in public spaces is the common default. The Public Produce

Project group offered to adopt the uprooted vegetables and replanted them in the public produce garden.

Due to the proximity of the garden near City Hall and the downtown business centre, city administrators, staff, councillors, and the general public were able to watch the progress of the garden during their daily commute. Prior to the Public Produce Project, edible landscaping initiatives in Kamloops were, for the most part, visually and spatially minimal.[5] Hence, the location of the garden was instrumental in demonstrating to the municipal government that it is feasible to use urban spaces to grow food, and simultaneously beautify the downtown urban landscape. The Public Produce Project is an excellent example of the way in which citizen engagement on a local level changed the municipality's approach to food policy. Edible landscaping, public fruit trees in parks, and public produce have entered the lexicon of Kamloops city planners. In fact, the city received a large grant for street improvement along the south shore of the Thompson River—the Lorne Street Improvement Project. At a KFPC meeting in May 2012, it was explained that the city's success in attaining the grant was due to the edible landscaping initiatives that were written into the application. The Lorne Street Improvement project, now complete, further demonstrates how urban agriculture and municipal planning can transform the way that Kamloops will look and taste in the future.

The municipality made great strides in demonstrating its willingness to grow public produce on municipal lands. Not only did the city place public produce into its budget, they set into action a municipally run public produce garden that was constructed 2012. On June 7, 2012, the City of Kamloops issued a press release announcing the brand new "Kamloops Showcase Community Garden" at McDonald Park, which was a formal partnership of the City of Kamloops and Interior Community Services (ICS). The McDonald Park showcase garden was Kamloops' first municipal-led and maintained public produce garden. It was planted in McDonald Park near a residential area and not far from the primary business district. The garden was fenced but not locked, and it was a combination of community garden plots (assigned plots) and public produce areas (not assigned and available to anyone). However, the municipality's configuration of social capital as it relates to bridging and mobilization of resources may be quite different from the grassroots approach used at the

Victoria Street garden. For example, to attain funding for this garden, the city applied for a grant with Scotts Canada. This funding was meant to initiate a "Showcase" community garden and a municipally funded and organized public produce garden. The application was successful and the showcase garden received a $5,000 injection of cash from Scotts Canada's "Gro1000 initiative" and another $5,000 in Scotts Canada products. The grant from Scotts Canada provoked important and challenging questions in terms of community collaboration and leadership at the municipal level. The benefits of the project were that Kamloops was only one of two cities in Canada selected to receive this grant. One could argue that the community benefits of a demonstration garden and a community garden in the park outweigh any of the associated negative perceptions of the partnership with Scotts Canada. Others question the city's choice of partners in developing the showcase community garden and demonstration gardens.

Because community gardens in Kamloops are organic by regulation, the Community Gardens Coordinator could not utilize any of the Scotts products. She chose to receive bark mulch, which was immediately buried under the gazebo, so that the mulch would not touch any of the plants. The Public Produce Project's initiative works within the same, deliberate politics of organic growing practices and supports sustainable, local economies when it is able to. Scotts Canada is the sole distributor of Monsanto's herbicide Roundup, and this fact alone does not jive with the political position of the Kamloops Food Policy Council. The city's acceptance of a very small injection of cash was troubling to members of the KFPC because it demonstrated how corporate donations can often derail the focus and purpose of local public spaces as sites of community collaboration and engagement. For a $5,000 cash donation (and $5,000 product donation, all of which remained unused) in a $70,000 garden site, Scotts was able to leverage their investment into a marketing opportunity for their gardening products. Brightly coloured T-shirts with Scotts logos were worn by children, City of Kamloops staff, and Communities in Bloom members involved in the opening of the showcase garden. The grand opening of this Scotts garden resembled the garden section of a big box store and, through both aesthetic and tone, emphasized the business partnership rather than the years of community efforts related to food security. As Dale and Newman point out, local networks are composed of social ties, and the structure

ROBIN REID AND KENDRA BESANGER

of those ties influences access to power and resources. Consequently, different sources of power offer different options as to how space is defined and used. The events that took place in the creation of the Victoria Street and Elm Street gardens were part of a grassroots initiative that helped to cultivate an ethos within the space. The experience at McDonald Park was very different. What questions can be asked about leadership and design of public spaces under the influence of corporate sponsorship? The increasing reliance on private funding to subsidize public services and spaces is a challenge that is too large to tackle in this chapter but is certainly ever present in conversations about community-engaged projects, food security, and grassroots politics, generally speaking.

While collaboration with community partners is paramount to the success of public produce initiatives, the role of volunteers on an ongoing basis is significant to grassroots initiatives trying to sustain pools of social capital in the long term. For example, as the summer progressed at the Victoria Street site and Elm Street relocation, there were fewer volunteers in the garden. While we do not have any concrete explanations for the decreased participation, we did note that while community partners are paramount to building social capital, the success of the public produce garden and gardening tasks rely on the continued support of volunteers. Without regular volunteers, responsibilities increase for the public produce coordinator, in particular. Responsibility also falls on other members of the group, who may have given extra time to the project on top of their designated roles. An observation regarding volunteers, offered by the public produce coordinator for 2013, was that people did not feel comfortable volunteering if they were not associated with the garden through a non-profit group or some other form of formal association with the garden. Drawing specifically from organizations that already have a strong base of volunteers is a consideration for future grassroots initiatives.

Conclusion and Reflection

Looking at the Public Produce Project through Dubinsky's lens of proximity has enabled us to draw important links between our approach to food security and public produce initiatives, as well as to the partnerships and community collaborations that are created along the way. If we are to

rethink city design and our way of being in urban spaces, citizen participation and dialogue that encourages diverse knowledge and perspectives
is central to city planning (Duxbury 2014). As Gieseking et al. (2014) have
pointed out, "cities are malleable, pliable and constantly changing and as
such the experience we have of urban spaces is always a negotiation between various powers and influences" (221). We see from Emery and Flora
(2006) the significance of cultural capital in driving the flow of other capitals in an upward spiral. However, the quality of the interactions between
social capital and local leaders (political capital and vertical ties) plays a
critical role in maintaining an upward spiral—particularly in the case of
projects such as the public produce garden, positioned to challenge public
and political perceptions of access, equality, and food security in urban
public spaces.

Montgomery's notions (2013) of what makes a city happy and healthy
have helped us frame the Public Produce Project as something that
belongs to a larger cultural shift in urban place making. Contributing
to this discussion, a number of authors have suggested that a relational
perspective of place allows for "a non-territorial way of viewing place
politics in an age of global connectivity" (Amin 2002, 397). As DuPuis
and Goodman (2005) have pointed out, "an inclusive and reflexive politics
in place would understand local food systems not as local 'resistance'
against a global capitalist 'logic' but as a mutually constitutive, imperfect,
political process in which the local and the global make each other on
an everyday basis" (369). As researchers, although we often are engaged
in traditional academic discourse within our respective disciplines, this
project has provided us with an opportunity to write a narrative from
an interdisciplinary position that is both pragmatic and personal. It
also has given us the opportunity to reflect on the process of initiating,
creating, and documenting the public produce initiatives that have been
created in Kamloops. Through the research and writing process, we
have encountered questions that should be taken up in future research.
These questions include a focus on the lack of funding, the limited role
of volunteers in community-engaged projects, and the corporatization of
community spaces, which raise further questions about where funding
should come from and what the future of "public spaces" might look like.
Through our shared experiences in and reflections on the garden, we have

FIGURE 4.6. Kamloops Public Produce Project. Artistic rendition of the Public Produce Project by Shelaigh Garson, 2013. Courtesy of Shelaigh Garson.

come to appreciate how public produce gardens can be instrumental in situating people in place and creating opportunities for community and political engagement in urban agricultural initiatives.

As Montgomery has suggested, the happy city is one that moves beyond meeting the basic needs of food, shelter, and security. It also builds conviviality, recognizes the city's natural systems, and creates individual and collective benefits across public and private spaces. The Public Produce Project, which truly extended beyond the physical garden, demonstrated the potential of urban sites to become beautiful, inviting spaces of collaboration. By creating a place of engagement, reprieve, and inclusivity, public produce gardens have the potential to demonstrate the viability of local food production, and actively invite people to participate in the kind of complex local civic engagement that belongs to the "think global, act local" phenomenon. As we have illustrated, "acting locally" is complicated, challenging, full of imperfections, and requires a lot of work (as per Shucksmith; Montgomery—see Introduction to this volume). This kind of local work and critique needs to come to the forefront of our thinking and practice when we consider what exactly we mean when we say *act local*. As researchers at a small university in a small city, the local particularities of where we live, study, and work become apparent, particularly when working with community partners in reimagining our urban spaces. Collaborative initiatives such as the Public Produce Project enable multiple perspectives of place and heighten our understanding of *equality of quality of life* issues in Kamloops (see Chapter 7: Conclusion on perpetuation of Public Produce idea on the North Shore).

NOTES

1   The Kamloops Food Policy Council is a group that has been bringing food and food security–related organizations and individuals together to network for over 20 years. The group meets monthly, over potluck dinner, to exchange updates, events, and opportunities.

2   The space is made up of three lots owned by two different owners. It faces north and runs along the south side of Victoria Street. The garden was built in the narrow lot on the west side of the lot (adjacent to the Cornerstone building). This lot is owned by Casey VanDongen, of TriCity Developments. The lot immediately to the east of the narrow lot is owned by a different resident and the lot on the furthest east end is also owned by VanDongen. The narrow lot, upon which the garden was built, measured approximately 4.6 metres (15 feet) wide and 36.5 metres (120 feet) long.

3   Given the climate in Kamloops, best practices for planting edibles suggest plants should go in the ground toward the end of May.

4   At that time, Kamloops Immigrant Services was the neighbour to the west of the garden.

5   In 2010, the City of Kamloops and the Kamloops Downtown Business Association held a competition in which downtown business owners planted the large flower planters along Victoria Street. Many of these planters contained edibles, but the edible nature of these planters was not made highly public. In 2011, a month before the Public Produce Project's "public plant-in," the same planters were planted with edibles.

References

Agnew, J. 2005. "Space: 'Place.'" In *Spaces of Geographical Thought: Deconstructing Human Geography's Binaries*, edited by P. Cloke and R. Johnston, 81–96. Thousand Oaks, CA: Sage.

Amin, A. 2002. "Spatialities of Globalisation." *Environment and Planning A* 34 (3): 385–400.

Cresswell, T. 2004. *Place: A Short Introduction*. Oxford: Blackwell.

Dale, A., and L. Newman. 2010. "Social Capital: A Necessary and Sufficient Condition for Sustainable Community Development?" *Community Development Journal* 45 (1): 5–21.

Dubinsky, L. 2005. "The Culture of Participation." In *The Small Cities Book: On the Cultural Future of Small Cities*, edited by W. F. Garrett-Petts, 65–84. Vancouver: New Star Books.

Dubinsky, L. 2006. "In Praise of Small Cities: Cultural Life in Kamloops, BC." *Canadian Journal of Communication* 31 (1): 85–106.

DuPuis, E. M., and D. Goodman 2005. "Should We Go 'Home' to Eat?: Toward a Reflexive Politics of Localism." *Journal of Rural Studies* 21 (3): 359–71.

Duxbury, N. 2014. "Culture and Sustainability: How New Ways of Collaboration Allow Us to Re-Think Our Cities." *Observatorio Cultural*, published by the National Council for Culture and the Arts of Chile, 1–9. Chile: Santiago de Chile.

Emery, M., and C. Flora. 2006. "Spiraling-Up: Mapping Community Transformation with Community Capitals Framework." *Journal of the Community Development Society* 37 (1): 19–35.

Garrett-Petts, W., ed.. 2005. *The Small Cities Book On the Cultural Future of Small Cities*. Vancouver: New Star Books.

Gieseking, J. J., S. Low, S. Saegert, W. Mangold, and C. Katz, eds.. 2014. *The People, Place, and Space Reader*. London: Routledge.

Harris, E. M. 2010. "Eat Local? Constructions of Place in Alternative Food Politics." *Geography Compass* 4.4:355–69.

Hinrichs, C. C. 2007. "Introduction: Practice and Place in Remaking the Food System." In *Remaking the North American Food System: Strategies for Sustainability*, edited by C. C. Hinrichs and T. A. Lyson, 1–15. Lincoln: University of Nebraska Press.

Johnson, L. 2011. *City Farmer*. Vancouver: Greystone Books.

Jones. H. 2007. "Exploring the Creative Possibilities of Awkward Space in the City." *Landscape and Urban Planning* 83 (1): 70–76.

Lim, W. S. W. (2002). "Spaces of Indeterminacy (Conference Presentation)." In *Bridge the Gap*, edited by A. Miyake and H. U. Obrist. Kitakyushu: Centre for Contemporary Art and Koln: Verlag der Buchhandlung Walter Konig.

Lippard, L. 1997. *The Lure of the Local, Sense of Place in a Multicentered Society*. New York: The New Press.

Lippard, L. 2013. "Small Cities, Big Ideas." In *Whose Culture Is It Anyway? Community Engagement in Small Cities*, edited by W.F. Garrett-Petts, J. Hoffman, and G. Ratsoy. Vancouver: New Star Books.

Massey, D. 1994. *Space, Place, and Gender*. Minneapolis: University of Minnesota Press.

Massey, D. 1999. "Spaces of Politics." In *Human Geography Today*, edited by D. Massey, J. Allen, and P. Sarre, 279–94. Boston: Polity Press.

Massey, D. 2007. *World City*. Boston: Polity Press.

Montgomery, C. 2013. *Happy City: Transforming our Lives through Urban Design*. Toronto: Doubleday Canada.

Nordahl, D. 2009. *Public Produce*. Chicago: Island Press.

Reid, R., K. Besanger, and B. Klohn. 2013. "The Kamloops Public Produce Project: An Edible, Artistic Site of Social Change." In *Animation of Public Space Through the Arts: Toward More Sustainable Communities*, edited by N. Duxbury, 209–29. Coimbra, Portugal: Almedina.

Tracey, D. 2011. *Urban Agriculture: Ideas and Design for the New Food Revolution*. Gabriola Island, BC: New Society.

Tuan, Y. F. 1974. "Space and Place: Humanistic Perspective." *Progress in Human Geography* 6:211–52.

Warburton, Nigel. 2013. "Doreen Massey on Space." [Podcast interview transcript]. *Social Science Bites*. http://www.socialsciencespace.com/wp-content/uploads/DoreenMassey.pdf.

Youds, M. 2011, June 17. "Guerrilla Garden Transplanted to Produce Project." *Kamloops Daily News*.

The Kamloops Adult Learners Society: Leadership through Organic Partnerships and Knowledge Support in the Small City

Ginny Ratsoy

Introduction

Established by local seniors in 2005 out of a perceived need for afford-able, flexible education, the Kamloops Adult Learners Society (KALS) is a non-profit, independent organization dedicated to improving the community's quality of life by furthering the education of the growing demographic of retired people. This chapter, after situating the organi-zation in the context of the third-age learning movement, examines the motivation for its creation, its leadership and structure, the motivation of its students, and the community partnerships—particularly the exten-sive but unofficial relationship with Thompson Rivers University—that KALS has established. Applying select ingredients of the "basic recipe for happiness" of urban studies theorist Charles Montgomery (2013), and drawing on the works of small cities researcher Lon Dubinsky (2006) and

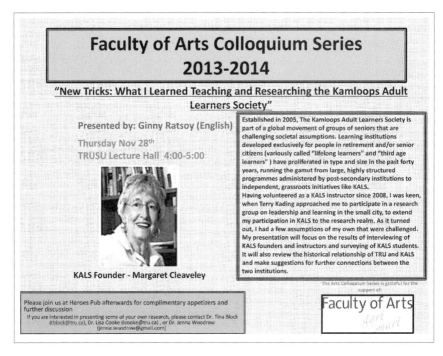

FIGURE 5.1. "Faculty of Arts Colloquium Series, 2013-2017," poster by Lisa Cooke.

rural leadership researcher Andrew Beer (2014), this study investigates the distinct challenges and successes of the leadership role of the Kamloops Adult Learners Society as a knowledge-support system in the small city and argues that the organization is a significant contributor to the quality of life of Kamloops.

When, in my third decade of teaching, I began to incorporate brief PowerPoint presentations and occasional YouTube videos into my classes, one of my students, apparently astonished, blurted out an old saw: "You *can* teach an old dog new tricks." I will, begrudgingly, acknowledge the "old dog" part, but, having taught retirees for over a dozen years, I have never for a nanosecond doubted that old dogs can learn, be taught—and teach—new tricks. The evidence goes well beyond the confines of my own experience and observation.

This chapter, after presenting a brief overview of the current global interest in various models of education for seniors, will provide a case study of the Kamloops Adult Learners Society by situating the organization in the context of third-age learner models and analyzing interviews with its leaders and surveys of its students to support the contention that KALS provides its students with transformational experiences. It will also explore a small-city relationship, best characterized as informal, between this vibrant group of seniors and selected constituents of the Kamloops community—particularly the Thompson Rivers University (TRU) community, a knowledge-support system with which no formal agreement has ever been drawn up—to support the contention that KALS' reach as a knowledge-support system in its own right extends into the larger community. I will employ components of models drawn from contemporary urban, small cities, and rural studies.

I borrow selected ingredients from "urban experimentalist" Charles Montgomery's (2013) "basic recipe for urban happiness" (43) (which, as Terry Kading indicates, can be extended beyond the urban design function to which Montgomery applies it). Montgomery (2013) envisions cities as instruments to improve individual and collective well-being: they should, for example, "maximize joy and minimize hardship," improve health, offer choice, and justly allocate space, services, and costs—to the ends of allowing individuals to build their lives as they wish—while fostering bonds "between friends, families, and strangers that give life meaning—bonds that represent the city's greatest achievement and opportunity" (Montgomery 2013, 43). Cities that celebrate commonality encourage the empathy and collaboration needed to face 21st century challenges, he maintains (43). I will argue that the Kamloops Adult Learners Society is a significant contributor to the happiness of Kamloops—of its students and various segments of the city as a whole, particularly the TRU community. As it offers educational choices for seniors, it improves the students' mental and social health; as it garners volunteers from the TRU community and, increasingly, a host of other organizations, KALS also forges bonds and enhances the lives of those volunteers. As it increasingly takes on a role of leadership within the community, KALS strengthens *equality of quality of life.*

I will also extend the provisional categorization of cultural community partnerships of small cities researcher Lon Dubinsky (2006) to the closely related educational sector in order to examine the KALS' connections with TRU and other community partners. Of the five partnerships Dubinsky identifies—mimetic, coercive, normative, self-interested, and organic—the last best reflects the relationship. Organic collaboration, often serendipitous, occurs when "organizations, through ongoing communication or by chance, might recognize that there are ways they can work together more effectively to accomplish goals than by going it alone." What begins by chance may remain informal, or over time, "require a formal framework" (99–101). Not only did the relationship between KALS and Thompson Rivers University begin organically—by chance, in fact—but it remains so. Although approximately two dozen TRU faculty and former faculty have instructed at KALS, no formal partnership exists between the two institutions—despite KALS' founder, the late Margaret Cleaveley, being well connected to the university (having served on the TRU Board of Governors) and several meetings between administrators of the two institutions having taken place (Cleaveley, personal communication, January 4, 2013). Yet the fact that several TRU faculty find it worth their while to instruct for KALS in an ongoing off-the-side-of-their desk relationship points to the strength of this organic collaboration. Over time, KALS has developed a number of partnerships with a variety of arts, sports, and cultural organizations that have strengthened both KALS and those partners. Andrew Beer's (2014) observations on leadership in rural communities, particularly his characterization of *transformational* leadership, which transcends limitations "in order to *guide* a process of change" (emphasis mine) rather than being top down (255), are also utilized in this paper. I will argue that the leadership of KALS has been characterized by flexibility; as the needs of their students change, so, too, do the curriculum and the organization's relationship with the larger community. As membership in the organization grows, KALS' leadership adapts its approaches.

In keeping with the pattern established by this volume, I will conclude with reflections on my experiences as a community-engaged researcher. I will contend that small collaborations can blur lines between the academic community and the community being researched, that universities can play varied roles as knowledge-support structures, and that knowledge support is multi-directional. Included in these reflections is an examination of a KALS-TRU interaction that illustrates community engagement at the micro-level.

Third-Age Learning

The Kamloops Adult Learners Society is part of a global movement of groups of seniors who are challenging old saws promulgated from societal assumptions. Learning institutions developed exclusively for people in retirement or senior citizens (variously called "senior learners," "third-age learners," and "lifelong learners"—although the latter term encompasses all learners returning to education as adults) have proliferated in type and size in the past 45 years, running the gamut from large, highly structured programs administered by post-secondary institutions to small, independent, grassroots initiatives. Membership in the University of the Third Age (but one indicator) suggests seniors' thirst for learning is global: the U3A, which started in a university in Toulouse, France, in 1972 and has come to be regarded as the pioneer of third-age education, now has affiliate member organizations on all five continents and in 23 countries (although it is likely more countries have organizations for third-age learners). For example, according to the website of the University of the Third Age, in April 2017, its UK branch had 1,010 affiliate organizations and over 380,000 individual members. The World U3A, a resource service connected to the University of the Third Age, indicates that Australia and New Zealand have over 270 affiliates, and that seniors from Reykjavik to Cape Town are engaged in lifelong learning forums (University of the Third Age 2015).

In Canada, universities that pioneered seniors' learning programs have, likewise, seen considerable growth, and third-age networks are established. The Université de Sherbrooke, among the first in North America to use the U3A model in 1976, had, by 2009, established programs in ten regions of Quebec. Simon Fraser University, which began its lifelong learning program in 1974, has experienced steady growth over a similar time period (Lusignan 2009, 114–17). The Third Age Network (n.d.) lists, in 2017, seniors' learning organizations in 70 towns and cities across Canada, ranging from university-affiliated groups to church-affiliated groups to independent organizations. From all appearances, Canadian senior learners are keen—not only to learn but also to organize and communicate with their fellow learners.

Reflecting their varying origins and mandates, programs for third-age learners are extremely diverse. As the University of the Third Age spread beyond France, where it tended to mimic a standard hierarchical university model, a second model—peer learning—developed and became the predominant model in the United Kingdom, for example. Formosa (2014) describes peer learning as embracing "a self-help approach based upon the principle of reciprocity, of mutual giving and taking. . . . people coming together to assist each other with common problems, providing mutual support and an exchange of information, whilst being typified by minimal social distance between them" (45). Currently, lifelong learning organizations tend to fall into one of two broad categories—university-controlled or independent. Independent models vary considerably: they may be closely affiliated with another community group, they may belong to national or international networks, and they may embrace peer learning models (in which courses are entirely planned, administered, and taught by fellow learners) exclusively, or rely entirely or partly on volunteer instruction from outside their membership—professors, teachers, or other experts in various subjects that interest their students. Although the social capital being built varies according to the specific configuration, it is, all told, considerable.

As the Kamloops Adult Learners Society is an example of the independent model, I will generalize based on my research of that model in Canada, with the cautionary note that—given the sheer numbers of such organizations, as well as their heterogeneity and the paucity of research on lifelong learning in Canada—I present tendencies only:

- Seniors themselves are involved in the administration of the programs: they may have been the founders, and they exercise considerable control, through board memberships and through day-to-day operations such as program coordination and facilitation

- Peer learning is quite common: not infrequently, the students are also the teachers, either drawing on their previous careers or researching and delivering on topics of interest to the larger group

- Courses vary considerably in duration: the content, rather than a pre-existing structure, dictates the length, but they are usually shorter than is typical in post-secondary institutions

- Small class sizes that promote optimum peer-to-peer interaction are the dominant model

- Accessibility of location is underscored: often, a single organization will have multiple public venues— such as libraries, seniors residences, churches, and community centres—to keep overhead costs low, facilitate parking, and maximize convenience

- Volunteers contribute the bulk of the work in administering these courses, although there may be paid employees

- Affordability is a fundamental consideration: tuition fees are considerably lower than in formal academic institutions, a situation encouraged by the fixed incomes of most participants and enabled by the fact that instructors are volunteer and by partnerships with and donations-in-kind from other community organizations

- Perhaps one feature is most prominent: the absence of course prerequisites, testing, and grading. Intellectual and social stimulation, rather than credentials, is emphasized. Learning for the sake of learning in a comfortable environment of one's peers is the motivation.

Leadership in the Creation, Structure, and Evolution of the Kamloops Adult Learners Society

Kamloops is a small city in British Columbia's interior with a population of just over 90,000 as of 2016 (Statistics Canada 2017a). As a service and cultural centre at a considerable distance from large cities (Vancouver, the nearest big city, is more than a four-hour drive), it has, as Dubinsky (2006) has observed, a wide range of cultural activities (anchored by four strong public institutions); furthermore, it is "distinguished by various and intersecting pools of social and cultural capital relative to its size and rather isolated population" (85). Kamloops also has a significant population of seniors. According to Statistics Canada's 2016 Census Profile, 20.1% of the population of the Kamloops Thompson region are aged 65 and over, and 2.2% are 85 or over (Statistics Canada 2017a). Against this backdrop, the Kamloops Adult Learners Society was created out of the desire for an independent, accessible, and affordable non-credit program developed solely for retirees. With a history of social capital and a sufficient representative population, Kamloops proved ripe for the initiative of a centre for seniors' education.

When, in 2005, the *Kamloops News* published an article about retired teacher and educational administrator Margaret Cleaveley's interest in starting such a program, over 60 people responded by attending an organizational meeting. One of the attendees, Dr. Anne Gagnon, volunteered to be the group's first instructor (Cleaveley, personal communication, January 4, 2013). Cleaveley and Gagnon, unknowingly, established a pattern of leadership that would serve to inform the organization—the Kamloops Adult Learners Society—that resulted. Grassroots and informal initiatives would characterize KALS.

The leadership that would form the organization was, certainly, as Kading (this volume) characterizes it, less visible than, for example, business leadership; however, it proved highly skilled and extremely efficient (1). By January 2006, that group of 60 had become a registered non-profit society with an objective of promoting "the physical and mental well-being and quality of life of seniors in the Kamloops/Thompson region;" an executive (president, vice-president, treasurer, secretary, and immediate past president), seven standing committees, and membership open to "any person who is retired, regardless of age, and lives in the Kamloops/Thompson region" (KALS 2015). The organization has also held self-evaluation workshops and developed a policy manual (KALS 2015).

Beer's (2014) lens of *transformational leadership*—"broad, strategic" leadership to "guide change" (255) is evident in the fact that KALS' leadership has proven to be both highly structured and highly flexible. At the time of writing, the organization has added the board positions

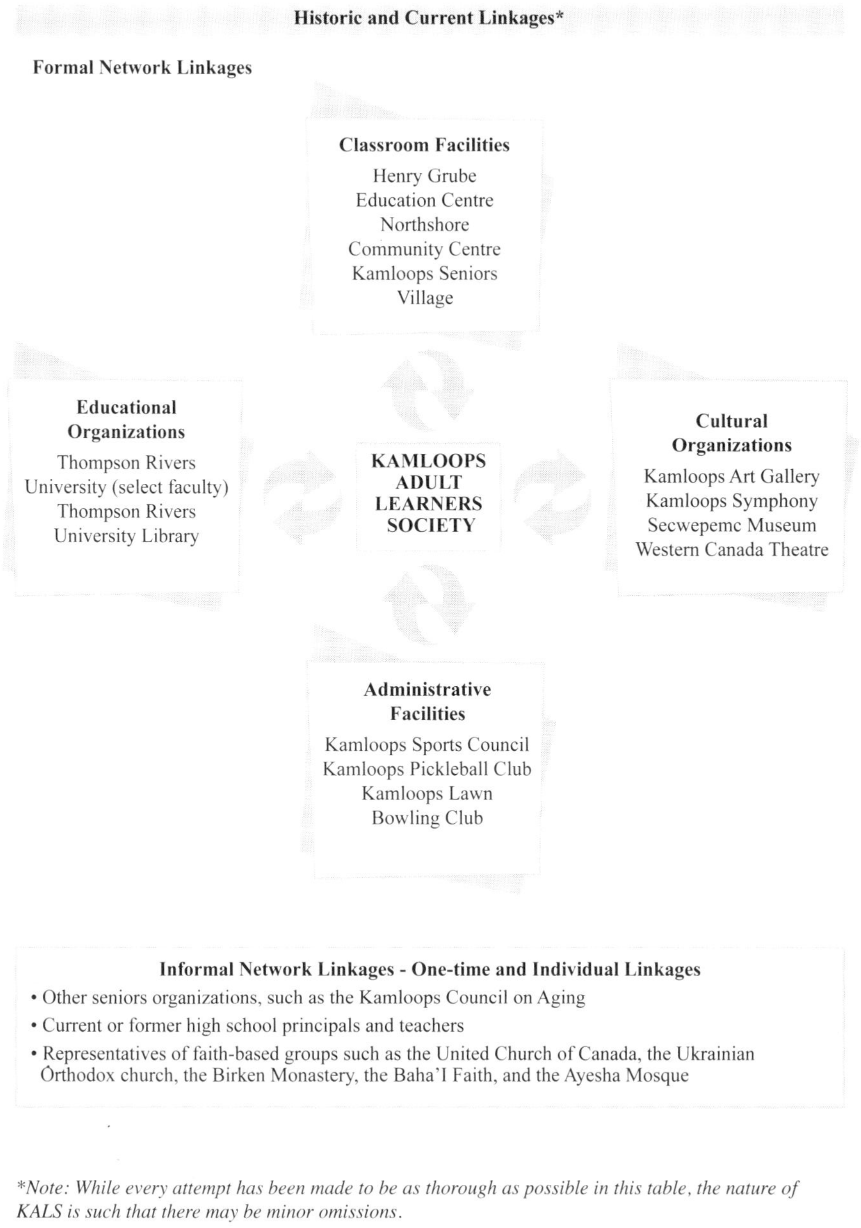
Historic and Current Linkages*
Formal Network Linkages
Classroom Facilities
Henry Grube Education Centre
Northshore Community Centre
Kamloops Seniors Village
Educational Organizations
Thompson Rivers University (select faculty)
Thompson Rivers University Library
KAMLOOPS ADULT LEARNERS SOCIETY
Cultural Organizations
Kamloops Art Gallery
Kamloops Symphony
Secwepemc Museum
Western Canada Theatre
Administrative Facilities
Kamloops Sports Council
Kamloops Pickleball Club
Kamloops Lawn Bowling Club
Informal Network Linkages - One-time and Individual Linkages
• Other seniors organizations, such as the Kamloops Council on Aging
• Current or former high school principals and teachers
• Representatives of faith-based groups such as the United Church of Canada, the Ukrainian Orthodox church, the Birken Monastery, the Baha'I Faith, and the Ayesha Mosque
*Note: While every attempt has been made to be as thorough as possible in this table, the nature of KALS is such that there may be minor omissions.

FIGURE 5.2. Kamloops Adult Learners Society Network by Ginny Ratsoy. Design by Moneca Jantzen, Daily Designz.

of program, publicity, and volunteer chair, as well as member-at-large. Structure, then, has become more complex. However, anyone who has sat on a volunteer board is keenly aware that practice is as important as policy; that flexibility is as important as structure; and that building personal connections is key to the successful operation of an organization. KALS is no exception. Though there are periodic vacancies in some board positions, they are usually short-lived, and the key responsibilities of such positions seem to be carried out by other members. For example, when, for a short time, it appeared as though the position of president would not be occupied, members remained confident that essential work could be carried out by those who filled other positions. This is a group whose experiences have led them to expect complexity and embrace flexibility. This is also a highly social, active group that collectively possesses a wealth of diverse experiences in varied public and private sector enterprises— and is keenly cognizant of the power of word of mouth and the strength of collective action. While the bodies occupying executive positions may change, the work deemed as vital continues to get done. In fact, the fluidity *within KALS* of the roles of the students, founders, and administrators blurs the lines within the organization.

The fact that Kamloops is home to a comprehensive university (where Dr. Gagnon was an assistant professor of history) opens up the question of partnerships between the two institutions. Thompson Rivers University was created in 2005, out of the merger of the University College of the Cariboo and British Columbia Open University; in turn, the University College of the Cariboo evolved from Cariboo College, which opened its doors in 1970. TRU is, therefore, uniquely placed to offer face-to-face and distance courses in a particularly wide spectrum—from vocational and trades diplomas and certificates to a variety of academic undergraduate degrees, as well as law degrees and a growing number of master's degrees. TRU also has a long history of offering continuing education courses, and its satellite campus, in Williams Lake, has had an ongoing affiliation with the Cariboo Chilcotin Elder College, which is committed to "meeting the lifelong learning needs and educational interests of older adults in Williams Lake and surrounding areas" (Cariboo Chilcotin Elder College 2013). A structured KALS-TRU partnership might seem fitting, in light of the latter's history and comprehensiveness. However, as we shall see, an organic partnership has evolved.

Cleaveley envisioned for KALS the peer learning approach modelled by a Kelowna organization with which she had been involved, and varieties of it have been instituted. In fact, peer learning was front and centre in KALS' initial vision statement, and the concept has, to some extent, been maintained. For example, a member has shared knowledge of stamp collecting, and students have moderated a popular movie club in which members select the materials for viewing. Occasionally, based on student feedback, members design courses in which students research and teach components of the course—peer learning at its purest. An ongoing discussion-based course, "News and Views," has been popular. In addition, members who are retired schoolteachers share their knowledge, and the KALS volunteer website manager has taught computing courses. The organization has certainly witnessed the benefits of the peer learning model in the promotion of engaged learning.

Nevertheless, KALS is nothing if not flexible and open and, as indicated, the Cleaveley-Gagnon encounter initiated a pattern: the program committee frequently seeks experts beyond their membership and allows them considerable flexibility in course content and delivery method, to the extent that, by 2017, the majority of KALS' courses are not peer-led. The current KALS vision statement reflects this evolution: "The rich expertise of the adult community—young and old—along with community partners is used to organize programs and instruct courses." The vision statement goes on to emphasize the role that KALS' students can play as volunteers in addition to teaching: "Volunteers are our lifeblood; as leaders, teachers, planners and organizers, they provide the skills and labour to create the program" (KALS 2017). Thus, the emphasis is on the varied roles—in addition to instruction—that KALS students can play. The need for volunteers beyond board positions is particularly high, as each course requires a coordinator, whose responsibilities include maintaining communication with both the instructor and the students and attending the course. At the time of writing, the organization has 50 members planning, organizing, and coordinating its courses and an additional 50 volunteer instructors. As KALS has grown, it has come to rely on its members increasingly for administrative functions and the larger community increasingly for instructional functions.

Methods of recruiting TRU instructors, a vital resource for KALS, reflect the typical dynamics of the small city. Although program coordinators select these experts based on surveys of student interest, their approach is often informal, frequently relying on intermediaries, word of mouth, and serendipity (Cleaveley, personal communication, January 4, 2013). For example, Dr. Gagnon was instrumental in developing the KALS-TRU connection by encouraging her TRU colleagues to follow her lead and by suggesting specific faculty who were likely fits with student interest. In an interesting example of the "intersecting pools" of capital that Dubinsky (2006, 85) writes of, a less direct path to a TRU Arts professor resulted in KAL's first course in a discipline its members had a long-time desire to study: early in 2012, two KALS members who engaged a stranger in conversation at the Kamloops Film Festival soon discovered they were talking to a philosophy professor; by the fall, KALS had its first introductory philosophy course, which proved extremely popular, and was soon followed by others on the subject (Jack and Pauline Braaksma, personal communication, January 11, 2014). The organization is increasingly enthusiastic for instruction beyond its membership, and TRU faculty are functioning as a knowledge-support structure in an organic fashion.

Increasingly in recent years, KALS has responded to its members' programmatic needs in two particularly innovative ways. First, they are extending the boundaries of traditional academic education by offering, for example, sessions on lawn bowling and Tai Chi, thereby taking a holistic approach to education that often incorporates Experiential Learning. A partnership with Kamloops' Big Little Science Centre has been a model for this: the KALS members travelled to the organization, and, thus, KALS' classroom space, which has periodically been scarce, was positively affected; the students received hands-on learning, and the science centre had the opportunity to generate new advocates. Furthermore, KALS' leadership has had the vision to capitalize on an existing strong cultural interest within its membership and deepen their students' knowledge of it by incorporating classes conducted by personnel at Kamloops Museum and Archives, Kamloops Art Gallery, the Secwepemc Museum, Kamloops Symphony, and Western Canada Theatre. Second, they are offering "single-session" courses (while maintaining a flexible model of multiple-session courses). These (usually) two-hour courses provide introductions to a wide variety of community resources. Recent topics have included Judaism, nutrition, stress management, entomology, and First Nations languages, to name but a few (KALS 2017). These two initiatives have resulted in, as Figure 5.2 at the beginning of this chapter indicates, a dramatic increase in KALS' outreach into many and diverse community sectors beyond TRU. By introducing these models into the mix, organizers have not only provided KALS members with a taste of community resources but have also provided the community groups with healthy models of aging, greater awareness of KALS, and potential membership growth. By increasing its flexibility for its students, KALS is further cementing its role as a knowledge-support structure in the community.

The hybrid model that has evolved for KALS embraces non-hierarchical learning and respects the wisdom of KALS members, while being open to more traditional models of education. The society's offerings reflect the practical, academic, and leisure interests of its membership: from computing and driving update courses through astronomy, sociology, and Canadian and Russian history and classical and contemporary literature courses to bird watching, drawing, travel courses and a variety of physically oriented courses, these classes are a marriage of internal and (increasingly) community expertise with student interest (KALS 2017).

Greater spatial needs have also resulted in further physical branching out into the local senior culture and larger community. In a move, due to spatial limitations, from its original location in a school district building, KALS now holds the majority of its classes at places where seniors live and recreate. At the time of writing, the organization has made inroads into the extreme south shore of the city, with a few classes being held at Kamloops Seniors Village and Ridgepoint Retirement Residence. If KALS has a physical centre, it is the North Shore Community Centre (with ample free parking and wheelchair accessibility). The centre is a large apartment complex geared to the senior population, with a coffee/gift shop and an array of facilities to accommodate such activities as socials, meetings, and exercise classes—an ideal location for making KALS' presence known to the population it wishes to continue to attract. KALS' administrative headquarters has recently moved from a north shore mall to a downtown (south shore) location run by the Kamloops Sports Council; while at first glance this partnership might appear an unlikely one, it has resulted in the addition of several single-session courses with pickleball, lawn bowling, and yoga groups under the Sports Council's umbrella. The Kamloops Adult Learners Society is taking incremental strategic steps, succeeding in its vision of "expanding educational opportunities for citizens in their retirement years" by physically locating in areas seniors frequent at the same time as it acts on its mission to better the community "through interaction and partnerships with other community groups" through outreach activities (KALS 2017).

While the initial focus on peer learning has been somewhat supplanted by a focus on volunteerism in every aspect of the organization, and while KALS has come to rely on the larger community to facilitate learning, KALS' autonomy remains secure. Rather than a transactional leadership, which is top down and limited in focus, KALS practices transformative leadership, which "transcend[s] organizational . . . limitations" and is "broad ranging and specific (Beer 2014, 255). By responding to the needs of its membership and drawing on the resources of the larger community in an organic fashion, KALS is practising a form of leadership that simultaneously strengthens the organization, empowers individual students, and supports segments of the larger community. At the time of writing, KALS is run by approximately 50 volunteers, employs a part-time secretary, has a membership of 285, occupies classrooms in community and seniors' centres, and takes diverse approaches to the over 100 different courses it has offered (McChesney, personal communication, June 14, 2017). From two initial courses (Gagnon's Canadian history course was accompanied by a course on safety for seniors) the offerings had grown to over 20 each semester by 2013 and 40 each semester by 2016 (KALS 2017). In just over a decade, the Kamloops Adult Learners Society has developed from a vision into a strong organization with a structure that adapts to the times.

Students' Quality of Life: "Come for the Intellectual Stimulation; Stay for the Socializing"

Quality and *equality of quality of life* are widely accepted as being fostered by third-age learning. KALS' current vision statement maintains that "participation in continuous learning adds to quality of life, supports good health in mind, body, and spirit, and provides a forum for sharing knowledge and ideas" (KALS 2017). Academic researchers such as Formosa (2014) support this assertion. Formosa effectively details the historical and ongoing contributions of Universities of the Third Age (U3As) to the lives of their students—emphasizing the health, independence, co-operation, and social bonding elements that also happen to be critical to Montgomery's (2013) happiness recipe (43). U3As "contribut[ed] strongly towards the ongoing construction of societies where people age positively" (Formosa 2014, 48). Enabling older members of society to continue learning, increasing their visibility, and empowering them to take an active role in society (even beyond their learning centres), these institutions have appreciably enhanced the social quality of life of seniors (Formosa 2014, 49). Formosa also maintains that U3As have also contributed to improved physical and mental health, pointing to multiple studies that demonstrate the power of mental stimulation to aid in the maintenance of physical and mental health (8), as well as those linking U3A participation and enhanced self-esteem and self-satisfaction, thereby alleviating symptoms of depression and anxiety (49). Furthermore, he reports on the positive effects on lifelong learners of "socializing, making new friends who share their interests . . . and finding a support group which helps them through difficult periods in their personal life" (9). U3As contribute much to the intellectual and social stimulation—and thus individual and collective quality of life—of their members, according to KALS' leadership and academic research.

In order to test some of these widely held beliefs about the holistic benefits of third-age learning, in 2013 I first interviewed four founders of KALS, and, subsequently, had written surveys administered to approximately 20% of KALS students. As a veteran instructor, I entered the process with an assumption of my own: because my classes have always been highly social (to the pleasant extent that I sometimes feel myself a mere appendage to their learning and have, on occasion, found it impossible to regain the group's attention after a break), I anticipated that the primary motivation for enrolment in KALS was socializing. However, founder Cleaveley's conviction (quoted in the subtitle of this section) that I would find students' primary motivation was intellectual stimulation proved, almost without exception, to be correct.

For the vast majority of these students—enrolled in such courses as astronomy, Canadian literature, introductory sociology, and "news and views"—intellectual stimulation was both their motive and their greatest satisfaction. These students are interested, above all, in both building on their existing knowledge of a subject and extending their learning to new fields. Although the survey did not test Cleaveley's assertion that socializing fosters retention in the group, the responses to open-ended questions indicate a deep appreciation of the power of group discussion and the friendships the classes have facilitated.

Course content affected selection to an impressive degree. Only a tiny minority ranked personal knowledge of the instructor or scheduling considerations above course content in enrolment decisions. Several students expressed enthusiasm for specific courses. "I am an astronomy addict" was one student's write-in response to the question of why he/she joined KALS. In open-ended responses, some students mentioned the fun and utility of the philately course, the practicality of computer courses, and the more directed reading facilitated by courses in history, politics, and Canadian literature. The new knowledge instilled by a philosophy course, as well as the broader understanding engendered by an Indigenous literature course, were also highlighted. In at least one case, a KALS course rekindled an old passion for theatre. Interestingly, general comments—positive, without exception—on the overall effectiveness of KALS instructors were frequent in the open-ended section; however, seldom were instructors named. Thus, the rankings were supported by the comments, and responses reflected satisfaction with the current curriculum.

Responses to the question "How has your life changed since you joined KALS?" and to the request to provide any further comments on the KALS experience were most enlightening. Those that focused on the intellectual development were more frequent than those that highlighted social benefits, although the latter was clearly recognized as significant. Perceptions of intellectual benefits were often indicative of the respondents' understanding of the transferability of knowledge—as well as running counter to myths that we become less open to change as we age. Several respondents perceived their reading as having both broadened and become more directed as a result of their studies. Improved reading potential and comprehension, directed reading, increased reading, and expanded reading were mentioned. More frequent were responses that indicated a broader sense of engagement, and sometimes transformation: "I realize how little attention I have paid to the world around me. Because of KALS, I am now sensitive to the wealth of knowledge and information that is yet to be amassed," was one thoughtful response. "Comprehension of local and world concerns" "understanding of our universe" "new perspectives and changing ideas," and more general reflections on mental and intellectual stimulation are further indications of the eagerness of students not only to build on existing knowledge but also to incorporate new thinking. In fact, several respondents selected courses based on a desire to be taken out of "comfort zones"; one student summarized these views succinctly, advocating "any experience which presents new ideas, new information, changes of view of the world and our place in it." These students deliberately seek out the opportunity to learn new tricks and embrace change: they are motivated by situations that challenge their world views—hallmarks of transformative learning.

The social benefits of the organization were addressed on several levels which, again, indicate that the seniors embrace new situations. A few respondents observed that the courses are an antidote to the isolation that can come with aging and appreciated the benefits of making new acquaintances. However, more frequent were comments that detected more than superficial or general connections: several opted for word choices such as "kinship," "like minded," "shared interests," and "kindred spirits." The respondents perceived a wider circle of friends "who also enjoy community engagement" as an important benefit of their involvement. The students also connected the intellectual and the social, evincing a recognition that their intellectual stimulation was fostered in considerable measure by "discussion and interaction" with "personable and knowledgeable people." Furthermore, the recognition of the growth and fluidity of the individual—even into the third age—evident in their perceptions of intellectual growth extends into the comments on the social benefits of KALS. As one student so eloquently stated, "I have made new acquaintances who are still trying to create themselves as I am." The frequent comments on social interaction indicate that, while not their stated primary motivation, it is a significant contributor to their satisfaction. Thus, while my initial sense that socializing was the foremost motivation didn't hit the mark, Cleaveley's sense that it is part of a complex whole—which includes awareness of the various benefits of structured and unstructured peer learning— is likely accurate.

Those surveyed and interviewed certainly reflect an appreciation of the novelty, joy, and choice KALS has afforded them. They express great enthusiasm for the mental stimulation and awareness of the social interaction with like-minded learners that Formosa (2014) sees as a major contribution of third-age learning organizations. KALS is certainly an antidote to the social isolation that Montgomery (2013) perceives as symptomatic of much urban life (54–55). The students perceive it as a catalyst for the "bonds between (former) strangers" that Montgomery (2013) includes as an ingredient in his happiness recipe—and perhaps even more so as an instrument for individuals to build their lives according to their desires, which he also sees as critical (43). By the time the Kamloops Adult Learners Society was just eight years of age, it had embraced the transformational leadership model—responding to the needs of its members by drawing on the expertise of the community. Not only was the leadership model transformative, the effect of the leadership on many of the students interviewed was life changing. KALS was clearly a significant knowledge-support structure for its members. As we shall see, those positive effects have, over the years, extended to the TRU community in myriad ways.

Reflections from (and on) the TRU Community: A Two-Way Street

Both TRU faculty and students have benefited from experiences with KALS students. Although my report on this aspect of the relationship is anecdotal and personal, indications are that TRU has received significant benefit from KALS interaction and that there is considerable room for expansion in this informal association. An interview in 2013 with a TRU professor relatively new to KALS indicated faculty stimulation from the connection as well as recognition of the potential for greater faculty and student benefit. Nan McBlane, a TRU sociologist, was recruited via the grapevine: a KALS coordinator asked her daughter, a TRU faculty member, to recommend a sociologist. The serendipitous nature of the organic collaboration is again evident. McBlane, whose research specialty was aging and who has always connected to older people, agreed to the request because she thought it would be challenging and interesting to talk to the group about sociology. She abbreviated, modified, and combined her TRU courses for KALS students, whom she described as "enthusiastic, well read, and curious." She was aware research shows that seniors are in many ways ideal learners, and the experience cemented things for her: "Their willingness to learn new things really impresses me," she said. "They reinforced the idea that you don't die when you retire, that aging is a state of mind," noting that her students were often physically, as well as mentally, active (N. McBlane, personal communication, February 19, 2013). The perspective of the social scientist newcomer was that the organization provides ideal classrooms.

Although she professed to little knowledge about the organization as a whole, apart from being aware of its flexibility, McBlane had a clear idea of what KALS contributes to the university community: "It brings together younger academics with an older learning audience that can teach us as much as we teach them" (N. McBlane, personal communication, February 19, 2013). Noting that most literature indicates that people who are employed past the usual retirement age work hard and have fewer absences than their younger counterparts, she believes societies that encourage early retirement are "throwing away a huge resource." "KALS," she said, "allows us to tap into that." McBlane envisioned further scenarios for "the interplay of ideas" between KALS and the university community; for example, she believed that "without formal bureaucracies, KALS can foster [TRU] department and instructor relationships," and envisioned some KALS students visiting TRU classes, engendering a reciprocal relationship between the two student groups that would erode societal silos (N. McBlane, personal communication, February 19, 2013). Clearly, McBlane saw much realized—and much potential—in the KALS-TRU relationship in terms of the cooperation and strengthening of community bonds that Montgomery (2013) advocates.

My own sustained relationship with KALS is historical and ongoing. I began teaching KALS classes in 2007, acting upon Dr. Gagnon's recommendation, because I was both appreciative of mature students in my TRU classes and eager to compare the lifestyles of the students with those of the older generation in my own family. I have subsequently taught one course most years, usually repurposing material that I have previously taught at TRU and condensing material for a time frame of five weeks. Occasionally I have repackaged and added to my TRU course material in a novel way; for example, in 2015 I taught, for the first time ever, a course on selected Massey Lectures, which arose out of ongoing KALS student interest. I have sometimes taught material to both groups concurrently, and thus been able to compare the responses of younger, graded students with those of older, non-graded students, and to share that comparison with both groups. Furthermore, on occasion both classes have studied a playscript that Western Canada Theatre or the TRU Actors Workshop produced; not only did this allow for comparing and sharing responses, but it also facilitated some cross pollination: KALS students attended guest lectures at TRU by theatre practitioners involved in productions, and several had their first exposure to TRU productions.

My KALS experiences have positively informed my professional and personal life in several ways. I have become more experimental and cognizant of different learning preferences in my instruction at TRU. I find it extremely rewarding to work with such an engaged, stimulated (and stimulating) student body. I am continually impressed by the students' wide reading and varied experiential perceptions on literature; for example, one pleasant outgrowth of the Massey Lectures course was a list of related recommended readings that we jointly compiled. In addition to reinvigorating my teaching, my KALS experience has come with social benefits that include a broadened community. For example, a Kamloops Museum and Archives exhibition, "Tried, Tested, and Proved—Cookbooks, Families and Tradition," was co-curated by a KALS student, the late Enid Damer, who solicited cookbooks for exhibition from several KALS participants—myself included. I was proud to attend the opening of that exhibit, particularly because one of my contributions, *The Can Lit Food Book*, compiled and edited by Margaret Atwood, was relevant to my teaching—at both institutions. Several of the students and I also have year-round communication by sharing information about events of mutual interest. On multiple levels, then, my KALS involvement has fostered the community bonds and cooperation that Montgomery includes in his happiness recipe.

KALS instruction also provides a healthy transition to retirement. McBlane rightly mentioned the potential for younger faculty that KALS offers; however, TRU faculty in the later stages of their careers are also well served by exposure to healthy, active, invigorating role models. It is worth noting the almost universally positive tone of the discourse of the KALS students' responses to open-ended survey questions: rather than perceiving their education as a refuge from the trials and tribulations of aging, for example, most students perceived it as adding to an already rich lifestyle. They are exemplars of well-rounded third-age life, not only pursuing life-long learning in the classroom but also continuing active involvement in other cultural and physical activity—as well as volunteering on boards in community organizations. In a reversal of the usual classroom direction, the student can be the teacher's role model.

McBlane's suggestion that TRU students work with KALS students is being acted upon and proving effective. By cultivating direct connections between the students at the two institutions with which they are affiliated, TRU faculty with KALS connections are extending "the build[ing] and strengthen[ing] the bonds between . . . strangers that give life meaning" that Montgomery (2013) advocates, beyond their own relationships with the two groups (43) and furthering TRU's role as a knowledge-support structure. For example, Gagnon enlisted a TRU student pursuing a degree in Education to present her research to a KALS class—a cross-pollination I was able to emulate in 2017. These encounters have the potential to bridge age gaps and "open the doors to empathy and compassion" (43), as Montgomery puts it, while providing TRU students with invaluable experiential learning opportunities. I had the opportunity to engage a fourth-year English major from TRU to co-teach "Nature in Canadian Poetry and Drama" as part of a service learning course. That student, who was concurrently auditing an extended version of the same course I was teaching at TRU, interacted with KALS students by presenting three short lectures on selected Canadian poets and joining in the group work that formed part of each week's class. I was impressed by how quickly she was accepted by the senior students, one of whom discovered the two of them have a shared hobby and provided the TRU student with some expertise in that area. I was also impressed by how quickly the TRU student understood and appreciated the opportunities afforded by intergenerational learning. What Tina Block (in this volume) notes about the Tranquille project is also applicable here: there are "ongoing opportunities for . . . student training."

KALS students are proving amenable to supporting and assisting in TRU students' learning, as well. In 2015, several KALS students accepted the invitation of the TRU Undergraduate Research and Innovation Conference to join them in the celebration of its tenth anniversary; some of them elected to spend an entire Saturday taking in student presentations on topics running the gamut from the application of Montgomery's *Happy City* principles to Kamloops to philosophical approaches to works by Canadian novelists—and contributing to discussion periods. I shall not soon forget the enthusiasm of a KALS student (who is well over 80) for the research findings of young undergraduate students; that student's only regret was that, with several concurrent sessions, attendees could not take in every presentation. At the 2017 conference, two KALS students were a highly engaged audience for my TRU students' displays related to their Nature in Canadian Literature course. The KALS students, while not familiar with all of the material the TRU students' displays were responding to, were able to bring to the table their own knowledge of the general subject, acquired in their course, as well as their years of broader experience. By opening TRU doors to KALS students, the conference organizers were not only fostering the empathy that Montgomery (2013) advocates, they were also acknowledging the significance of the seniors' expertise and cooperation in tackling a variety of societal challenges (43). The ground work for what Emery and Flora call (2006) "inter-generational transfer" and deem an important component of "healthy happy communities" has been laid (27).

The KALS-TRU relationship is also an evolving illustration of what Emery and Flora (2006) call "bridging social capital: loose ties that bridge among organizations and communities" (21). Clearly, the existence of the Kamloops Adult Learners Society has fostered *equality of quality of life* that extends far beyond its membership. As these selected examples of

TRU-KALS interactions indicate, the flexible, organic, and non-hierarchical leadership structure of the latter and the willingness of its membership to embrace the knowledge of TRU faculty and students have facilitated a variety of enriching experiences in the community. Increasingly, various segments of the TRU community are embracing the potential of collaboration with KALS in various forms. Particularly as some forms of traditional university education—notably humanities—come under increasing societal scrutiny, advocacy by respected community members becomes ever more valuable. TRU faculty would be wise to continue to replicate and to intensify this community engagement.

As Kading reminds us, contemporary university mission statements and plans profess to promote "diversity, equity, inclusion, tolerance, addressing societal challenges, and engagement with new ideas and peoples" (see Introduction to this volume). While TRU faculty have admirably stepped up to the plate by contributing vital volunteer teaching to KALS, the contributions are not evenly distributed across faculties, and, arguably more significantly, TRU administrative and service wings are conspicuously absent in TRU-KALS collaborations. As I argue in "The Roles of Canadian Universities in Heterogeneous Third-Age Learning: A Call for Transformation," our university administrations need to dissolve disconnects with third-age learning institutions and "consider multi-pronged forms of collaboration," being motivated "not by short-sighted financial concerns but by their core obligation to serve the public good by fostering community engagement" (Ratsoy 2016, 76). TRU faculty have laid a solid foundation upon which administration can build.

However, as I stated in that article, I would not recommend a formal partnership between KALS and TRU; when two organizations of unequal size enter a contractual partnership after a history of a horizontal relationship, what begins as an equal relationship may well evolve into a hierarchical one (86). The existing relationship—healthy and in keeping with KALS' independent spirit—could be strengthened through a variety of arms-length collaborations. For example, TRU's educational administration areas, which currently do not have any connections to KALS, could support and encourage more faculty to consider volunteering as a way to foster bridging social capital, pilot new courses, and enhance their scholarship of teaching and learning—while adding diversity to KALS' curriculum.

Other areas of the university could be encouraged to follow the example of faculty librarians, who have conducted library tours for KALS and invited their students to take advantage of a free (for seniors) community borrowers' card. Furthermore, interdisciplinarity, a hallmark of research at TRU, could be encouraged: faculty in Sociology, Nursing, Education, Social Work, and Law, for example, have in the Kamloops Adult Learners a ready pool of well-educated and active seniors from which to draw—and with whom they could collaborate. Experiential learning is highlighted in TRU's Academic Plan; co-op and service learning courses at TRU offer the potential for further intergenerational learning. KALS students have proven open to attending TRU lectures and other events—whether or not they are directly connected to their own studies; if TRU administration were to take the initiative of sharing communication about such events it would be furthering bridging social capital. Perhaps, above all, an ongoing commitment by TRU to grant access to even a single classroom on the main campus each semester at a time when room and parking utilization are not at a premium would alleviate space concerns for KALS, while broadening KALS' accessibility on the city's South Shore (Ratsoy 2016, 85). The potential is there for educational administrators, from Deans to Marketing and Communications, Research Office, and Provost's Office personnel, to foster these connections. With relatively little effort and virtually no cost, the bonds created by Gagnon could be strengthened. As the only university in the city, TRU administration could do more to heed Montgomery's (2013) suggestion that opening doors of cooperation is instrumental to meeting societal challenges (49).

Conclusions

Trends and demographics indicate that interest by Canadian seniors in third-age learning programs will only increase. According to Statistics Canada, although in 2011 most Canadian baby boomers were still part of the working-age population (aged 15–64), the number of seniors had risen by almost 1% from 2006, and, as the 2011 census counted nearly 3 in 10 people as baby boomers, "population aging will accelerate" (Statistics Canada, 2013) By 2017, more Canadians were 65 years or older than under 15. Statistics Canada has also estimated that by July 1, 2024, those 65 and older would constitute over 20% of Canada's population (2017b). As baby boomers enter their third stage often healthier, more highly educated, and with a longer life expectancy than any previous such generation in history, every indication is that third-age learning organizations are not only sustainable but also have growth potential. They are a burgeoning resource with which the larger community in general and universities specifically—especially those in Canadian small cities such as Kamloops that may be experiencing quite different trends and demographics— would be wise to collaborate.

KALS is a vibrant example of what a small group of passionate, dedicated, adaptable individuals can accomplish in a small city—not only for their fellow members but also for that city's academic and larger communities. The society's independent model, with its history of organic collaboration, is well suited to small cities, where social networks are, enviably, large enough to be vibrant but small enough to lend themselves to informal communication and collaboration. Especially considering how recent its creation is, KALS has built up considerable social capital and is contributing significantly to our city's happiness (see Chapter 7: Conclusion on local impact).

It is important to recognize, as Formosa (2014) notes, the larger benefits of U3A learning to the greater society. The volunteer approach of many of the institutions makes a financial contribution, and, he asserts, the lifelong learning institutions enable nations to "spend less on welfare and civic programmes targeting the improvement of quality of life in later years" (51). He also indicates an indirect benefit: those who are lifelong learners tend to take on helping and other volunteer tasks in the larger community (52). A recent study indicates that Canadian seniors in smaller cities, specifically, form an important component of the culturally active population. Jonathan (2012) has found that seniors in small cities are more inclined to both consume cultural activities *and* produce cultural products, concluding that they "often play a central role in . . . community life, including in heritage preservation and the local art scene" (10). Informal surveying and anecdotal evidence confirm that KALS members are cultural—as well as educational—contributors to their small city. As seniors debunk stale stereotypes when they expand their knowledge base, they are not only enhancing their individual and collective quality of life; they are also improving the quality of life of those—of all ages—around them. As it enters its 13th year, the Kamloops Adult Learners Society is proving a significant knowledge-support structure and, thus, a vital ingredient in the recipe for happiness in Kamloops.

Reflections on Community-Engaged Research in the Small City

The Kamloops Adult Learners Society has evolved into a knowledge-support structure for a host of reasons—among them a strong and visionary leadership, a ready supply of seniors interested in third-age learning, *and* an established infrastructure of knowledge support within the small city. For several decades, for example, Kamloops has had a professional theatre, art gallery, symphony, two museums, and an institution of higher education that have contributed to the "various and intersecting pools of social and cultural capital" of which Dubinsky wrote in 2006 (85). These resources have provided an infrastructure of knowledge and history of collaboration upon which newer organizations can build. KALS' founding and ongoing relationship with TRU faculty and its more recent collaborations with the theatre, art gallery, Secwepemc Museum, and symphony serve as evidence of this.

As an educator/researcher with a history of various levels of community-based and community-engaged research, dating from 2005 and ranging from an analysis of local literature to a study of the success of the professional theatre company in Kamloops, I have come to (a) see these small collaborations as blurring the lines between the academic community and the community being researched, (b) appreciate the variety of roles that universities can play as knowledge-support structures, *and* (c) understand that knowledge support is not unidirectional but reciprocal. I view the KALS students I interviewed in 2013 more as active participants than as subjects—likely because I have come to know them well and because, having also taught them, I am aware of how much they have taught me. I have both observed and participated in the organic growth in the distinctive relationship between TRU and KALS. I have witnessed and experienced the reciprocal exchange of knowledge and the resultant *equality of quality of life* of the partners.

A close examination of my initial public sharing of the results of the surveys I devised and of the interviews supports these three points. I should add that when I first disseminated those results in an on-campus public lecture, as part of the TRU Arts Colloquium Series—to which I invited KALS students—I had an ulterior motive or two: to further contact between the KALS and TRU communities, to the ends of *both* attracting more TRU faculty as KALS instructors *and* drawing more KALS students to the rich campus life at TRU. I did have some success in those aims. Little did I know that further consequences would ensue.

Approximately one dozen KALS representatives and an equal number of the TRU community attended the presentation, which would prove to engage the two contingents in the ways I had intended and beyond. Although I began the talk as a lecture, I soon involved some of the KALS members, who, after all, were the subjects of the research and could offer experiential knowledge to supplement my research. The participatory and fluid tenor of the talk carried over into the question period, which immediately evolved into a discussion period between the two contingents. The first question, from a young TRU student, was directed not at me but at the KALS attendees. Could he, were he to win a lottery before he began a career, become a KALS student? The draw for him was a fundamental difference between the KALS and TRU systems: the absence of grading—a feature subsequently praised by the KALS students. A KALS student then raised the issue of administrative hurdles (financial and logistical) to seniors enrolling in TRU courses, which in turn, revealed that all of those present were unclear about TRU policy on third-age students. Some TRU faculty present then issued invitations to KALS students to circumvent the bureaucracy and informally attend their classes. I found it significant that communication among the two groups, which seemed to evolve naturally, was centred around the liberating effects of a grades-free education and the less-than-liberating effects of bureaucracy. As well as being somewhat envied and invited into the university, the subjects—the KALS students— became direct—rather than indirect—suppliers of knowledge to the university community.

Equally enlightening, in terms of blurring the lines of circumscribed roles and the serendipitous ways in which universities can act as knowledge-support structures, were the post-talk interactivity and the ensuing publicity. Among the small groups who went off to continue the discussion were two neighbours—one a course coordinator for KALS and the other a TRU Political Science professor—the latter of whom is also the editor of this volume. Among those who remained behind was a local newspaper reporter, who had previously published an article on KALS. After asking me and the series organizers a few questions, the reporter spent the bulk of her time interviewing several KALS members. The subsequent newspaper article, entitled "Lifelong Learning Equals Longevity: University Study of Kamloops Adult Learners Society Purports Benefits of Classroom Later in Life," was quite extensive and considerably focused on the Kamloops Adult Learners Society. The reporter apparently saw her obligations to follow up on previous articles on KALS published by her paper and to provide her readership with information on how to connect with the organization as more significant than providing her readers with details of the colloquium series—or, indeed, of my research results. It should also be noted that proximity can lead to an interesting circularity. A TRU internal publication—*Bridges*, an alumni magazine—contacted me after reading about the presentation in the city newspaper. Thus, the written documentation of the event came from *outside* the university and focused on KALS, rather than the university, as a knowledge-support structure, and precipitated interest in the research from *within* the university.

My original aim of sharing my research findings was accomplished, and my ulterior purposes of attracting KALS students to campus and TRU faculty to KALS were largely fulfilled by my first public talk on my research. The KALS contingent had a pleasant learning experience in campus access and were welcomed by faculty to extend their relationship with TRU to classrooms. The TRU attendees learned more about both third-age learning and the bureaucracy in their own system. The KALS course coordinator (a former TRU faculty member) followed up by contacting professors present at the talk who had expressed an interest in teaching for KALS. Communication between the two groups was enhanced. There is much evidence of fluidity and the power of proximity.

An unforeseen consequence of my talk also points to the power of proximity in an organic partnership. As a result of my research and talk, I was contacted by a KALS student, who is also a founding member of the Kamloops Council on Aging (KCA). Isabelle Allen, a retired nurse (who had been involved in a research project on aging when she was employed in Ottawa), invited me to join the KCA. In fact, Allen had suggested several years earlier that KALS was a promising site of investigation. She was apparently cognizant not only of the significance of research into third-age learning but also of the value of involving researchers on aging in activism on aging.

A final unforeseen consequence of that initial talk was that it motivated me to take more of an activist approach to my research than I had originally intended. The apparent disconnect between Thompson Rivers University's administration and third-age learners, identified by a KALS student and discussed by several of those present, precipitated this turn in my research. At a national university teaching conference in 2014, I made the case that universities should adapt multiple flexible platforms—beyond the Elder College and Continuing Studies—with which to engage seniors. Specifically, I advocated for university administrations offering informal, "no strings attached" assistance to independent learning organizations, as well as establishing mutually beneficial opportunities for cross-pollination. In turn, the conference presentation generated my 2016 article in the *Canadian Journal of Higher Education,* wherein I argue that "Universities have a civic duty to assist in maximizing the benefits of education for seniors for mutual benefit—and for the greater public good" (Ratsoy 2016, 85). Thus, a subject of the research stimulated a change in direction in the researcher.

A single talk generated a host of varying responses among and between the individuals and groups present. As I hope the preceding paragraphs make clear, the small city is fertile territory for organic partnerships between knowledge-support systems that transcend boundaries and transform participants.

NOTE

I am grateful to the wonderful Kamloops Adult Learners Society (KALS) students I have taught for well over a decade for inspiring this chapter—and for much more personal and professional growth. I also thank the students who completed my surveys for their insights. The invaluable contributions made to this article by Isabelle Allen, Jack Braaksma, Pauline Braaksma, Lois Hollstedt, and Janet McChesney are appreciated. For her support, survey assistance, and wisdom, I am indebted to Susan

Duerden. For both her assistance with my research and the vision that resulted in the creation and ongoing success of the Kamloops Adult Learners Society, I dedicate this chapter to the memory of Margaret Cleaveley.

References

Beer, A. 2014. "Leadership and the Governance of Rural Communities." *Journal of Rural Studies* 34:254–62.

Cariboo Chilcotin Elder College. 2013. https://www.wleldercollege.com/.

Centre for Seniors Information. 2015. *About Us.* http://www.csikamloops.ca/.

Dubinsky, L. 2006. "In Praise of Small Cities: Cultural Life in Kamloops, BC." *Canadian Journal of Communication* 31 (1): 85–106.

Emery, M., and C. Flora. 2006. "Spiraling-Up: Mapping Community Transformation with Community Capitals Framework." *Community Development: Journal of the Community Development Society* 37 (1): 19–35.

Formosa, M. 2014. "Four Decades of Universities of the Third Age: Past, Present, Future." *Ageing & Society* 34 (1): 42–66.

Jonathan, D-J. 2012. "Cultural Industries in Small-Sized Canadian Cities: Dream or reality?" *Urban Studies* 49 (1): 97–114.

KALS (Kamloops Adult Learners Society). 2015. *Lifetime Learning for Seniors.* http://www.kals.ca/.

KALS (Kamloops Adult Learners Society). 2017. *Lifelong Learning for Adults in the Daytime.* http://www.kals.ca.

Lusignan, Y. 2009. "For the Pleasure of learning." *University Affairs* 50 (7): 14–17.

Montgomery, C. 2013. *Happy City: Transforming our Lives through Urban Design.* Toronto: Doubleday Canada.

North Shore Community Centre. 2015. *About Us.* http://nsccs.webs.com/.

Ratsoy, G. 2016. "The Roles of Canadian Universities in Heterogeneous Third-Age Learning: A Call for Transformation." *Canadian Journal of Higher Education* 46 (1): 76–90.

Statistics Canada. 2013. *2011 Census: Age and Sex.* Ottawa: Government of Canada

Statistics Canada. 2017a. *Census Profile, 2016 Census.* Ottawa: Government of Canada.

Statistics Canada. 2017b. *Population Trends by Age and Sex, 2016 Census of Population.* Ottawa: Government of Canada.

Third Age Network. n.d. http://www.thirdagenetwork.ca/canadalist.html.

University of the Third Age. 2015. *The U3A Story.* http://www.u3a.org.uk/.

6

The Tranquille Oral History Project: Reflections on a Community-Engaged Research Initiative in Kamloops, British Columbia

Tina Block

Introduction

In recent years, the field of public history has grown significantly in Canada. Although there are ongoing debates about the scope and purpose of public history, most historians agree that the term refers to "historical practice carried out of, by, and for the public" (Dick 2009, 7). Public history encompasses a wide range of practices, including the work of preserving heritage sites, using technology to bring the past to life, and commemorating local historical figures and events. In this chapter, I reflect on the development of one public history initiative in Kamloops, British Columbia: the Tranquille Oral History Project (TOHP). Established for a two-year period beginning in June 2012, the TOHP involved representatives from private industry, the non-profit sector, and the university. Although the project benefited from the support of the university, it was—like many

FIGURE 6.1. "Tranquille Sanatorium," photograph by Willian George Lothian, 1920. Wikimedia Commons, Canadian Copyright Collection, British Library, image HS85-10-38188.

other collaborations discussed in this collection—primarily led and sustained by members of the wider community. The TOHP reflected a broader interest in heritage preservation and restoration across British Columbia and Canada, but was grounded in the distinct history and culture of the small city of Kamloops. Despite varied backgrounds, participants in the project shared a mutual interest in Tranquille, a site of historic significance located west of Kamloops. This public history initiative offers a useful lens on certain challenges common to collaborative research, particularly that which involves multiple stakeholders with different motivations, priorities, and expectations. Such challenges were, however, outweighed by the rewards of a project that helped not only to create and share new knowledge about Tranquille's complex past but also to enhance student engagement and establish connections between the university and wider community.

Located on the north shore of Kamloops Lake, Tranquille has a rich and varied history. Not only was the area an important meeting place for early Aboriginal communities, it also became significant to gold seekers during the 1850s. Tranquille has a long agricultural history, and was the site of the Cooney and Fortune homesteads during the 19th century. In 1907, it became home to the King Edward VII Sanatorium, established to treat tuberculosis patients; the location was chosen, in part, due to the favourable climate of the region, an important consideration in early tuberculosis treatment and care (Harris 2010; Norton 1999). The facility closed its doors in 1957 and was reopened in 1958 as the Tranquille Medical Institution, a training school for intellectually and developmentally disabled people (Spark 2012). In 1983, the training school employed

TINA BLOCK

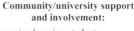

Tranquille Oral History Project

Thompson Rivers University
(Small Cities CURA)

Tranquille On the Lake
(Tranquille Ltd Partnership)

Kamloops Heritage Society

**Community/university support
and involvement:**

• service learning students
• former residents/employees of
  Tranquille
• local media outlets
• community members and TRU
  faculty with an interest in heritage
• TRU Library

Kamloops Museum and Archives; Kamloops Heritage Commission; Friends of Tranquille

FIGURE 6.2. Tranquille Oral History Project Network by Tina Block. Design by Moneca Jantzen, Daily Designz.

approximately 600 people, many of whom lived on the site (Purvey). The school was important not only to the students and their families but to the wider Kamloops economy. Given its importance, it is not surprising that many Kamloopsians raised their voices in protest when the institution closed down in 1984. The closure of the Tranquille Medical Institution was not an isolated event, but rather part of a nationwide movement to deinstitutionalize mental health facilities and reintegrate patients into the broader community. The closure of Tranquille was carried out in an unexpectedly abrupt and rushed manner, which caused dismay and concern among residents, workers, and the wider community (Purvey). In a recent interview, a former employee of the Medical Institution reflected on the closure: "I didn't want to leave. I thought I was going to be there till sixty-five, you know? I never ever dreamed that they would ever close it" (C. Anderson,[1] personal communication with Francesca Lucia, July 5, 2012). During the 1990s, Tranquille was purchased by private interests who planned to turn the area into a high-end, Italian-themed resort named Padova City. Such plans were soon derailed, and the site remained vacant for several years. Following the closure of the training school in the mid-1980s, the site gradually deteriorated as the gardens became overgrown and the buildings dilapidated. Over time, Tranquille (or Padova, as it was and is known to many) came to be associated with trespassing, partying, and vandalism. A cursory internet search reveals that the site also became popular among ghost seekers, and gained a reputation as one of the most haunted places in Canada.

In 2005, the new owners of the site, British Columbia Wilderness Tours, put plans in motion for the establishment of a "sustainable agri-community that combines an urban farm and working waterfront with a mixed use village community" (Tranquille on the Lake 2012, 1). In the years that followed, the developers of the proposed community of "Tranquille on the Lake" (TOL) engaged in ongoing conversations with municipal officials, sought environmental assessments, and consulted with the wider community.[2] Kamloops residents took advantage of such consultations and made their voices heard. As many of the contributions to this volume make clear, the small city of Kamloops does not lack for community engagement. According to Lon Dubinsky (2006), Kamloops is distinguished by a "culture of participation" (86) that extends into several realms, including that of heritage. "Kamloops is little more than 100 years old," Dubinsky notes, "but for a relatively young place it is very conscious of its heritage" (90). Such consciousness is evident in the existence of a thriving museum, two local heritage societies, an active Heritage Commission, and ongoing community support for activities such as heritage fairs.

Given this broad-based interest in heritage, as well as the more specific attachment of many Kamloopsians to the Tranquille site, it is not surprising that residents of the city urged Tranquille on the Lake to protect and preserve the site's heritage. Through consultations with the community, it became clear to the developers that it would be neither possible nor desirable to disassociate present-day Tranquille from its unique past. Many of the original sanatorium buildings are still standing, and the developers were open about their commitment to honouring this built heritage. In an interview, TOL development manager Tim McLeod detailed efforts to incorporate "the history directly into the development plan. Interpretive signs throughout the development will give passers-by bites of relevant information, and buildings are being renovated to preserve glimpses of the site's history" (Spark 2012, 20). Tranquille's rich past lives on, not only in the run-down buildings, historic gardens, and well-worn pathways of the site but in the memories of the people who lived, worked, and visited there. The significance of these memories very quickly became apparent to McLeod, who "has long been getting calls and emails from people around the world who had a connection with Tranquille's past" (Spark 2012, 18). Though less tangible than buildings, memories of Tranquille are central to understanding its history, and were the focus of the Tranquille Oral History Project.

As activity at Tranquille has increased over the past several years, so too has storytelling about the area. Many people have expressed great interest in sharing their memories as well as their Tranquille-related photographs, artifacts, and memorabilia. Recognizing the importance of this oral and material heritage, McLeod approached the Kamloops Heritage Society (KHS) for expertise and assistance. Representatives from the KHS were keen to get involved and, together with McLeod, invited other organizations such as Thompson Rivers University (TRU) to come on board. As a faculty member in history at TRU, I was drawn to a project that not only fit nicely with my research and teaching interests in British Columbia history but seemed ideal for engaging students in the practice of public history.[3]

At early meetings, it was clear that we all shared a sense of the significance of Tranquille's history, wide-ranging as it is, but there were various thoughts on how best to capture, preserve, and disseminate that history. These initial, exploratory meetings resulted in a Memorandum of Understanding (MOU), signed in June 2012, establishing a two-year research collaboration between the Small Cities Community-University Research Alliance (CURA, a research unit based in Thompson Rivers University), Tranquille Limited Partnership (on behalf of Tranquille on the Lake), and the Kamloops Heritage Society. The MOU states that collaborators agreed to the following:

- To work together on projects that document, study, and archive local history research—especially oral histories related to Tranquille

- To work toward the creation and maintenance of a 'Tranquille Interpretive Centre' (a physical space located on the Tranquille site as a community educational resource)

- To create opportunities for student research experience
- To seek further partnership opportunities through external grants. (MOU 2012, 3)

As indicated in the MOU, one of the larger objectives of this initiative was the establishment of an interpretive centre—an archival and educational space—on the grounds. At early meetings, it was agreed that while this should be a long-term goal, our most immediate objective should be to record and archive the memories and stories of "Tranquillians"[4] themselves (Youds 2013, June 10). Although not formally part of the MOU, other organizations, such as the Kamloops Heritage Commission and the Kamloops Museum and Archives, participated in efforts to define the project and set it in motion. The collaborators agreed that as the project moved forward, they would encourage other "stakeholders with common interests" to join (MOU 2012, 2). Keeping in mind the longer-term objective of establishing an interpretive centre, our goal during this initial, two-year collaboration was to conduct, transcribe, and archive oral histories of Tranquille.

Tranquille on the Lake is not unique in incorporating heritage preservation and restoration directly into its development plan. Across British Columbia, several former provincial institutions have been remade into housing developments, and have retained aspects of that institutional heritage.[5] For instance, in 1995, a townhouse development was established on the site of the former Provincial Industrial School in Vancouver. In that case, many of the original buildings were rehabilitated and restored, and new construction was made compatible with the "Spanish Mission Revival" architectural style of the original 1914 structure (Dewhirst Lessard Architects 2009). Similarly, the Prince of Wales Fairbridge Farm School at Cowichan Station, originally established in 1935 as a school for underprivileged British children, was purchased by developers in the 1970s. Now a residential area, Fairbridge includes many of the original Farm School buildings, and the Fairbridge Chapel Heritage Society plays

TINA BLOCK

a key role in administering and maintaining this built heritage (Fairbridge Canada 2017; Vancouver Island Beyond Victoria 2017).

In addition, over the past few years, the large housing development of Victoria Hill has been gradually taking shape on the site of the former Provincial Lunatic Asylum in New Westminster. Established in 1878, the asylum was renamed the Provincial Hospital for the Insane in 1897, and Woodlands School for the Developmentally Disabled in 1950. The institution closed in 1996 and was purchased by Onni Group of Companies in 2003. While many of the original buildings were destroyed by a fire in 2008, a few of the smaller buildings that survived the fire were restored. When it came time to determine the fate of the last remaining major building on the site—the Tower portion of Centre Block—conflict erupted. While the city initially approved plans to restore the Tower, this decision was reversed in 2011 in response to the demand of former patients that the building be demolished "in order to assist in their healing process" (Spitale to Wright and Members of Council 2009, 2). Over the past several years, countless stories of physical, mental, and sexual abuse at Woodlands have surfaced; for the survivors of such abuse, the Woodlands Tower represented not an opportunity for heritage preservation but a site of deep, irrevocable hurts (Hall 2011). The decision to demolish Woodlands Tower suggests the extent to which heritage developments depend on community support and are grounded in specific historical contexts. The "development of heritage and the promotion of heritage sites," Paul Shackel (2011) aptly notes, "are essentially political acts" (2). To date, there have not been any public claims of abuse at Tranquille (Purvey). Most Tranquillians have not only supported but actively encouraged efforts to preserve the institution's heritage. Although the Tranquille development is not unique in its incorporation of heritage, such incorporation was and is made possible, in part, by wider community support and the distinctive history of the institution.

Like other initiatives discussed in this collection, the TOHP involved various stakeholders with distinct motivations for participating. The project was propelled by the countless individuals who, from the outset, expressed their eagerness to share memories of Tranquille. Early on, the developers learned of the strong emotional attachment that many people, both within and outside of Kamloops, have to the Tranquille area. Recognizing the importance of these personal histories, the TOL development manager approached the Kamloops Heritage Society (KHS) with a request that the society become the "gatekeeper" of Tranquille's oral and material heritage (Spark 2012, 20). The KHS is a non-profit organization with a mission of "preserving the past for the future" (MOU 2012, 2); KHS members thus had a distinct motivation for joining this collaborative project. With their focus on preserving heritage buildings and artifacts, KHS members welcomed the opportunity to take on both the oral history and archival components of the Tranquille project.

While the TOHP emerged in response to the needs and desires of the community, it was also driven, in part, by self-interest on the part of the developers and academics (Dubinsky 2006). The significance of Tranquille's historic ties are acknowledged in the TOL neighbourhood plan (TOL 2012), which lists "heritage recognition" as one of the development's guiding principles: "The Tranquille On the Lake property has a rich history of uses including First Nations hunting and fishing activities, ranching, farming, gold mining, and several provincially significant health institutions. Tranquille On the Lake will respect previous uses and peoples who are part of the site's heritage in a meaningful and sustainable manner" (22). Of course, TOL is a business venture, and the commitment to heritage is likely motivated, in part, by an understanding that such a commitment will enhance the appeal of the proposed development. As well, the developers presumably recognize that the success of their venture partially depends on the extent to which they can nurture and maintain a positive relationship with the wider community. While some stakeholders see Tranquille primarily as a business venture and others see it, firstly, as a heritage site, TRU CURA faculty see it as a place rich with research possibilities. Given the importance of its relationship with Kamloops, Tranquille fits nicely with the CURA focus on small cities. More generally, community partnerships such as the TOHP appeal to faculty concerned to make their research more relevant and impactful both within and outside academia. While this is not a new concern, scholars are under increasing pressure to demonstrate the relevance and impact of their research in order to secure external funding, tenure, and promotion.

As a specialist in British Columbia history with an interest in local history and experiential learning, I saw the Tranquille project as an opportunity to offer a unique, hands-on research experience to undergraduate students.[6] Given that it was based in the community, the project seemed an ideal endeavour for undergraduate service learning. According to Ginny Ratsoy (2008), service learning "is experiential learning that actively engages students in projects that connect them to a community and, significantly, requires them to reflect upon that engagement" (2). Although they differ somewhat across institutions, service learning courses typically include both an experiential and reflective component. Service learners receive course credit (on a pass/fail basis) for their work with community organizations, which can involve a range of creative, administrative, or other types of service. Service learning is not reducible to volunteer work, as students are required to critically reflect upon the meaning and impact of the experience within their own lives and the wider community (Ratsoy 2008; Weber and Sleeper 2003). According to Mark Chupp and Mark Joseph (2010), "without structured critical reflection, it is possible that students do not consider their service experience in its larger social and political context, nor determine implications for how to apply the experience to future action" (194). Service learning is increasingly appealing to instructors searching for innovative ways of enhancing undergraduate student engagement and of moving beyond the "passive classroom learner" model (Chupp and Joseph 2010, 193). Research has shown that service learning can help to at least partially resolve the "disconnect" between the university classroom and the so-called "real world" (Post 2012, 414). Historians are not well represented among the advocates of service learning, which, observes A. Glenn Crothers (2002), is somewhat "ironic," as "many historians claim that their teaching aims to help produce individuals who are highly engaged in civic and political life" (1447). Service learning enhances both student and faculty engagement, and can help history instructors in their quest to make studying history about more than just memorizing the dates and details of the past (Carpio, Luk, and Bush 2013; Lyons 2007). In the case of the Tranquille Oral History Project, service learning not only allowed my students to engage with the past in new ways, it inspired me to get out of the classroom and into the community.

In the summer sessions of 2012 and 2013, I invited a total of four students (two each summer) to become involved in the TOHP through service learning. Each student completed a 13-week course that included both an experiential and reflective component. In addition to reading some key works on the history of Tranquille and oral history methodology, students were required to complete a minimum of 65 hours of hands-on work. While the students did everything from assisting the Kamloops Heritage Society to undertaking some preliminary archival and heritage display work, their focus was on conducting interviews with former employees and residents of Tranquille. The students learned about the research ethics process and were actively involved in the creation of the interview questions. They located potential interviewees with the assistance of the KHS and were responsible for coordinating and carrying out the interviews. I structured the course loosely and gave the students the freedom and flexibility to carve out their own research path—to become historians in their own right. As Patricia Mooney-Melvin (2014) remarks in her reflection on a public history initiative in Chicago, "when students are actively engaged in the process of inquiry they are more committed to learning, work collaboratively toward a larger goal, and take ownership of the knowledge they are producing" (470).

In the end, each student conducted three in-depth interviews, most of which were with former employees of the medical institution, and completed full transcriptions of those interviews. Several studies indicate that students benefit immensely when they are actively involved in all aspects of the research process (Healey 2005). Although arduous and time-consuming, transcription is a critical step in oral history research; through the process of transcribing the interviews, my students deepened their connection to the participants and their stories, and learned first-hand what it means to create primary source material. As service learners, these students not only became involved in the community but gained practical experience in the historian's craft. Those who agreed to be interviewed for the project were informed that the transcriptions of their interviews would likely be deposited, at a future date, into an archives and interpretive centre. The students recognized that their work would constitute an invaluable resource not only for themselves but for others, and that it would contribute to a "permanent historical resource for the community" (Crothers 2002, 1447). If established, this permanent resource will also include the students' reflective papers on the TOHP and the history of Tranquille. I required that the students not only contribute their written work to the archives but that they present their research to a conference,

TINA BLOCK

class, or community group. Such presentations not only enriched the students' own learning but allowed them to share their newfound knowledge with their peers and the wider community. Through their work with the TOHP, students learned that the work of the historian extends beyond the classroom. As Peter Knupfer (2013) notes in his analysis of a local history project in Michigan, the "students discovered that the learning and sharing of history need not be confined to classrooms and formal works of scholarship, that it need not arise from cutting-edge research into a recently opened gap in the literature, and that it can instead be taken into a community to serve a community's needs" (1162).

All collaborations bring certain challenges, as the contributions to this volume make clear, and the Tranquille Oral History Project was no exception. As a primarily organic collaboration that evolved from "emergent conditions or opportunities" (Dubinsky 2006, 100), the TOHP brought together participants from varied social locations with a common interest in preserving Tranquille's heritage. At the same time, each stakeholder had somewhat distinct motivations for joining the project, and varied expectations about priorities and outcomes. During the course of my involvement in the TOHP, I became ever more cognizant of the reality that "community organizations and universities do not necessarily speak the same language or hold the same objectives and values" (Garrett-Petts 2005, 4). To KHS members, the recording, though not the transcribing, of the oral histories was of utmost priority, especially given the advanced age of many interviewees. Despite sharing with other stakeholders a concern for heritage preservation, my central focus was engaged learning and student training. I was therefore less concerned with the timely completion of all possible interviews than I was with ensuring that my students received a rigorous and hands-on experience in the practice of oral history. It was important that the students learn the skills of effective transcription, even though "this is a time-consuming and difficult process that can be burdensome" (Mills et al. 2011, 42). Given the immense time commitment, the students were able to complete far fewer interviews than originally anticipated. There are still possibly hundreds of interviews to conduct, in spite of the efforts of KHS members and volunteers to complete them.

Although it was established by a Memorandum of Understanding, the TOHP was loosely structured and lacking in any formal or defined leadership. As Dubinsky (2006) notes, organic collaborations are often quite informal and "guided by inherent trust and clarity about expectations and responsibilities" (100). While the informality of the TOHP was not in itself an issue, such informality was not balanced with a clear, shared understanding regarding expectations and responsibilities. The initial impetus for this collaboration came from the developers, but it was the KHS that took a leadership role in the day-to-day work of the project. While the TOHP would have floundered without the energetic leadership of KHS members, such leadership was limited, and likely frustrated, by a relative lack of clarity around roles, objectives, and anticipated outcomes. From the outset, I considered the initiative to be a long-term project with ongoing opportunities for research and student training; others seemed to envision it as a short-term endeavour with a firm completion date. It was challenging to negotiate and reconcile such competing expectations, which reflected a lack of consensus about the pace and timeline of the project. Chupp and Joseph (2010) note that "real limits exist to the alignment between the role and functioning of the academy and the workings of the real world." They go on to suggest that such limits, which include the "artificial constraints of the academic calendar," should be made clear through "proactive communication with community partners" (206). The TOHP would have benefited, at the beginning, from an open discussion regarding academic priorities, requirements, and constraints. Furthermore, a formalized leadership structure and succession plan would have helped to guide and sustain this research partnership in the long term.

Like the Public Produce Project discussed in Chapter 4 of this volume by Robin Reid and Kendra Besanger, the TOHP struggled to maintain a stable cadre of volunteers and to secure adequate funding. The momentum and energy that characterized the project in its initial stages proved difficult to sustain. As is common in collaborative work, there were varying levels of commitment to the TOHP, and some participants were willing and able to devote more time to it than others. Despite the "culture of participation" characteristic of Kamloops, volunteer participation in the TOHP was sporadic and inconsistent. While this is to be expected, those who made this project a priority, and who were anxious to see it completed, risked becoming overwhelmed by the workload and frustrated by the relatively slow progress. Such challenges were not unique to this particular collaboration and, as with most volunteer projects, would have been at least partially mitigated by access to external funding. Limited funds exist for community-engaged collaborations and heritage projects, and efforts to secure external funds for the Tranquille project were unsuccessful (Dick 2009). As such, TOHP participants relied largely on their own or borrowed equipment and on volunteer and student labour. The developers provided access to the site and potential interview contacts, but the project would have greatly benefited from stable funding for equipment, archival expertise, and transcription.

Genevieve Carpio, Sharon Luk, and Adam Bush (2013) note that community-university collaborations often flounder due to a lack of consistent, sustained support; the success of such collaborations, they argue, requires "universities to make more time, energy, and resources available for them" (1187). Thompson Rivers University offered important support in the form of student and faculty participation, but such participation was somewhat limited due to time and resource constraints. The particular environment of TRU—a comprehensive, learner-centred, primarily undergraduate university—both facilitated and challenged the development of the TOHP. In his work on the linkages between research and teaching, Mick Healey (2005) draws on findings that suggest "it was easier in less research-intensive universities to develop the linkages than in more intensive ones because a wider definition of what counts as research was taken in the former" (194). TRU recognizes a broad concept of research, encourages the scholarship of teaching and learning, and provides wide-ranging support for community-engaged research. It is also home to a thriving culture of undergraduate research, which is reflected in two vibrant, annual undergraduate conferences and numerous funding opportunities for undergraduate students to pursue original research. At the same time, unlike most large universities, TRU has neither an archivist nor a special collections, both of which might have helped to expedite the management and preservation of Tranquille-related records.[7] In addition, while TRU faculty are free to engage students in service learning, such work is not factored in a concrete way into teaching workloads, which may dissuade some from participating.[8]

Despite certain challenges, the Tranquille Oral History Project was a worthwhile and rewarding initiative. With their involvement in the project, and their inclusion of heritage recognition in the Tranquille on the Lake plan, the developers engaged the wider community and acknowledged the importance of Tranquille's unique history. For their part, the students discovered a history of Tranquille that is far more compelling and complex than popularly imagined. As Natalie Ames and Stephene Diepstra (2006) note, intergenerational oral history service learning projects give students the opportunity to "understand the impact of the social environment on human development, and to develop an empathetic understanding of another person's reality" (733). In their conversations with people who lived and worked at Tranquille, students learned about the long-lasting friendships forged between workers and patients, and about the deep impact that the medical facility's closure had on many Kamloops families. With its focus on heritage, the TOHP departed from the traditional service learning emphasis on social issues such as poverty. But, as Ratsoy (2008) suggests, service learning "can equally effectively engage and influence students when the placement is with artistic, cultural, and academic organizations" (3). The TOHP service learners became actively engaged in preserving the heritage of their community, gained valuable, hands-on experience in public history, and discovered a past that was more "immediate, tangible, and relevant" than that found in any textbook (Crothers 2002, 1447). In giving students the opportunity to conduct oral histories and create primary source material, the TOHP "turned students into knowledge producers rather than just consumers" (Mooney-Melvin 2014, 474). The project also enabled Kamloops Heritage Society members to branch into a new area of heritage preservation—oral history—and to deepen their ties with TRU students, faculty, and other community members. Thompson Rivers University is part of, rather than separate from, the Kamloops community—but it doesn't always feel so. Public history projects, such as the TOHP, can be used to "breach the traditional walls between 'town and gown'" (Coles and Welch 2002, 229). Scott Casper (2013) observes that "town and gown"—or the community and the university—"have often existed in tension, typically surrounding the different sorts of economic, social, and cultural capital they represent" (1159). Like Ginny Ratsoy in her work with the Kamloops Adult Learners Society, my involvement with the TOHP revitalized my teaching and research and deepened my engagement with the wider community. As a historian accustomed to researching, writing, and preparing lectures in relative isolation, I was energized by new connections with local non-profit organizations and private industry, and inspired by their enthusiasm for exploring and understanding the past.

The benefits of the TOHP extended beyond the official stakeholders to the wider Kamloops community. The potential impact of the Tranquille project on quality of life in the small city of Kamloops is perhaps less obvious than other important initiatives discussed in this volume, such as a public produce garden or an accessible shower for the homeless. Heritage projects such as the TOHP can, however, help to fulfill one of Charles Montgomery's (2013) central requirements for a "happy city": the city "should enable us to build and strengthen the bonds between friends, families, and strangers that give life meaning, bonds that represent the city's greatest achievement and opportunity" (43). Heritage projects are about more than preserving buildings and collecting memories; as in the case of the TOHP, such projects can "build and strengthen bonds" between people with shared interests, connect students with seniors, and make for a more caring community. In effect, they can help to nurture and sustain a sense of community. The impetus for, and significance of, the Tranquille project at least partly reflects the social proximities within this small city (Dubinsky 2006). When word got out about the emergent development at Tranquille, Kamloopsians made their voices heard about the importance of protecting the heritage of the site. In part, this outpouring reflects the "power of proximity" at work, as Tranquille, along with its history, looms larger in Kamloops than it might were it situated in a more populous urban centre. A large number of people from the Kamloops region have, or know someone who has, some connection to the history of Tranquille. The site was and is, Diane Purvey notes, "intimately linked to Kamloops through a web of well-travelled connections." Such connections persist, at least in the collective memory, and reflect Tranquille's history as a major employer, residence, and economic driver for Kamloops. In a recent interview, a former employee of the medical institution described her enduring attachment to Tranquille: "You still have that attachment. It's still there . . . Just, I don't know, it's just a part of your life" (G. Crowston, personal communication with Brandon Frederick, July 25, 2013). From the perspective of many former and current Kamloopsians, then, the history of Tranquille is inseparable from the history of the city itself. The small-city context is not tangential here. In contrast to many large urban centres, with their plethora of provincial institutions and heritage developments, Tranquille's historic prominence in the social and economic landscape of Kamloops seems to be relatively unmatched.

As Diane Purvey notes, although the institution has been closed for many years, "the memory of Tranquille remains embedded in the Kamloops psyche, a testament to its enduring influence." Over the years, it has been common to hear those who used to live, work, or visit at Tranquille express their sadness and dismay at the site's deterioration. One former employee of the medical institution recently recalled her sadness at the site's decline: "And then one day, we drove out there, just to drive out there, and it was really sad because, well the way I put it was watching an old friend deteriorate, you know. It was the grounds were getting overgrown with weeds, and the buildings were starting to deteriorate." (G. Crowston, personal communication with Brandon Frederick, July 25, 2013). The many people who lived and worked at Tranquille are honoured, and the value of their history affirmed, by recent efforts to preserve the oral and material heritage of the site. There is a growing emphasis in community-engaged research on approaches that seek to reduce the power imbalance between "the researcher and the researched" and that are "marked by local stakeholders being directly engaged in the research process itself" (Boser 2006, 10). Likewise, there has long been a movement in oral history toward "shared authority" between interviewer and interviewee, and calls for more careful attention to power relations inherent within the interview context (Frisch 1990). By making their voices heard about the importance of the site, and eagerly sharing their memories, Tranquillians played a key role in initiating the TOHP. As well, during the interviews, participants were asked relatively open-ended questions and encouraged to take an active part in directing the conversations. Nonetheless, unequal power relations remained, as the project was largely designed, directed, and carried out by community and university-based researchers, rather than by former residents and employees of Tranquille themselves.

While the TOHP did not subvert conventional power relations in the research process, it did help to challenge popular caricatures of Tranquille and to foreground stories that might not otherwise have been told.

Historian Chad Reimer (2000) notes that local history is, in some ways, "inherently democratic," based as it is in "the claim that history is not just the story of great men and wars, but also of ordinary people making a living" (111). The TOHP focused on the "ordinary people" of Tranquille, and in so doing offered a rich, compelling view of everyday life at the medical institution. The interviewees generally shared fond memories of the medical institution, and of the relationships they established there; one interviewee described the employees and residents of the medical institution as a "large family" (D. Richard[9], personal communication with Brandon Frederick, August 13, 2013). Tranquille emerged in the oral interviews, not as eerie and haunted, but rather as a place where ordinary people worked and played, lived and died. The popular preoccupation with ghost stories disrespects these people and detracts from their histories. By inviting them to share their memories, be they happy or sad, exciting or mundane, the TOHP helped to uncover a history that is far more nuanced than rumours suggest. This project also helped to give a voice to those who were deeply affected by the abrupt closure of the medical institution in 1984. One interviewee recalled feeling "devastated" by the closure, a sentiment that was echoed by others (F. Walker,[10] personal communication with Justin Potestio, July 22, 2013). The unexpectedly rapid closure had a significant impact not only on the residents and their families but on the workers. According to Diane Purvey, some of the workers "found that their work was not valued, and they became ashamed to tell people that they had worked at Tranquille."[11] In offering an outlet for people to share their recollections of the closure, the TOHP helped to shed new light on the process of deinstitutionalization and the personal, often emotional impact of that process on those who lived in small cities.

According to historian James Opp (2011), the production of heritage is "inherently dissonant and contested." We need to be cautious, he urges, about "totalizing the experience of place" (243). Thus far, the oral history of Tranquille that has been captured is selective, partial, and centred on the medical institution. Efforts need to be made to capture the many other voices and histories of the area, which will require branching out beyond oral history to incorporate a range of methodologies. Despite the conclusion of this oral history collaboration, research on Tranquille continues. Given such ongoing interest, it is likely that over the next few years

FIGURE 6.3. Present-day Tranquille, photograph by Tina Block.

FIGURE 6.4. Panoramic view of Tranquille, photograph by Tina Block.

new research collaborations will emerge, resulting—it is hoped—in the establishment of a permanent Tranquille archives and interpretive centre. Although it was not without challenges, the Tranquille Oral History Project benefited those directly involved and enhanced quality of life in the broader Kamloops community. For my part, I learned first-hand that "good things happen when historians broaden their mandate, seeing the university as an integral part of the community in which it functions" (Crothers 2002, 1450). There are, I suspect, more "good things" to come at Tranquille, as researchers and community members continue their work of exploring the site's unique landscape, aesthetics, and history.

Notes

I would like to thank the Kamloops Heritage Society, the TRU Small Cities CURA, and Tranquille on the Lake for their contributions to the Tranquille Oral History Project. I am grateful to my service learning students (Debra Andrews, Brandon Frederick, Francesca Lucia, and Justin Potestio) for their dedication to the project. Finally, I would like to extend a special thanks to those individuals who so generously shared their memories of Tranquille.

1   Pseudonym.

2   As of January 2016, Tranquille on the Lake was listed for sale. According to the development manager, Tim McLeod, the current owners seek to either sell the property or find a development partner (CBC Kamloops 2016).

3   I am grateful to both Dr. Terry Kading and Dr. Will Garrett-Petts for inviting and encouraging me to become involved in this project.

4   TOL development manager Tim McLeod uses the term "Tranquillians" to refer to people with historic ties to the site.

5   I would like to thank Dr. Christopher Walmsley for drawing my attention to several former provincial institutions in BC that have since become housing developments.

6   I am grateful to Ginny Ratsoy for introducing me to, and inspiring me to try, service learning. The service learning program at TRU was originally developed by Dr. Will Garrett-Petts.

7   TRU is now home to TRUSpace, an institutional repository which digitally archives research materials created by the TRU community.

8   The literature on service learning suggests that TRU is not unique in this respect.

9   Pseudonym.

10   Pseudonym.

11   According to Purvey, former employees of Tranquille express varied, and sometimes competing, views about the closure of the institution and the broader process of deinstitutionalization.

References

Ames, N., and S. Diepstra. 2006. "Using Intergenerational Oral History Service-Learning Projects to Teach Human Behavior Concepts: A Qualitative Analysis." *Educational Gerontology* 32:721–35.

Boser, S. 2006. "Ethics and Power in Community-Campus Partnerships for Research." *Action Research* 4 (1): 9–21.

Carpio, G., S. Luk, and A. Bush. 2013. "Building People's Histories: Graduate Student Pedagogy, Undergraduate Education, and Collaboration with Community Partners." *Journal of American History* 99 (4): 1176–88. doi:10.1093/jahist/jas601.

Casper, S. E. 2013. "Shared Histories: Teaching Outside the Classroom 'Box.'" *Journal of American History* 99 (4): 1159–60. doi:10.1093/jahist/jas649.

CBC Kamloops. 2016. "Manager Talks about the Sale of Tranquille on the Lake. 2016." Kamloops CBC, *Daybreak Kamloops*. January 31. http://www.cbc.ca/news/canada/kamloops/manager-talks-about-the-sale-of-tranquille-on-the-lake-1.3427722.

Chupp, M., and M. Joseph. 2010. "Getting the Most Out of Service Learning: Maximizing Student, University and Community Impact." *Journal of Community Practice* 18:190–212.

Coles, D., and D. Welch. 2002. "Bringing Campus and Community Together: Doing Public History at Longwood College." *The History Teacher* 35 (2): 229–35. doi:10.2307/3054180.

Crothers, A. G. 2002. "'Bringing History to Life': Oral History, Community Research, and Multiple Levels of Learning." *Journal of American History* 88 (4): 1446–51. doi:10.2307/2700608.

Dewhirst Lessard Architects. 2009. *Provincial Industrial School for Girls: Conservation Plan*. Vancouver: Vancouver Heritage Foundation (Copy of report in possession of author).

Dick, L. 2009. "Public History in Canada: An Introduction." *The Public Historian* 31 (1): 7–14. doi:10.1525/tph.2009.31.1.7.

Dubinsky, L. 2006. "In Praise of Small Cities: Cultural Life in Kamloops, BC." *Canadian Journal of Communication* 31 (1): 85–106.

Fairbridge Canada. 2017. Accessed June 12. www.fairbridgecanada.com/.

Frisch, M. 1990. *A Shared Authority: Essays on the Craft and Meaning of Oral and Public History*. Albany: State University of New York Press.

Garrett-Petts, W., ed.. 2005. *The Small Cities Book: On the Cultural Future of Small Cities*. Vancouver: New Star Books.

Hall, N. 2011. "Woodlands School Survivors Say Good Riddance to Final Building." *Vancouver Sun*. October 19.

Harris, A. 2010. "Tranquille Development: Past Influences, Current Realities." *Small Cities Imprint* 2 (1): 3–11.

Healey, M. 2005. "Linking Research and Teaching to Benefit Student Learning." *Journal of Geography in Higher Education* 29 (2): 183–201.

Knupfer, P. 2013. "Consultants in the Classroom: Student/Teacher Collaborations in Community History." *Journal of American History* 99 (4): 1161–75. doi:10.1093/jahist/jas602.

Lyons, J. 2007. "Integrating the Family and the Community into the History Classroom: An Oral History Project in Joliet, Illinois." *The History Teacher* 40 (4): 481–91.

Mills, A., S. Schechter, S. Lederer, and R. Naeher. 2011. "Global Stories of Citizenship: Oral History as Historical Inquiry and Civic Engagement." *Oral History Review* 38 (1): 34–62. doi:10.1093/ohr/ohr042.

Montgomery, C. 2013. *Happy City: Transforming our Lives through Urban Design*. Toronto: Doubleday Canada.

Mooney-Melvin, P. 2014. "Engaging the Neighborhood: The East Rogers Park Neighborhood History Project and the Possibilities and Challenges of Community-Based Initiatives." *Journal of Urban History* 40 (3): 462–78. doi:10.1177/0096144213516076.

MOU (Memorandum of Understanding). 2012. Research Collaboration between *The Small Cities CURA*, *Tranquille On the Lake*, and *Kamloops Heritage Society*.

Norton, W. 1999. *A Whole Little City by Itself: Tranquille and Tuberculosis*. Kamloops, BC: Plateau Press.

Opp, J. 2011. "Public History and the Fragments of Place: Archaeology, History, and Heritage Site Development in Southern Alberta." *Rethinking History* 15 (2): 241–67. doi:10.1080/13642529.2011.564830.

Post, C. 2012. "Objectives and Prospects for Bringing Service-Learning into the Memory and Heritage Classroom." *Southeastern Geographer* 52 (4): 413–28. doi:10.1353/sgo.2012.0030.

Purvey, D. 2018. "Like Building a Bridge that Missed the Other Side by Five Feet: The Deinstitutionalization of Tranquille and the Small City of Kamloops." In *Small Cities, Big Issues: Community in a Neoliberal Era*, edited by C. Walmsley and T. Kading. Edmonton: Athabasca University Press.

Ratsoy, G. 2008. "The Small City as Classroom: Academic Service Learning Participants Reflect." *Transformative Dialogues: Teaching & Learning Journal* 2 (2): 1–11.

Reimer, C. 2000. A Sense of Place: The Local in British Columbia History. *BC Studies* 127:109–15.

Shackel, P. 2011. "Pursuing Heritage: Engaging Communities." *Historical Archaeology* 45 (1): 1–9.

Spark, J. 2012, May/June. "Wanted: Memories from Tranquille Lake." *Kamloops Currents*, 18–20.

Spitale, L., to Mayor W. Wright and Members of Council. 2009, June. *The Tower at the Centre Block, Victoria Hill* (Development Services Department, Report, File No. 2608.20.19). City of New Westminster website: http://www.newwestcity.ca/council_minutes/0615_Jun15/CW/Reports/7.pdf.

TOL (Tranquille On the Lake). 2012. *Tranquille On the Lake Neighbourhood Plan*. http://www.tranquille.ca/neighbourhood-plan/.

Vancouver Island Beyond Victoria. 2017. Blog post. Cowichan's Bucolic Splendour Reveals an Historic Footnote at Fairbridge Farm School. Accessed June 12. http://vancouverislandbeyondvictoria.com/?p=3141.

Weber, P., and B. Sleeper. 2003. "Enriching Student Experiences: Multi-Disciplinary Exercises in Service-Learning." *Teaching Business Ethics* 7:417–35.

Youds, M. 2013, June 10. "Fresh Approach: Tranquille Farm Fuses Past, Present, and Food-Centred Future." *Kamloops Daily News*.

Leadership Initiatives and Community-Engaged Research: Explorations and Critical Insights on "Leadership and Learning" in the Small City of Kamloops

Terry Kading, Lisa Cooke, Dawn Farough,
Robin Reid, Kendra Besanger,
Ginny Ratsoy, and Tina Block

Introduction

We believe this collection offers experiences and insights on "leadership and learning" and community-engaged research that will inspire more faculty, students, and citizens, in Kamloops and other locales, to take up this transformational exercise within their respective communities. In our individual and collective engagement with this subject we have learned much about the challenges and opportunities for leadership and learning in the small city of Kamloops. We present in this chapter a collaborative assessment of the varied initiatives examined in this collection; how they have contributed to *equality of quality of life* in the small city; the resulting

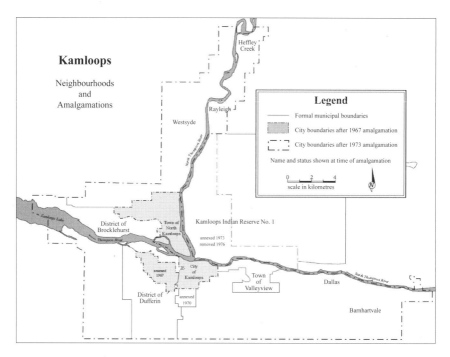

Kamloops

Neighbourhoods
and
Amalgamations

Heffley Creek

Rayleigh

Westsyde

North Thompson River

Legend

——— Formal municipal boundaries

City boundaries after 1967 amalgamation

City boundaries after 1973 amalgamation

Name and status shown at time of amalgamation

0   2   4
scale in kilometres

N

District of Brocklehurst

Thompson River

Town of North Kamloops

Kamloops Indian Reserve No. 1

annexed 1973
removed 1976

annexed 1967

City of Kamloops

District of Dufferin

annexed 1970

Town of Valleyview

Dallas

South Thompson River

Barnhartvale

FIGURE 7.1. Municipal Boundaries of the City of Kamloops past and present. From *The Small Cities Book: On the Cultural Future of Small Cities*, edited by W.F. Garrett-Petts (Vancouver: New Star Books, 2005). Courtesy of W.F. Garrett-Petts.

practice of a community-engaged research model as a response to the local learning conditions under the new model of governance; and the small university as a knowledge-support structure. As a complement to the individual case studies, this synopsis contributes to understanding "the heterogeneity of structural and everyday activities of all cities," and furthers the "critical dialogue with urban studies" on "the ways in which small cities have particular physical landscapes and are spatially organized" and the "cultural lives, mindsets, values and goals of small cities" (Bell and Jayne 2009, 692). And while individual chapters have identified the local participation in formal and informal collaborative networks, we provide here a spatial-locational, contextual, and cumulative assessment of the significance of these leadership initiatives and reveal the unexpected linkages among them all, despite their bases in disparate areas of study. This chapter addresses an acknowledged gap on leadership from within the

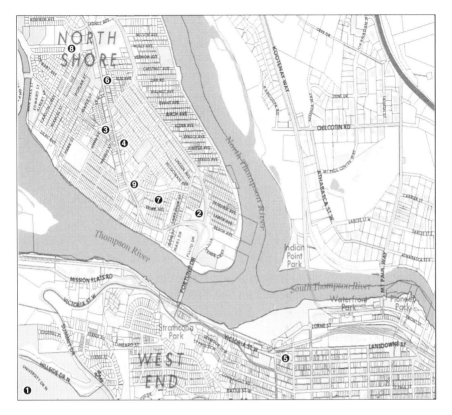

1. Thompson Rivers University (TRU)
2. Changing the Face of Poverty (CFP)
3. ASK Wellness
4. Theatre Project
5. Public Produce Project I

6. Public Produce Project II
7. Public Produce Project II
8. Northshore Community Centre
9. Small City Change Lab

FIGURE 7.2. Spatial-Locational Placement of Network Activity, City of Kamloops. Contains information licensed under the Open Government Licence – Kamloops.

literature on *urban and regional governance* in accounting for "agency" and "who, how, and why provides these systems, processes, and relationships with future directions" (Sotarauta, Beer, and Gibney 2017, 188–89).

In this chapter we will analyze how the qualities of Kamloops may limit or expand opportunities for bridging and vertical knowledge and social capital linkages, identifying strengths and weakness in the overall social, creative, and cultural capital—in moving from transactional leadership to transformational leadership outcomes through the "practice of power" (see Introduction). The analysis will include a set of evaluations on the outcomes and challenges flowing from the different types of leadership initiatives, and provide an understanding of the learning and dynamics within particular leadership initiatives and collaborations, or combinations of collaborations, in achieving intended goals. Finally, we examine the role of Thompson Rivers University as a knowledge-support structure, and the leadership and learning challenges from within this institution. This deepens what is recognized as an incomplete understanding of how institutional capacity emerges to be a critical "facilitating agent" in achieving transformational leadership and equality of quality of life outcomes at the local level (Sotarauta, Beer, and Gibney 2017, 189). Drawing on contributor experiences with these local initiatives on the practice and challenges of research, writing, and interrogating local leadership, we will explore the peculiarities and challenges of community-engaged research in a small city, and the varied forms and outcomes from university engagement that may be facilitated in the community and beyond. In concluding, we demonstrate the significance of community-engaged research to the small city, and to the trajectory of our university—as an emergent and integral feature of leadership and learning at the local level.

Local Capacities and Equality of Quality of Life

Is the small city an ideal setting for addressing *equality of quality of life* goals? Like large urban centres, the small city has the challenges of poverty, homelessness, marginalization, and increasing dispersal that express deep inequities and may generate feelings of exclusion and inferiority. As in small towns and rural areas, the small city has persistent economic insecurities and population growth and investment challenges. The main purpose of this collection has been to reveal and challenge understandings of *quality of life* in the small city by providing diverse perspectives and analyses of local leadership initiatives in advancing *equality of quality of life*. As demonstrated, in addition to separate community groups, there are both established networks and a variety of initiatives minimizing hardship, leading us to health, building resilience, increasing fairness, strengthening bonds, and opening doors to empathy and cooperation in Kamloops. By applying the categories of "leadership and learning" under the new forms of governance to the areas of homelessness and marginal residents, food security and sustainability, heritage preservation, and adult education, we have offered a rendering of the local leadership initiatives and unlikely alliances that counter the trends that diminish the *equality of quality of life* in this small city and serve as examples of transformational leadership outcomes. It is these leadership initiatives, which support other small-city qualities, that we explore in more detail, with particular attention to whether these qualities may mitigate or even prevent the negative individual and community outcomes documented by Montgomery (2013) in large urban centres. And as emphasized in the literature on *governance*, we pay particular attention to the local Kamloops context in which these leadership and learning initiatives occur in relation to provincial and federal efforts to "govern through community." The types of capital identified by Emery and Flora (2006) in creating a local inventory, and Bryant and Marois' (2010) recognition of networks as formal and informal organizations generating particular local orientations, observed and latent, frame our assessments of what has been attained, and what might have been or is yet to be realized, within the existing matrix of capitals.

The overall trajectory of Kamloops, after the economic instability of the 1980s to the early 21st century led first to out-migration and then to stagnant population growth, has been a gradual diversification and stabilization of the local economy, of which the city's status as a regional centre serving a much larger area has been an important feature in attracting provincial and federal investments. Within this trajectory, particular forms of local capital have become more evident and enhanced in shaping orientations: *natural capital*, "those assets that abide in a particular location, including weather, geographic isolation, natural resources, amenities and natural beauty"; *cultural capital*, "the way people 'know the world' and how they act within it" and how "creativity, innovation, and influence emerge and are nurtured" (and acknowledged as *political capital* within a particular local political culture—*our refinement for this chapter*); *human capital*, "the skills and abilities of people to develop and enhance their resources and access outside resources and bodies of knowledge"; *social capital*, "connections among people and organizations or the social 'glue,' to make things, positive or negative, happen"; and *built capital*, "the infrastructure supporting these activities" (Emery and Flora 2006, 20–21). These forms of capital, in relation to Montgomery's remedies for the challenges of our largest urban centres of biophilia (access to nature), conviviality (increasing connections and closeness), and mobility (opportunities beyond vehicle ownership), reveal that Kamloops has particular strengths.

Perhaps the city's greatest advantage, though little recognized in its contribution to facilitating "community," is the abundance of natural capital, from which other benefits in social-creative capital emerge. With mild and short winters (in contrast to the rest of Canada) and hot, dry summers, "weather/climate" has been consistently identified in citizen surveys as the main feature making Kamloops a "good place to live" and contributing to overall quality of life, followed, in a 2016 survey, by "location/proximity to other places," "recreational/sports activities and facilities," "size of community," and "friendly/nice people" (Trawin 2016, 9). This climate is matched with considerable natural assets, ranging from the hillside/mountain views to the natural vegetation and numerous parks throughout the city and along the confluence of two major rivers (North & South Thompson) in the downtown core. In combination with nearby skiing/snowboarding , numerous local and regional golf course options, and limitless opportunities for fishing, boating, and other water activities, the city is well-placed to attract and retain residents from an aging population and those desiring an active lifestyle. The local government has contributed significant built capital in this area, with a $55 million commitment in 2003 to new and revised parks and facilities throughout the city, justified as generating "sport tourism, sport development, athlete development, health and wellness, and civic pride development" (McCorkell 2011). The centrepieces of this project are the new Tournament Capital Centre and fields (next to TRU) and the revamping of lands and facilities at McArthur Island Park on the North Shore. There have been continuous expenditures to expand activities for biking, year-round programming in facilities, and the introduction of new activities responsive to different age groups (e.g., skateboarding and long board parks for youth, and pickleball courts for seniors), from which the city has received notable recognition. "Highest satisfaction ratings were recorded for: programs and services for recreation and sport (93%), availability of green spaces for recreation and enjoyment (92%), as well as the overall aesthetic appearance of the city (92%)" (Trawin 2016, 13). In addition to this observed orientation, the "health and wellness" aspect of this investment may be seen as a latent orientation from which to further engage the city in advancing *equality of quality of life* goals (as per Bryant and Marois—see Introduction).

Climate and nature contribute to a long, yearly engagement with a wide variety of outdoor activities, events, venues and sports, and address a critical feature observed by Montgomery (2013) in reviving the fortunes of large urban centres and facilitating the creation of social-creative capital: "We know that nature in cities make us happier and healthier. We know it makes us friendlier and kinder. We know it helps us build essential bonds with other people and places in which we live" (123). This has been borne out in Kamloops, where in 2016 the "majority of respondents said quality of life in the City of Kamloops was either good or very good," adding that this "is significantly higher than quality of life ratings in other British Columbian municipalities"[1] (10). Thus, a combination of climate, ease of access to nature, and official local support and promotion of an active lifestyle has contributed to local conviviality. As Montgomery (2013) observes, "People who say they 'belong' to their community are happier than those who do not. And people who trust their neighbors feel a greater sense of that belonging. And that sense of belonging is influenced by social contact. And casual encounters (such as, say, the kind that might happen around a volleyball court on a Friday night), are *just as important* to belonging and trust as contact with family and close friends" (134). And while one of the lowest levels of citizen satisfaction was recorded for "alternative forms of transportation," Kamloops continues to provide a context for multiple and ongoing casual encounters, further enhanced by not having to contend with the traffic congestion and lengthy commute times of large urban centres that may dramatically reduce social time.[2] Such qualities as friendliness, kindness, and trust that arise through these natural and built forms of capital foster local opportunities for multiple and complex encounters, and continue to preserve the "power of proximity" / ease of contact and engagement identified in several chapters (as per Dubinsky, 2006) that allows for the development of social capital and creative initiatives. Kamloops has the added advantage in *human capital* over smaller towns and rural areas as the regional base of a number of well-established community organizations, several with provincial or national links and recognition (as evident in the formal and informal network linkages in each chapter). Whether in terms of local social challenges, heritage, sustainability, or creating age-friendly communities, these entities (of which the university has become an important example) have provided ongoing bridging and vertical knowledge, and have grown in scope of assets, services, and programs.[3]

There is little doubt that climate, size, and ease of contact facilitate both the monthly meetings of the Changing the Face of Poverty Network (CFP) and the generation of subcommittees and informal discussions within the network to address the immediate needs for clients or to examine and assess the local resource capacities to initiate new services, such as coordinating shelter and food services or supporting events to provide for the homeless or fundraise for member initiatives—events that often have an outdoor component or take place in the evening or on weekends. Such continuous multi-sectoral representation and engagement beyond monthly meetings confirms that the context allows for more *social time* than in large urban centres. For the Kamloops Adult Learners Society (KALS), the medial position of the small city plays an important role in the success of the organization, with enough residents who are of retirement age to provide KALS with a sufficient number of students and most Kamloopsians living within a 15-minute drive to most parts of the city. As Ginny Ratsoy notes, the sufficient population base and accessibility of location are favourable attributes of this small city—advantages it may have over its village and metropolis counterparts. KALS is succeeding in its vision of "expanding educational opportunities for citizens in their retirement years" by physically locating in areas seniors frequent and gearing publicity toward them, at the same time as it acts on its mission to better the community "through interaction and partnerships with other community groups" through outreach activities. Climate, size, and proximity all facilitate this success—which is crucial in the collaboration of older people, such as those involved in the Kamloops Adult Learners Society, for whom travelling great distances and contending with parking mazes hold little appeal. Those who were instrumental in founding KALS, making the attempt in a large city with a less accommodating climate, might have found more obstacles in their way requiring more resources to address these limitations.

The contributions by Lisa Cooke on the "culture of giving" and Dawn Farough on the homeless theatre project provide more evidence of this small city adaptability and openness, or fluid "social space," that advances and enhances new leadership initiatives. What I (Lisa Cooke) can say is that my involvement in the project is directly relational to this particular urban setting. I first learned of the Shower Project from Dr. Will Garrett-Petts, a colleague at work who had learned about it in a conversation with Jim McCarthy at a completely separate community event. The two men knew each other from some other context, got to chatting, and the story of the showers came up. These kinds of serendipitous encounters that lead to conversation which leads to research projects happen in all kinds of communities. What is specific about this particular project is that not only is it more likely that people know people and then bump into people in a smaller city context—but this small city has a university in it. Dawn Farough's research through the No Straight Lines theatre production has provided the clearest understanding of the advantages of the small city to developing new leadership initiatives. Group members believe that closer proximity leads to better and closer connections between community members: "I feel like we have the right size of community where it's easier for people to feel connected. We are only a very few degrees from everyone else in the community. You know someone who knows someone who is related to someone."[4] There was also a feeling that *status* or elitism were not as evident in Kamloops as they might be in larger urban centres, serving to facilitate awareness, mobilization, and interaction across a larger cross-section of the community, and a strong sense that the community was open to engaging with new initiatives.

This familiarity and knowledge of multiple contacts across the community, and the varied resources they may provide, reveals the depth of *human* and *social capital* in particular areas. For the theatre project, "If we need or want help from Western Canada Theatre, enough of us know people at Western Canada Theatre well that that might happen. It might not happen in Toronto, for example."[5] Considerable social capital has been developed in the area of sustainability and food security, as the Kamloops Food Policy Committee (KFPC) had been working in the community for over 15 years as a non-profit, grassroots advocacy group before initiating the Public Produce Project. The KFPC had developed an elaborate network of important partners, including the City of Kamloops, Interior Health, Interior Community Services (ICS), and the Kamloops Farmers Market. As an umbrella organization, the KFPC's success as a non-profit, grassroots organization relates to the broad representation of food-related groups that it works with. As Robin Reid and Kendra Basinger observe, "the ability of the small Public Produce Project to access such a network of resources and partnerships had to do with its willingness to engage locally and work within pre-existing frameworks. It is certainly the case that relying on partnerships of trust and collaboration was essential to the success and continuation of the project." The Tranquille Oral History Project partly reflects the fact that the city is "very conscious of its heritage" (Dubinsky 2006, 90), a consciousness supported by the work of two heritage societies, a Heritage Commission, and a local museum. As Tina Block observed, "when word got out about the emergent development at Tranquille, Kamloopsians made their voices heard about the importance of protecting the heritage of the site," and in part, this outpouring reflects the "power of proximity" at work, as Tranquille, along with its history, looms larger in this small city than it might were it situated in a more populous urban centre. Concerns about protecting Tranquille's heritage are grounded not only in the specific history of the site but in a more general awareness of heritage in this city. It is indeed possible to speak of a heritage culture in Kamloops—a culture that is reproduced and disseminated in both organizational and everyday spaces. This culture has a positive impact on *equality of quality of life* in this small city by nurturing unlikely alliances among the private, public, and non-profit sectors, shedding new light on local histories, and bringing together people with shared interests.

These insights capture other facets of proximity in the small city that contribute to successful initiatives, notably the numerous and close linkages between community members and a variety of established organizations, the weaker emphasis on status (or lack of an evident elitism), and the fact that this urban context offers a space to promote new initiatives, as there is more opportunity for *social time* than in larger urban centres. Ginny Ratsoy, who has done considerable research into smallish cities—particularly Kamloops (largely in the context of the success of its professional theatre company, Western Canada Theatre)—has had several occasions to reflect on the question of whether or not Kamloops' small to mid-size facilitates the formation and success of organizations:

> I do not believe this question can be answered in isolation from other factors. Specifically, Kamloops's location, I would argue, must be taken into account. It is a relatively isolated small city: the nearest large city, Vancouver, is a four-hour drive away. As such, it has a distinct identity—a luxury it might well not have if it were a one-hour drive from a large city. So, while I do believe that the size of Kamloops facilitates a certain ease of communication—getting from place to place is relatively easy, and, for example, one can go to an unfamiliar organization or social setting and pretty well be assured of already being acquainted with at least one person one encounters—I also believe that the clear boundaries that demarcate the city –figuratively and metaphorically—are as much responsible for the energetic arts and social culture of the city. Thus, at least two factors (and likely many more) are at play in making Kamloops the culture-rich small city it is.

These observations serve to support our earlier assessments that the small city may more readily foment initiatives and long-standing collaborations, as it is less constrained by challenges of distance and silos that are more evident in larger urban centres, but also advantaged by its regional status and numerous established community organizations. The dual advantage of distance from larger urban centres and the "proximity" within the small city clearly generate particular features that support the principle of *equality of quality of life*. On the one hand there are better and closer connections between community members who are less encumbered by status or class concerns. Within this context, initiatives and opportunities may arise more informally—including unlikely alliances—and there is a sense that there is the space to try new things. On the other hand, Kamloops has a substantial and diverse enough citizenry to sustain a wide variety of collaborations which aid in public awareness and mobilization behind initiatives. Whether considering local social challenges, heritage, sustainability, or the creation of age-friendly communities, the small city is fertile ground for the face-to-face contact that is an important, and perhaps a necessary, element for strong partnerships among individuals and organizations, particularly in fostering successful leadership initiatives, and, as we will see, supporting community-university engagement (Tremblay and Hall 2014).

Despite the evident strengths and advantages of the small city over large urban centres and smaller towns and rural areas, there are serious challenges. From the 2016 Citizen Survey, those residents who felt that the quality of life in Kamloops had declined "blamed it on a higher cost of living, high unemployment / lack of job opportunities and economic downturn more generally" (Trawin 2016, 14). Their concerns are not without merit, as data from the 2011 census revealed that 18.1% of homeowners (compared to a provincial average of 23.8%) and 47% of renters (compared to a provincial average of 45.3%) were spending more than 30% of their income on shelter (Government of BC 2014). Since then, local housing costs and rental rates have continued to rise dramatically, generating an "affordability crisis" by 2016, wherein "the lack of affordable housing in Kamloops has reached a level not seen before. The number of homeless and working poor has increased, and over the last several months shelters and non-profit organizations have seen more and more people turning for help" (Cronin 2016, February 10).[6] Thus, with respect to the local government and social issues, "the largest proportion of respondents said children and youth at risk, mental health, homelessness, as well as people living in poverty should take priority"—a persistent concern observed in earlier surveys (Trawin 2016, 28). And although the observed orientation of the City of Kamloops is toward many *equality of quality of life* outcomes (best expressed through the local Sustainability Plans),[7] like many small cities it has limited financial resources and is highly cognizant of local concerns over raising property taxes or imposing bylaws that may deter investment and growth, and this reinforces a cautious approach to governing. These challenges and concerns relate to our spatial-locational analysis of network activity and initiatives, which feature predominantly on the North Shore of Kamloops and represent a continuing weakness of the local political culture / *political capital* and the structural integrity of Kamloops' social fabric. North Shore Kamloops residents have retained a long-standing grievance regarding their place in the trajectory of the city, going back to the late 1960s / early 1970s when the Town of Kamloops (North Shore) was amalgamated with southern shore communities to form the City of Kamloops. Since this time there has been a strong sense that their voice has not been heard and that later developments (commercial, professional, retail, and housing) and investment by the local government have advantaged the South Shore over the North, accounting for the dearth in services, inadequate infrastructure, stagnant population growth, and visible social challenges (poverty, homelessness, addictions, and petty crime). In the late 1990s, in response to a proposed halfway house for parolees by the John Howard Society, Deutschmann (2005) observed:

> The North Shore is currently the area demonstrating the greatest amount of resistance to the placement of new social service facilities, and the controversy has typically been framed in terms of the North Shore being increasingly and unfairly disadvantaged relative to the expanding, and wealthier, South Shore neighbourhoods. A comment that was repeated in various ways at the public meetings on halfway and social housing issues: "When you have something good, you put it on the South Shore; when it's bad you dump in on us." This expression of resentment was even more pronounced in private conversations, which often mentioned the way the "night-time lights shine down on us from the hills of the South Shore, getting brighter every year." The university and the largest retail stores are "up the hill," in contrast to the many failed or threatened family-owned small businesses on North Shore. While there are important pockets of poverty and social problems in other parts of the city (especially the downtown South Shore), the heaviest concentrations are found in North Shore communities (341–42).

The North Shore has long been stigmatized locally as more "working class" and an "undesirable area" to locate (Brady et al. 2013), and this division in status has had significant implications for the *built capital*, and by extension the overall political culture / *political capital* by limiting "how creativity, innovation, and influence emerge and are nurtured" (Emery and Flora 2006, 21). Whereas the 2003 referendum on the Tournament Capital proposal was passed (by demonstrating a commitment to direct investment in North Shore parks and recreational facilities), the 1987 referendum on a $50 million waterfront project that proposed a convention centre, sports coliseum, arts museum, and performing arts centre, and the 2015 referendum on a $90 million performing arts centre[8] (both to be located in the downtown South Shore), failed due to the strong "no" vote from North Shore communities—and were seen as opportunities to voice the latter's continued discontent. Both projects comprised sizable provincial and federal financial commitments linked to a local increase in property taxes, with significant potential to access ongoing provincial and federal monies for activities and spinoff benefits (and thus their rejection represented major losses in *vertical capital*). The inability of City Council to address this division and fund North Shore redevelopment (beyond existing incentives in property tax and development cost breaks), remains a persistent challenge, and is testament to a local weakness in City Council engagement with this issue and *financial capital*, the "financial resources available to invest in community capacity-building, to underwrite the development of businesses, to support civic and social entrepreneurship, and to accumulate wealth for future community development" (Emery and Flora 2006, 21). Thus, advantages in climate, proximity, social time, and established community organizations in this small city provide only a context, or preconditions, for this ease of engagement and to initiate change. For instance, it is not hard to envision small and mid-sized cities where the limited goals set by the Government of Canada in addressing homelessness have prevailed over a broader vision being taken up by a separate leadership such as the Changing the Face of Poverty network, or where there are no shower facilities, theatre productions, public produce, KALS, or collaborative heritage initiatives. Only the efforts and success of leadership initiatives that have emerged locally can explain these outcomes. The activities, initiatives, and leadership from various community organizations, as identified in earlier chapters, have been decisive in preventing the exacerbation of this north–south division, and are the bases of addressing this weakness in the political culture and *political capital*. They are testament to the increase in *human* and *social capital* that has taken place in Kamloops generally, in which the small university has played an increased role, supporting *equality of quality of life* outcomes.

From Transactional Leadership to Transformational Outcomes under the New Governance Model

Success in achieving goals through collaboration requires a particular type of leadership style, as the "authority to lead" is not granted by a predetermined job description, and leadership is a shared and cooperative responsibility. Trust, respect, and the credibility of the leaders are recognized as the critical components for collaborative success, with a supportive leadership style that promotes involvement, increases members' satisfaction and participation, resolves conflict, and encourages commitment, different viewpoints, and group achievement, whether in local initiatives or community-engaged research (Tremblay and Hall 2014, 399–400). Dubinsky (2006) has observed that the origins and nature of particular collaborations are important "if collective understanding is a desired goal" (99). From these observations we have revealed the backgrounds and goals of different leadership initiatives in the small-city context in facilitating or limiting these leadership qualities, with an emphasis on what has been learned by and through these collaborations and how this knowledge has contributed to *equality of quality of life* outcomes. As the chapters in this collection have demonstrated, Kamloops has particular qualities that have facilitated a variety of networks, generating a variety of leadership initiatives and the development of *social capital*. There are also persistent and emerging challenges with implications for the overall political capital / *cultural capital* of the city. In this section we examine the varied collaborative leadership initiatives in relation to the new governance / "governing through community" model adopted by higher levels of government (see Introduction to this volume), a model which has established important limitations and constraints and fostered new opportunities to draw on local resources and the expansion of bridging social capital. The emphasis is on (1) the extent to which transactional forms of leadership have become transformational, leading to outcomes that move the city toward improved *equality of quality of life*, and (2) the potential, or latent, orientations that reside within Kamloops in creating a more inclusive trajectory for the city. An assessment of these efforts in addressing the recognized weaknesses in *political capital* reveals surprising linkages between all of the initiatives analyzed in this collection in relation to this goal, despite their varied foci, when examined from the new governance perspective.

There is also the opportunity to challenge aspects of the existing literature on what constitutes transformational leadership success, which tends to prioritize the longevity of collaborations over recognizing the impact or power of smaller, one-off leadership initiatives in contributing to *equality of quality of life* outcomes. For instance, the collaboration on this collection may be understood as a *coercive collaboration*—to meet the requirements for a specific publication, and a *self-interested collaboration*—in order to fulfill research expectations of our academic positions and meet the benchmarks for tenure and promotion within our university. On the surface, a collaborative initiative based on coercion and self-interest might strike many as unsound grounds from which to achieve a successful result; however, since the goal has consistently been about a specific and tangible outcome—the creation of a publishable collection—coercion and self-interest have served to keep our collective focused, reach particular standards based on continued feedback, and work toward integrating disparate themes into a cohesive collection. Further, the opportunity to read, review, and assess works on different issues from varied academic fields has provided for each of us deeper insights into our academic community and the city in which we live. The initial workshop to examine individual contributions and determine common terms of integration was significant in revealing the multiple connections between the different themes covered and the similarities and the variations in the local collaborations under review. Discussions also evoked memories and experiences of past efforts by contributors engaged in community initiatives as well as recognitions of particular places, changes, and the dynamics of our small city due to these and other local initiatives. Thus, this coercive and self-interested collaboration has had unintended consequences in which there has been a high level of cooperation and a rich learning environment. Nevertheless, the nature of this collaboration is exclusive (rather than broadly inclusive). And it entails particular limits in content, where the narrative of the editor becomes more pronounced in framing and integrating this venture toward the goal of a particular product, after which the shared leadership, dynamics, and reflective learning from this collaboration will fade. But the collective learning outcomes may endure and be articulated through new or follow-up research, or under new forms of local leadership in Kamloops or elsewhere—important qualities that are evident in similar collaborations with short-term aims at the community level or in particular collaborations involving the university. Thus, we initially examine the prospects for two leadership initiatives with large, open-ended and long-term goals—the Kamloops Adult Learners Society and the Changing the Face of Poverty network. Then we look at the short-term leadership initiatives—the Shower, Theatre, Public Produce, and Oral History projects, revealing these projects as expressions of a much broader and deeper *social capital* emerging under the new governance model, and how these projects continue to have an impact at the local level.

From the inception of Kamloops Adult Learners Society, transformational leadership outcomes in the lives of retirees were the goals of the early founders. Intentionally formed as an independent organization free from formal linkages to other institutions, KALS has demonstrated adaptability and resourcefulness, and enjoyed significant success in expanding linkages and offering a variety of learning options to its membership. Originally envisioned in terms of a peer learning approach where the learners would teach and learn from one another, it has embraced a hybrid model, welcoming instruction from those outside its membership from a wide range individuals, groups, and organizations with varied backgrounds and knowledge. Despite the leadership and organization being highly structured and becoming more complex (an executive with president, secretary, treasurer, and past president, and specialized committees for facilities, programs, policy and planning, fundraising, and membership/recruitment), as Ginny Ratsoy observes, this is "a group whose experiences have led them to expect complexity and embrace flexibility." KALS remains a highly social, active group that collectively possesses a wealth of diverse experiences in varied public and private sector enterprises, and with the wisdom of age, and more *social time*, the personal connections within this structure ensure that all essential tasks are carried out even when vacancies arise due to unforeseen circumstances. "Thus, this collaboration reveals a broader form of leadership that has emerged due to the experience and commitment of the members—which allows for a less formalized structure to persist as a successful initiative." The position held by KALS to retain its independence as an organization not reliant on other entities may be interpreted as the desire of the membership to affirm their individual power and continued resilience against the prevailing stereotypes of seniors as an increasingly costly and needy demographic in a "larger narrative of decline" (Chappell 2016, June 10). The informal and intimate structures underlying the formal structure further express this collective empowerment in generating security through connections and supporting individual independence, community engagement, and active living as *equality of quality of life* outcomes. In addition, the *political capital* as a voter bloc linked to this demographic change will continue to facilitate provincial investments in healthcare and other services in the city.

KALS is also active in an urban environment that is optimal for growth and outreach prospects, as 20.1% of the Kamloops population is presently 65 or over, with the potential to rise to some 30%+ over the next 25 years based on demographic projections and the high preference of retirees to "age in place," in their existing home or community.[9] And while only a very small number of retirees report being socially isolated, a significant percentage (25%) would like to participate in more social activities. KALS offers not just an activity to "fill time," but a life-affirming organizational structure with a range of responsibilities and duties that reinforce and expand community contacts on multiple fronts within an environment free from the paternalistic or discriminatory practices evident in other spheres of life for retirees (e.g., employment opportunities) (Chappell 2016).[10] Notable in this regard is the locational base of most KALS activities, operating primarily out of the North Shore Community Centre, a local multi-use facility situated within a block of the very area historically fraught with the most visible forms of poverty, petty crime, addictions, and homelessness. Thus KALS, drawing on a membership from across the city with ample choices for alternative venues, has bucked local stereotypes regarding "personal safety issues" on the North Shore in favour of practicality and convenience, in an area where the most growth in retirees is occurring.[11] With the increase in built and planned senior facilities on the North Shore, most of them proximate to the North Shore Community

Centre and offering a range of housing options (from independent to supported living), the placement of KALS is a significant contribution to the
local *social capital* and overall *political capital* of the city in making the
North Shore an attractive area to "age in place" and contribute to the local
economic and social revitalization (and potentially attract retirees from
other areas of the city and region). Transformational leadership qualities
are not evident just in the membership of KALS but also in redefining the
spaces in which they are active, which is further demonstrated in other
long- and short-term leadership initiatives.

In the face of a lack of concern or resolve by the federal and provincial
governments to address homelessness and poverty in a meaningful manner,
the transformational leadership goals of the Changing the Face of Poverty
network (CFP) may appear illusive and unrealistic from a leadership perspective. The *Five Year Plan to End Homelessness* has been met by an affordability crisis in local housing, continued visible and hidden homelessness, and the prospects for increased poverty and housing insecurity due
to the rising living costs and stagnant provincial rates of social assistance
and wages for those most in need. The considerable local learning and ac-
cumulated knowledge about local homeless needs in housing and services
has not resulted in the vertical supports in resources, thus confirming the
most negative assessments of the new governance / "governing through
community" model as entailing no meaningful devolution of power and
resources, facilitating new inequalities among and within communities,
and placing an increased burden on local community groups, while creating a "confused set of accountabilities" (see Introduction to this volume).
Despite local awareness of all these facets, the CFP and member organizations have persevered and continue to expand local and external linkages and envision improved programs and services to address the needs of
marginalized residents. The Sub-Committee on Anti-Poverty Strategies
of the CFP continues to research initiatives (programs and policies) in
other cities of similar population size to reduce prices and improve access
of public transit, study incentives for increasing the availability of low-
cost childcare spaces and after-school supports, engage local employment
agencies on services, expand representation within the group, and conduct
surveys on local needs, encouraged by efforts in other cities (see Carlton
and Born, 2016). As a testament to ongoing support within the network

and the flexibility among dominant members, volunteers of the Jubilee Urban Movement and Partners (JUMP) Kamloops program, initiated in 2012 to fill the weekly gaps in food service provision for homeless residents, have been embraced for their generous frontline outreach efforts and organizational skills, and integrated into directing the programs for the Life Skills Project—which they have expanded through access to city facilities and support from CFP members.[12] Stronger overlap and coordination has been established with the *community entity* of the HPS through cross-representation on the various committees of the HomeFree Collective that inform and guide the use of HPS funding. And while the initial enthusiasm and prospects for the HomeFree Collective to act as a cohesive and engaged vehicle for local change have been dampened considerably due to the lack of affordable housing to exercise the principles of "housing first," a division of labour has emerged in which the CFP is focused on coordinating services for the homeless and strategies to prevent homelessness and housing insecurity, while the HFC is focused specifically on the issue of housing affordability and increasing the local housing stock. This has led to the increased recognition of barriers in municipal policies and of the need for stronger advocacy by the local government in accessing resources for affordable housing (Williams 2017, June 20).

Perhaps, though, the most dynamic leadership has emerged out of the action plan on youth homelessness. A passionate group of young leaders (several with lived experience) have created the A Way Home Committee, now a nationally recognized organization for embracing a Housing First approach to youth homelessness (ages 13–24) by leveraging access to housing through existing community organizations and the private sector (paying rents / set-asides in rental properties) and "breaking down" silos among the many service providers for youth. Confronted with the same constraints in housing availability and the capacity to provide sufficient support services, A Way Home Committee continues to deepen local connections in raising funds and creating educational and employment opportunities for formerly homeless youth. They are also responsible for developing and implementing the first youth homeless count in Canada, and are solicited by other communities and national organizations for advice and progress reports.[13] Along with providing younger membership in the CFP network and HomeFree Collective, they represent the emergence of a substantial and knowledgeable youth leadership with established connections to a variety of local, provincial, and national organizations, provincial and federal government ministries, the private sector, and the university (and acquiring unmatched entrepreneurial skills in these areas, as per Emery and Flora 2006, 24).

Over the last ten years there is evidence of increased bridging and vertical linkages within the CFP and in concert with other organizations and networks, as well as increased services and programs, while the CFP explores further options with the school district, Ministry of Children and Family Development, and the City of Kamloops. Despite the resource limitations in achieving local goals in reducing poverty or ending homelessness, resolve is maintained in the recognition that their efforts have been part of broader local and national efforts to have the Government of Canada acknowledge the human and financial costs of the ineffectual measures to date (Schwan 2016). The 2015 federal election of the Liberal Party of Canada, on an agenda for a more active government role in addressing urban issues, has seen increased and long-term financial commitments through the HPS and to affordable housing for the provinces. The 2017 election in BC has resulted in a new New Democratic Party–Green Party coalition government in response to insufficient action on housing and related urban social issues by the former provincial government. And while the efforts of the CFP have not been able to "transform governance itself" to arrive at commensurate goals with the provincial and federal governments on homelessness and poverty (as per Shucksmith 2010), local leadership has developed institutional capacity in knowledge resources, relational resources, and mobilizing capacities on a number of fronts. Community advocates and visiting speakers from other centres have noted the strong collaborative dynamic in Kamloops, and formerly homeless residents have mentioned the significant number of services and support compared to other cities. These aspects and their transformational qualities are further evident in the short-term leadership initiatives, strengthening the local *political capital* and moving toward *equality of quality of life* outcomes.

In the case of the Shower Project, one need only to look at the relationships between the groups that have come together for guidance on this initiative. ASK Wellness had worked hard to nurture a working relationship with the North Shore Business Improvement Association long before a group of United Steelworkers from Local 7619 turned up offering to build a shower. Three self-interested groups came together organically to accomplish a common goal. Despite the focused nature of the project, success was never guaranteed. As Lisa Cooke observes, affirming Shucksmith's critical insights on strategies as "emergent" rather than conforming to a rigid development plan, "the lesson for researchers in this is that the strengths of the collaborations are in the nuanced ways that all of the complexities are negotiated." Thus, it is easy to imagine many "good-intentioned" leadership efforts failing due to this inability to negotiate complexities, particularly a shower project as a visible service that would attract and congregate marginalized residents to the North Shore, an environment recognized for being hostile to this outcome from social initiatives (as per Deutschmann 2005 above). Although the leadership of the Northshore Business Community and the United Steelworkers is to be commended for their openness, flexibility, and resolve, there is little doubt that the mediation skills and reputation of ASK Wellness facilitated the completion of the shower project—revealing the surprising level of generosity toward our most marginalized residents by all parties—as each organization had the collective power to derail or prevent this outcome if confronted by local resistance. Underlying this result, though, is the voice of one individual—Bob Hughes—who took a small storefront organization offering counselling and referral services to residents with AIDS and turned it into a multi-million dollar housing and service provider for thousands of marginalized residents. Openly critical of the federal and provincial government response to homelessness, Hughes is quick to give credit when due, and collaborates with and supports numerous other community organizations and leadership initiatives (e.g., the A Way Home Committee).

Ever present in the local media informing the public as to local affordable housing, addictions, and homeless issues, ASK Wellness has ensured a visible and publicized homeless count every year for over a decade and tirelessly promoted the benefits to the community of adopting the latest harm reduction strategies (such as the shower project). This local (and national) credibility has been built on mediating and revising the trajectory of the North Shore. As gentrification of the South Shore began occurring between 2004 and 2006, residents of low-cost housing were displaced to the North Shore (with related drug and criminal activity), leading to what Hughes refers to as a "war zone" between 2006 and 2010[14] (see also Chapter 2 of this volume). ASK Wellness, in collaboration with local residents and community organizations, the North Shore Business Association, the RCMP, and the City of Kamloops, gradually introduced the service supports and physical infrastructure that altered the social environment.[15] Hughes later observed, "I'm quite proud to say that it didn't result in the condemnation of and eradication of some of the more marginalized or troubled people. I think they became more embraced" (Brady et al. 2013). Thus, ASK Wellness has played a decisive role in reversing what had become an extremely negative setting for the North Shore (even worse than observed in the 1990s by Deutschmann) while reducing the stigmatization of local residents in need. Acting at an opportune time, when the provincial government was more willing to provide money for affordable housing and services, ASK Wellness has redeveloped several sites on the South Shore for marginalized residents (thus preserving their presence and accommodation in this area), established cordial relationships with property owners in providing housing options throughout the city, and has been a strong advocate and supporter in encouraging other community organizations to make the leap to housing provision despite the risky terms established by BC Housing.[16] Hughes has demonstrated that it is possible to be an innovative risk taker while challenging the power behind existing policies and practices to further *equality of quality of life* outcomes. This is most evident in his belief that even a successful Housing First strategy is not the solution, and that formerly homeless residents need more than "supported shelter." These residents deserve to be fully integrated into the community as working and contributing members of society, and to have the discriminatory impressions attached to addictions, mental health challenges, or being previously homeless erased.

Evidence of this trajectory is demonstrated through the power and the impact of the Theatre Project. The highly challenging but transformative qualities of the collaborative leadership model have been revealed through the insights of Dawn Farough, as both researcher and active participant in the unique theatre project working with at-risk individuals to stage a play. Complexity and uncertainty are apparent in negotiating the outcome, made more difficult by the demands of preset dates for the opening of the play. Nevertheless, even besides the fixed dates for achieving goals, several other factors contribute to complexity and uncertainty and are important in determining the success of any collaboration—particularly if it is a highly original initiative bringing together partners and leaders working together for the first time. With production, rehearsals, and performances sited within the area of the North Shore, with the most obvious social challenges,[17] everything—from managing available space, accommodating research requirements with the safety and comfort of at-risk participants, communication among individuals from within organizations unfamiliar with each other, and the terms of all engagement—needs to be negotiated and practised for the power of this collaboration to be fully realized. In addition, the uncertainty surrounding the ability of at-risk residents to adapt and remain engaged with this onerous schedule, not to mention the local response to this theatre opportunity, heightens the insecurities surrounding the success of this leadership initiative.[18]

At a micro-level, the challenges of forging and completing a collaborative project among a leadership and participants unfamiliar with each other, with aspirations that the homeless / formerly homeless will be the dominant voice in the enterprise, are the same challenges confronted at the community level. There is an awkward space among individuals with such different life experiences in which common ground may be difficult to attain without building bonds of trust, mutual respect, and mutual value. The main difference at the community level is that "mutual avoidance" is the norm: the homeless consciously avoid the community through hidden camps along the shorelines, the parks, or the underused or rarely observed spaces of downtown urban centres, with contact only through instances of panhandling, bottle collection, or accessing food services. These terms of engagement are usually heavily regulated by police, local bylaw officers, and private security firms; only the intervention of certain individuals and community groups, backed by the support of concerned citizens, is able to moderate this context through ongoing contact, developing an understanding, expressing empathy and concern, and responding to recognized needs in a meaningful manner. The strong local support (see Table "Outside the Rehearsal Hall") and sold-out performances for the No Straight Lines production of *Home/Less/Mess—Bringing Stories of Homelessness out of the Dark* demonstrated not just the local interest in theatre but also the interest in hearing the creative voices of residents rarely heard, and confirmed the value of years of work by community groups in raising awareness and fostering a general understanding of the local homeless challenge. Further evidence of the enhanced power of these voices arising from this successful series of performances has been the re-organization of the Home Free Collective, now built on the input of those with "lived-experience" through the Lived Experience Committee, to participate in and inform all decisions by subcommittees and the council; several of the No Straight Lines actors are regularly present.[19] To accommodate the participation of these voices, various forms of assistance are provided, with all meetings taking place in city venues near the South and North Shore waterfronts. At a community level, there are no open voices calling for municipal tactics to foster discomfort or expulsion of homeless residents, even though there has been a noticeable increase in their numbers. And results of an anonymous research survey of local business owners and managers, investigating their willingness to employ formerly homeless residents, revealed near-unanimous support for offering these residents a "second chance" in collaboration with mediation and skills development by a community organization.[20] Thus, while the success of the theatre project has not been matched at the community level in addressing homelessness, the local learning and resulting *social capital* have increased, creating a social context amenable to long-term solutions should adequate resources arrive.

Perhaps the most surprising post-project outcome has been the fate of the Public Produce Project. As Robin Reid and Kendra Besanger have stressed, the success of the Kamloops Public Produce Project was enhanced by links with and support from larger existing local associations, in particular the already nationally successful Kamloops Food Policy Council (KFPC) and the well-established Thompson-Shuswap Master Gardeners Association. The vocabulary of "strategic alliances, shared resources, co-productions, co-sponsorships, and cross-sectoral partnerships" made for successful grant applications to emphasize that the project would amount to more than "just a garden" and that the reach would extend beyond the physical space and into the community dialogue of food security. Facing three large challenges—putting forth a new, untested idea in the community; raising adequate funds for the project; and acquiring credibility as a new community initiative—the KFPC provided the legitimacy and mentorship for a young project, still in the early stages of conceptualization, and this initial legitimacy granted by larger local associations strengthened the prospects for the project and its ability to establish broader collaborations. Since this project, the City of Kamloops has developed the *Food and Urban Agricultural Plan: Harvesting Our Future* based on broad consultation (and in which Robin Reid was a primary member), with the vision of Kamloops being "a leader in sustainable food and urban agriculture systems" (City of Kamloops 2015). City efforts have resulted in continued expansion of Community Gardens due to high demand, fulfilling Montgomery's (2013) observations as to increased health and social benefits of this even greater proximity to nature, as "extreme intimacy—not just looking at nature, but actually touching or working with plants and dirt—is good for us in ways we never imagined"[21] and "every time a slice of urban land is transformed into a community garden, the salubrious effects flow through the brain and bodies of the people who work it and those who just pass by" (121–23). As the profile and support has increased for gardening generally, so has the focus on urban food production to meet the immediate needs of local residents and raise awareness of the "hunger crisis" around Kamloops and surrounding areas. Sponsorship and volume have grown as the "Grow a Row" campaign encourages citizens to expand garden production for the Food Bank (which further distributes food to another 45 agencies), and some 29 local businesses have now established raised beds on their properties for these ends (Cronin 2016, June 7; *The Echo* 2017, 1–2). Whereas the Public Produce Project served to visually, verbally, and physically engage residents around food security issues, while challenging perceptions as to the uses of urban space in the downtown South Shore (in the finest spirit of Montgomery), its most significant impact is emerging on the North Shore because of the leadership within the JUMP program. Initially relocated to an undeveloped and degraded vacant lot on the North Shore at the centre of Kamloops' most visible social challenges, the Public Produce Project struggled to acquire local traction and interest. However, the leadership in the JUMP program, with support of the KFPC and its membership, has gradually transformed this site into a thriving garden area with raised beds and cement pathways (for wheelchair access), and developed a second public produce site across from the Food Bank on 6,000 square feet of land (and through donations, added an irrigation system and hired a TRU student to develop and maintain the property). The Public Produce Project further demonstrates the potential long-term impact and ripple effects of short-term projects in moving from *quality of life* features (community gardens) to *equality of quality of life* outcomes (public produce, "Grow a Row"). It also illustrates the role of community leaders in advancing imaginative initiatives that contribute to the local *cultural* and *political capital* under the new model of governance.

Of all the projects, the Tranquille Oral History Project (TOHP) best symbolizes and articulates the challenges, limitations, and lost potential under the new model of governance. As Tina Block observed, the "TOHP was loosely structured and lacking in any formal or defined leadership. Initially propelled by the energy and enthusiasm of its participants, the project would have benefited from a more formalized agreement and the establishment of a more consistent leadership to guide and sustain this research partnership in the long-term." The developer continues to preserve and promote Tranquille's heritage, TRU faculty are drawn to Tranquille as a space of creative inquiry, and the site remains rich with possibilities, but "securing stable funding would help to mitigate such issues as limited volunteer capacity and inconsistent leadership"—revealing the importance of particular resources (e.g., time, money, and support) in determining and achieving collaborative goals. Thus, the Tranquille site, despite long being replete with opportunities, also offers considerable space for critical reflection on what has occurred to date in relation to broader local dynamics. The provincial government in the 1980s closed a large and fully functioning government facility employing and addressing the needs of hundreds of individuals. Located in a stunning natural area on the North Shore with access to the vast Kamloops Lake (whereas South Shore access has been restricted by massive pulp and lumber facilities), these elaborate facilities were allowed to go into complete disrepair rather than being repurposed, and access for citizens was limited. While the facility was ostensibly closed to move toward a more progressive community-based model of support for those with mental health challenges, these individuals would eventually appear on the streets as a high percentage of the homeless population.

Combined, these outcomes would be further testament to the decline experienced on the North Shore. Various private sector efforts to redevelop and redefine the area would be found to be uneconomic, and thus sporadic, without government support. But with the financial resources of the local government unable to bear the expense of a major brownfield redevelopment project, and the province repeatedly failing to take responsibility for the increasing costs of the decline, in 30 years there has been limited success in transforming the site into a larger vision of local economic and urban renewal. Again the fate of the site remains precarious, as the "vagaries of the market" and costs of redevelopment have led to the site being placed up for sale—even though a comprehensive, community-engaged, and sustainable vision has been articulated and advanced by the developer. Thus, the commendable leadership skills revealed in preserving this important heritage have been blunted by severe resource constraints, limiting the transformational potential of the site.

In conclusion, collective reflection on these case studies yields several insights on the types of leadership initiatives, the challenges they confront, the importance of local learning, and their transformational qualities and outcomes under the new model of governance and "governing through community." And while Montgomery provides important indicators as to what transformational success should be comprised of, and the local qualities that may facilitate these outcomes, numerous other factors have to come together to foment this transformation—of which leadership and learning are critical and central components. Successful leadership may be broadly understood as a committed core of individuals and organizations who are credible, trusted, flexible, and able to facilitate the advancement of particular goals. There is little doubt that individuals with local experience, knowledge, and contacts—whether in supporting and advising particular initiatives, or as active participants—are a considerable asset in contributing to and negotiating the success of an ongoing initiative. Perhaps what is just as important are the types of goals of leadership initiatives (with or without a university role), as challenges of time, resources, and volunteers require a high degree of flexibility in achieving outcomes. Short-term and precise goals accommodate a variety of forms of collaboration, whereas more general and ongoing goals require higher levels of trust and flexibility in leadership to ensure that participants remain active and engaged to the overall project, as in the CFP network and KALS. It is also apparent that categories of analysis for understanding potential success, such as the different types of motives for collaboration, grass-roots or government-initiated leadership, the number of networks or local organizations, short-term versus long-term goals, or proximity, only partially assist in unravelling local intricacies and the impact of leadership initiatives. As Lisa Cooke points out, affirming assessments by Shucksmith (see Introduction to this volume):

> Collaborations in practice do not fit into tidy categories. As this overview highlights, no leadership initiative is without complexities and complications. As researchers, when we evaluate the kinds of collaboration, ally-ships, and projects presented in this collection we are confronted with one of the primary difficulties of participatory and collaborative research initiatives—critically engaged honesty. None of us can fault the efforts of those with whom we work. Building showers for street involved and vulnerable people is an incredible gesture of generosity and caring. As are public produce gardens, adult learning programs, public heritage projects, homelessness action initiatives, and theatre productions with homeless and recently housed peoples. But these are also complicated projects that require constant negotiation. We argue here that it is precisely the kinds of creative collaborations that come together in each of these projects that make any of them possible at all. It is these same collaborations that complicate the process. Our critical gaze often leads us to focus on the problems. By using the motivations for collaborations as Dubinsky outlines them as the starting point, we can shift that critical gaze beyond the inter-intra politics of organizations to the broader contexts of the conditions that leave the kinds of gaps that the efforts we examine here are attempting to address. And this is how we as researchers stand to contribute to these collaborations. These more intangible qualities take us beyond the actual dynamics we have observed within the

collaborations to the broader urban environment they are active within.

Contrasting the local transformational leadership outcomes against "what was" in relation to the research categories on *governance* serves to highlight the level of significance from these initiatives and assess their ongoing potential (even if they originated as short-term collaborative initiatives). This is most evident in the small city of Kamloops, where numerous indicators as per Montgomery and the governance literature on small rural towns suggest a wealth of qualities and advantages (supported by local citizen surveys and observed orientations), yet the overall *political capital* was recognized as severely weak, based on earlier research and the spatial-locational recognition as to where our case studies either largely took place or would become focused—the North Shore of the city. What we have been able to expose are important local gains in *natural, human,* and *social capital* that have reduced hardship and improved the health, well-being, circumstances, and opportunities for thousands (perhaps tens of thousands) of residents, either directly or indirectly across the city, and how the voices of formerly marginalized residents have emerged, or been preserved for posterity. Most importantly, due to the varied forms of leadership initiatives identified, the North Shore is no longer opposed to "social service facilities" and has become a stimulating area for ongoing activity, new programs, and specialized services—with the appearance of numerous other community organizations focused on affordable housing, youth issues, Indigenous peoples, and retirees (and whose challenges and successes remain to be investigated, assessed, and supported). And while a "performing arts centre" on the South Shore may not yet have traction on the North Shore, what was an area that saw a decline in population during 2005–2011 now has quite positive and recognized growth prospects for the future (Brady et al. 2013; City of Kamloops 2017). There is little doubt that the leadership and learning identified in this collection has led to this transformational outcome and increased *equality of quality of life* for all residents. It is evident that Kamloops has developed significant "space" for new local leadership initiatives, with a university role in a variety of areas (as per evident latent orientations). There are, however, thought-provoking challenges for community-engaged research from within the university, and in relation to the small city context, to fill an important role as a knowledge-support structure in developing transformational leadership and advancing *equality of quality of life* outcomes.

Leadership and Learning within the Small University and the Intricacies of Community-Engaged Research

Richard Florida identified the university as a necessary component to *quality of life / quality of place* in fostering a creative community. His sense of how the university contributed to this was through "technology, talent, and tolerance," with the link between the inventiveness of the hard sciences and private companies as the critical factor (Florida 2002, 291–93). As we have seen through this collection, though, a broader sense of "the university"—comprising faculty and student researchers from many other fields who are also instigators of creative acts, participants in initiatives, accumulators, and purveyors of "community learning"—plays an active role in generating novel forms of "creative capital" and enhancing not just local *quality of life* but the *equality of quality of life*. Whether in response to the observations by Richard Florida and the effects of global economic change, or to government and parent-student pressures, universities are increasingly challenged to be more active in fostering connections and opportunities with the broader society for faculty and students, placing a higher premium on community-university engagement. Contemporary university mission statements and plans often emphasize diversity, equity, inclusion, and tolerance, addressing societal challenges and promoting engagement with new ideas and peoples.

The emerging intersection between the ideals of the university and the transformational goals of *equality of quality of life* as per Montgomery establishes fertile ground for diverse partnerships in addressing contemporary urban challenges under the new governance model. This has brought to the foreground an emphasis on *community empowerment research* or *action research* (Bryant 2010, 147–50). More formally referred to as Community-Based Research (CBR), this term refers to a particular form of community-university partnership in which the community partners are equal collaborators or co-creators in all aspects of the project: identifying the issues, determining the research questions, guiding the research, and benefiting the most from the project and research outcomes. Whether addressing community-health issues, housing, poverty, sustainability, discrimination, or exclusion, CBR has a documented history of academic collaborations with local community leaders with respect to particular local concerns. "Although not a panacea, the methodology of community-based research (CBR) provides a feasible and long-standing framework for generating the kind of boundary-crossing knowledge and community organizing strategies necessary for addressing multifaceted issues in the real world" (Etmanski, Dawson, and Hall, 2014, 3). The definitive "gold standard" in community-university partnerships, CBR is not without its challenges in implementation and practice, particularly under the new governance model of "governing through community," in which there are severe constraints in resources and discretionary powers at the local level that may arise depending on the province, the size of the population, and prospects for the local economy. Our recognition of these limitations within local community organizations, and within our own university as a knowledge-support structure, has resulted in a more flexible set of relationships and a more nuanced support role we define as *community-engaged research*. Our collection offers insights into the forms and degrees of university-community engagement that may occur in the small university in support of *equality of quality of life*. Community-engaged research is both an expression of the multiple ways in which faculty and students may be engaged with local leadership initiatives and a flexible response to limitations recognized within local organizations and local networks. Most importantly, community-engaged research, as this collection attests, can take a variety forms beyond the terms established through formal funding agencies and Community-University Research Partnerships (CURP). These may range from documenting community initiatives and outcomes in relation to larger themes (e.g., "small city–big city" debates, federal/provincial governance, sustainability, heritage, social challenges, or an aging population), to participation at meetings and activities of local community groups, to direct roles in establishing new initiatives with community partners—all of which, as will become evident, may evolve and unfold over time in unanticipated and surprising directions. This broader understanding of "research opportunities" may also address a recognized shortcoming of formal CURPs in supporting the standards of Community-Based Research—which tend to require community "partners" with "dedicated research and evaluative staff" for a "truly vibrant and respectful practice of co-creation to exist" (Tremblay and Hall, 2014, 401). Within this formal framework, many lesser-resourced community groups and initiatives may be spurned despite their greater need for partners and research to support initiatives—which is not uncommon in the small city where funding sources from both private and public institutions (i.e., TRU) are more limited. These chapters attest not only to the varied types of leadership initiatives in the small city but also to the diverse role of "the university" in supporting and initiating a variety of opportunities that may reduce this inequality in community groups—opening up new spaces and horizons in this urban setting for faculty, students, community organizations, and local government. The following examples illustrate these points, and how the specific research outcomes in this collection represent but one facet of the potential benefits from community-engaged research.

There is little doubt that there are unique challenges and rewards with community-engaged research in the small city. It is a very different kind of research from the more objective and distanced approach encouraged and promoted through academic methodologies, because of the extremely close proximity of the researchers to the community participants and the likelihood of repeatedly meeting with participants in multiple settings outside of the initiative. An important aspect of researching and evaluating collaborative initiatives in the small city is what may be called the *predicament of proximity* for us as researchers: because of the close affiliation of all the contributors with the very initiatives under investigation, standards of objectivity are necessarily compromised. However, because of "active observations" and "researchers as participants," there is a deeper appreciation of the small city context, and of the varied interests, dynamics, and challenges that foster community understanding through leadership initiatives. This raises the question as to whether what is lost in foregoing a more objective set of evaluations is balanced by the advantage of subjective measures—measures that perhaps contribute to a richer understanding of the challenges local initiatives confront and highlight the local learning outcomes (from which new ideas and leadership initiatives may emerge). We have found that community-engaged research in the small city establishes a distinct research context, as the intervention in the subject matter is often due either to direct participation in the generation or sustaining of a response to a local challenge or gap in service, or in documenting and assessing a local response that has tangible benefits, directly or indirectly, for the researcher. As members of the very community, we have a vested interest in the success of these leadership initiatives. Thus, the types of critical engagement that may be directed at more abstract and distant subjects from our immediate lives, such as institutions, public personae, societal practices, and structures, are more difficult to maintain when assessing the actions of fellow community members whose efforts and accomplishments rarely receive much attention, let alone "researchable status." In this process of engagement, then, a certain degree of self-censorship is necessary, as one may be privy to occasional outbursts of frustration, heated disagreements, or personal jibes relayed discreetly, which, while interesting at the time, do not detract from the overall goals of the initiative. However, from this it is apparent that numerous leadership initiatives may have struggled, collapsed, or become dormant, because of personality conflicts or the inability of members to work together to achieve similar ends—an inability to negotiate the inherent complexities of collaborations. Understanding the internal pressures and the external constraints (i.e., time commitments, resources, volunteers) is critical to providing a fair and balanced assessment of achievements, while recognizing that the firm research standards of the university may just not fit. A further unexpected challenge relates to differences between how "research" is understood at the university and by members within the community. Whereas university research ethic boards place a premium on anonymity, confidentiality, and security of information, often community participants have no problem with their name being openly associated with an interview (and do not understand the "secrecy"), even when they are freely being critical of institutions and practices that have hampered their efforts. This can be even more challenging when community members avail themselves of the opportunity to solicit and relay to the researcher opinions and evaluations from other members of the community—regardless of the ethical guidelines put in place by the university (e.g., consent procedures). There is little doubt that an open, accepting, and flexible approach can quickly facilitate informal ties and conversations that endure into other local contexts because of proximity, and become important bases of awareness of new initiatives and efforts by local organizations.

These observations are supported by Dawn Farough, whose rich account of her experience with the No Straight Lines theatre project revealed some of the initial challenges, discomfort, and surprising insights from engagement with marginalized residents:

> I expected the participants to be somewhat shy or reticent. This is the case for only a small minority; most of our participants loved to talk and had no trouble taking centre stage for as long as possible. The stories varied but there were the expected similarities: dysfunctional childhoods involving foster care, abuse, and neglect; addictions to drugs and alcohol; and few support systems outside of the homeless community and subculture. Some participants were temporarily housed but feeling nervous that they would be back on the street eventually. Others were "camping" . . . I wonder if this process will simply confirm their already firm ideas about mainstream society and their place within it, or will further self-reflection ensue? They certainly aren't submissive and don't seem to lack the "soft life skills" of confidence and communication which No Straight Lines wishes to impart to this group. Perhaps the idea of the disadvantaged as submissive is simply an ivory tower stereotype? Or, perhaps these three men came from more privileged backgrounds than the rest of the group? It's impossible to tell.

These qualities are increasingly apparent at the HomeFree Collective as representatives from community organizations seek to advance the voice of those residents with lived-experience in formulating local responses to homelessness and the housing crisis. Research on homelessness, both local and national, and on the Changing the Face of Poverty network has been particularly rewarding. Outcomes from small research projects with students are being used to shape local government policies and priorities, to support local funding initiatives for critically necessary facilities and services, and to generate deeper student interest in municipal government and community issues. The largest advantage, though, has been the shift from "researcher" to "active participant." From attending monthly meetings of the Changing the Face of Poverty network, ongoing discussions with councillors and staff from the City of Kamloops, and participation in the HomeFree Collective overseeing HPS funding, there is no longer the need for the formal interview process as a means to acquire an understanding of the homelessness and housing challenges in Kamloops, as these community partners provide more up-to-date information and insights than could ever be acquired through a formal research process. As Ginny Ratsoy observes on the close proximity and relationships maintained with the "research subject":

> In my own experience as a TRU educator and researcher who has also been an educator for the Kamloops Adult Learners Society, fluidity in terms of the researchers' perspectives on those being studied is also worth examining. Those interviewed and surveyed were viewed as active participants rather than subjects. In fact, the fluidity of the roles of the KALS students, founders, and administrators—several of them have been former TRU faculty and students—blurred the lines in other ways. I have long believed that, in all of my teaching, I learn as much as I teach, and never more so than with a group of often well-educated and usually highly life-experienced individuals; perhaps in this case my teaching carried over into my research in that way. In this light, it is revealing that one of the surveys—designed to be completed by KALS students—was in fact completed by a KALS instructor from the perspective of both teacher and learner. A rethinking of the polarization that can result from a traditional researcher-subject relationship may be in order.

Thus, the destruction of established impressions, assumptions, and categories is a natural outcome of this knowledge-sharing experience, and most evident the longer or more in-depth the engagement, challenging certain academic or societal assumptions while offering new and compelling insights into the lives and thoughts of fellow residents. As Dawn Farough states, in considering the Theatre Project,

> I reflect on the arguments in political theatre and the social sciences about using theatre as a method to allow for a critical self-reflection and consciousness raising that challenges mainstream thinking and common-sense knowledge. Disadvantaged people become less submissive; they start to advocate and envision a different kind of democracy. Three of the homeless men are already very critical of mainstream society; they discuss the divisions between the poor, the middle-class, and the wealthy, analyze racism and the lack of spirituality in mainstream society, and comment on the average Canadian's total disregard for the environment. They seem more politically aware than the majority of my sociology students. They are also very critical of their own families. Ironically, their family backgrounds, to my way of thinking, seem to be less abusive than that of the average participant in the group. Rather than tales of foster care, physical abuse and rape, they talk about family members judging them or not being able to understand their lifestyles. All three have battled addictions. Their identities are very strongly tied to a certain way of life which they see as superior to that of the mainstream. They are devoted champions of the homeless and "would never want to become like the rich people they know."

These insights generate new and unique opportunities for new understandings and research, and a richer and further productive engagement with participants, but they also provide a more focused societal critique of the local needs or gaps giving rise to particular initiatives. As Lisa Cooke highlights from the Shower Project:

> Thinking about the critical role of volunteers in the delivery of programs in Kamloops led Bob Hughes from ASK Wellness, Will Garrett-Petts, and me to submit an

application to the Vancouver Foundation for funding to support a more detailed inventory and analysis of the reliance of health-based agencies on volunteer labour for the delivery of their programs. The seeds for this research question are found in the very roots of the Shower Project—how is it that there was no free and safe shower facility in Kamloops for street-involved people and what does it mean that it took a group of volunteers to build one? What other gaps are government institutions able to overlook because volunteer efforts fill them?

These insights are revelatory not only in re-examining one's own community from a new perspective (as per Montgomery) but also in understanding the kinds of severe inequities among marginalized citizens between communities resulting from "governing through community." These more critical reflections arising from community-engaged research may also be directed at the role of the university, as highlighted by Dawn Farough's experience in which the "elitist image"[22] of the university can also be matched by arcane understandings of what constitutes "research":

> One of the more perplexing aspects of this process for interdisciplinary research was revealed in seeking approval for the No Straight Lines theatre project. The ethics committee is not concerned with how the homeless / recently housed are recruited for the purposes of the "artistic" side of the research, but it is concerned about recruitment for the purposes of ethnographic observation and formal interviewing. Since the same participants are involved, this has left members of the research team scratching their heads as to how to comply. A letter of instruction from the ethics committee states: "This application would be far easier for the PI [Principal investigator] and for the REB [Research Ethics Board] to manage if it was focused only on the research component instead of being interwoven with the theatre section." Apparently, "art" is not research and "artists" are not researchers. Therefore the theatre faculty can decide for

themselves how to proceed "ethically" without bureaucratic guidance or interference.

This challenge is not without significance as, increasingly, local initiatives are linked to utilizing a variety of artistic forms and mediums in fostering community-university engagement while simultaneously assessing the effectiveness and challenges of these new techniques in fostering creative citizens (CUVIC Conference 2014). This is also significant in engaging our students, whose facility with the latest technologies only needs to be encouraged and fostered to inspire new and creative leadership initiatives with *equality of quality of life* goals. Thus, from community-engaged research new voices surface from both within the community and within ourselves, bringing about the critical reflection that better serves our research and our students, opening up novel opportunities.

Opportunities to personalize and enrich our own teaching practices to reflect these connections are exemplified by the experience of Tina Block. The Tranquille Oral History Project nurtured connections between the university and the community, and provided TRU undergraduate students with unique opportunities to explore and disseminate Kamloops' public history. Student participants in the TOHP shared their research findings, and their experience with community-based research, in presentations to my classes and those of my colleagues. Such presentations have inspired other students to visit the Tranquille site and to investigate its history, and the knowledge from such presentations now weaves its way through my courses on British Columbia history. Other students may develop a more critical stance, as Dawn Farough recounts, where "one of the service workers, in telling her story at rehearsal, made a point of saying that she enjoyed her sociology classes at TRU but decided to become a social worker since she couldn't stand the idea of being out of touch with people and 'ivory tower' in her thinking and behaviour." It is from such insights, and with an increased confidence in my understanding of "Kamloops," that I (Terry Kading) completely changed the content of an upper-level course on *Local Government in Canada*. The standard text on local government, filled with large urban administrative experiences (e.g., from Toronto and Montreal), was replaced by a critical engagement with Charles Montgomery's *Happy City* in relation to the lived experience and the personal observations of students being in Kamloops (the first essay question was—"Is Kamloops a Happy City as per the ideals of Charles Montgomery?").[23] Numerous students have relayed to me how the book and class assignments had fostered a unique experience at TRU—sitting around outside of class endlessly discussing with fellow classmates and other students *equality of quality of life* and what that meant for their own life goals and for Kamloops. Similar experiences with research grounded in local content is found more generally in a variety of forums. As Lisa Cooke observes on the Shower Project:

> Because collaborations in all of their complicated forms spur new kinds of configurations of people and ideas, there are a number of things that have evolved out of my research on the Shower Project. Dr. Will Garrett-Petts and I have presented this work on two occasions, once as an informal Research Cabaret at the Thompson Rivers University Campus and once at an academic conference. In both cases our presentations evolved into fascinating conversations with and between research participants on the complexities, challenges, rewards, and successes of the Shower Project. Arriving to both events prepared with notes and presentation slides, as good academics do, we found ourselves swept up in wonderfully rich discussions that added to our data collection (as opposed to reporting on it!). This has been one of the great lessons for me from this project—grounded community-engaged research just keeps going as collaborations form and reform, new relationships emerge, goals shift, and those out there "doing" keep doing.

All contributors can attest to the unique and dynamic discussions that emerge in response to presentations "on the local" by students, faculty, and visiting scholars, in which community members of varied backgrounds feel comfortable relaying insights and experiences, extending the "question period" well beyond allotted times. This affirms (as per Montgomery) that there is a passionate interest by residents in the fate of their communities;

they are looking for opportunities or "spaces" in which to participate and be engaged with ideas on *equality of quality of life.*

From these experiences, it is possible to reimagine the university as a site of broader community engagement—expanding the local impact of this established learning area. Ginny Ratsoy, with such aims, elected to disseminate her research in a face-to-face setting, as part of the TRU Arts Colloquium Series—which, while its location was an academic campus, was inclusive of the representatives of the subject of her research—with the intent to further contact between the KALS and TRU communities in order to attract more TRU faculty as KALS instructors and draw more KALS students to the rich campus life at TRU. In the ensuing question period, "a KALS student raised the issue of administrative hurdles (financial and logistical) to seniors enrolling in TRU courses, which in turn, revealed a lack of certainty among all present about TRU policy. This issue also resulted in invitations to KALS students from TRU faculty to informally join their classes and thus avoid administrative hurdles altogether. Communication among the two groups was facilitated during this discussion, interestingly, around the liberating effects of a grades-free education and the less-than-liberating effects of bureaucracy." The subsequent newspaper article, entitled "Lifelong Learning Equals Longevity: University Study of Kamloops Adult Learners Society Purports Benefits of Classroom Later in Life," contributed equally to KALS and the university. Research on this topic for this collection has served to mobilize knowledge in ways that have generated multiple learning outcomes and new leadership initiatives in advocating for adult learning,[24] and reveals the unexplored potential of the university in supporting less visible or unrecognized leadership initiatives within the community.

These responses, questions, reflections, and critical examinations demonstrate the real power of community-engaged research—a heightened level of introspection and revelation as to how we understand and may redefine the role of the university where we work and the community within which we reside. As is evident from these accounts, there is no easy way to categorize the varied responses and observations arising from engagement, and what may be more "cut and dried / black and white" categories and assessments in an academic framework become much more nuanced and "grey." This more open format of sharing and learning also flips on its head the question as to who is being studied and researched, and who is learning the most from the experience—the local resident or the academic. What determines what is or is not "research" in this engagement? The challenges of this type of research require constant reflection and examination, as the "knowledge" gained from multiple vantage points (interviews, observations, discussion forums, and individual conversations) does not easily serve to confirm or deny a particular theory or hypothesis. This supports the idea of a "knowledge democracy" comprised of "helpful theoretical discourse" in "building a new architecture of knowledge" (Tremblay and Hall 2014, 377), and relates directly to the requirement to understand the local social terrain before it may be transformed to the advantage of all residents.

It has been critically observed that university-community partnerships have assumed "a somewhat functional character, that is, it is adopted in order to gain access to funding. . . . Partnership could thus be viewed as a hoop to be jumped through in order to attain funding and/ or legitimacy" (Storey 2010, 157). And while such instrumental purposes may not lend themselves to greater participation, the recognition of new voices, or transformational leadership outcomes, we have found that engagement with university faculty and researchers is grounded in quite diverse motives depending on the community organization / network and their goals. Certainly among larger, well-established organizations there is a recognition of the significant "status" of the university in both enhancing the prospects for initiatives and advancing opportunities for research and further funding. As identified by Robin Reid and Kendra Besanger, the Kamloops Food Policy Committee (KFPC) co-chair explained that the relationship between the KFPC and Thompson Rivers University adds validity to KFPC project endeavours. Research on food security–related projects is essential because it helps frame grassroots actions in language that can be used in documents, presentations, and grant proposals. The partnership worked to articulate the significance of the project and thus added institutional legitimacy to the work being done on the ground. For these organizations, then, grant applications require "deliverables" or "outcomes," and research becomes important. For some collaborations, awareness of the skill set in the university leads to the success of the initiative (as in the Theatre Project and the Tranquille Oral History

Project). For other organizations there is simply the quality of "pride in accomplishments" in which university research is seen as validation, with the possibility of publicity and the opportunity to promote activities and events to engage a larger audience (as with KALS and the Shower Project). With respect to the Changing the Face of Poverty network there have been no expectations from the university, but there has been enthusiastic support for participation and research projects by undergraduate student researchers—a recognition of the value of mentoring a new generation as to local social challenges. What is evident is that funding opportunities are not the primary motive for engaging with university faculty and students, and that for numerous local organizations, confronted with significant resource and time constraints, the value of engaging with the university is unclear and yet to be determined. Committed leadership from within the university is required to reveal this dimension.

The chapters in this collection study the interactivity of representatives of various community and professional organizations. As is apparent, a clinical, detached approach is less likely to capture the nuances, essences, and insights inherent in such complex social interactions; and not all data is easily—or best—reducible to numbers or terms. For instance, given the persistence of high numbers of visible homeless and hidden homeless since the initiation of the National Homelessness Initiative in 2001, it would be easy to suggest that there have been few meaningful gains made by the local leadership in resolving this challenge. However, such a harsh assessment would be at the expense of recognizing the countless lives that have been enhanced, even spared, through local initiatives from the leaders and participants in the Changing the Face of Poverty network, the Shower Project, and the No Straight Lines Theatre project, or enriched through the Kamloops Adult Learners Society, the Public Produce Project, and the Tranquille Oral History Project—unrecognized benefits on a regular basis that have supported *equality of quality of life* for a wide variety of residents. Thus, a less critical gaze is cast as one engages with the local initiatives, replaced by a deeper appreciation of the ongoing contributions, commitment, and talents of a much broader set of unrecognized local leaders in one's own community. This observation extends to understanding the pivotal role the university has (or may have) in the community, in which it can lend considerable credibility to an initiative and strengthen the human and political capital (i.e., local influence and support for a project). Exposing this rich and complex collaborative web that underlies *equality of quality of life* is not without its challenges—but this research also reveals the critical role the university plays in inspiring, supporting, and shaping the dynamics and outcomes of local leadership initiatives. Our explorations and methods of analysis of these local leadership initiatives are also an expression of a long process of capacity building within TRU as a knowledge-support structure.

At first glance, the university may appear as a natural source for the role of knowledge-support structure, but to be substantive and offer transformational leadership outcomes at the community level requires the same leadership and learning initiatives as are found within the local community. In developing "collaborative modes of governance" to support local collective agency—recognized as the "key to successful place-based development" (Wellbrock et al. 2013, 420–22)—the "university" occupies a complex position as its own "learning area" with a designated space for "grassroots development initiatives" (student and faculty research projects, student clubs, and organizations), a knowledge-support structure with "facilitating agents and agencies" (courses, programs, faculty, administrators), and a public administration with "supporting policies" (student services, student loans, and awards). However, this learning area, while appreciated by the local community for the potential career opportunities for local youth (*quality of life* features), is ordinarily insular and isolated from the larger community, and thus the "ivory tower" caption is not without validity. From the perspective of the university, our mere presence can be accepted as a significant "community role" in offering both higher education, and, in the case of Kamloops—as the third largest employer, with expanding facilities and employment opportunities—a sizable contribution to the local economy. And for faculty and students, what is a unique environment from most real-world forms of employment is also a maze of policies, practices, and funding arrangements that defy easy comprehension on their face, let alone understanding how they might lend support to the local community. Thus, despite the advantage in spatial proximity to facilitate a larger local "learning region" (421), a concerted effort to develop bridging linkages and *human* and *social capital* is needed to move from the *quality of life* features of a university for a community to *equality of quality of life* outcomes at the local level. This capacity, or power, is subject to the same foibles as confronted by leadership initiatives within the local community, and involves the same process of learning and advocacy in order to develop institutional stability and resilience as has been evident at TRU.

All of us as contributors to this collection are representative of a particular knowledge-support structure that stems from fortuitous outcomes by several internal leadership initiatives to facilitate ongoing community-engaged research. Without this prior collective agency, each of us would have likely maintained (as per "publish or perish" requisites) a focus on traditional research issues within our respective disciplines, with only casual connections to the community and the challenges of Kamloops. However, in 2000, and after eight months of negotiation, a sizable group of university-college and community leaders submitted what would be a successful grant proposal to the Social Sciences and Humanities Research Council of Canada (SSHRC) under the Community-University Research Alliance (CURA) program, entitled *The Cultural Future of Small Cities* (Garrett-Petts and Dubinsky 2005, 3).[25] This initiative was audacious at the time, for as a teaching-centred undergraduate university-college—with no established research office or graduate programs—neither in institutional nor cultural capacity did the University College of the Cariboo (UCC) appear as a likely contender for a million-dollar federal grant. The majority of faculty did not have PhDs, and those who did were advantaged with a slightly lower course load of six classes for a Fall/Winter term (versus eight for those without a PhD), with the expectation of perhaps attending or presenting at a conference every couple of years. At the time, the president of UCC and the other top administrators, demonstrating leadership, actively endorsed and supported the application even though the prospects for success were low.

Having secured a CURA grant, we would experience constant constraints in matching resources (funding, space allocation, research support services) as UCC adapted to the demands of a new research mandate. For many UCC faculty with PhDs, the CURA themes of "culture" and "small cities" did not readily resonate or inspire, but the flexible leadership within the CURA actively recruited faculty from a variety of disciplines to join in and collaborate on research projects (not just as observers of knowledge outcomes). This established very strong bases for a renewal of the CURA from 2006 to 2011–12 as more faculty better understood the research potential and their niche within the themes, and strove to understand what was going on within Kamloops and other small and mid-sized cities. The attainment of university status for the institution in 2005 served to open up new funding opportunities and place individual research agendas in higher regard; however, despite a course load reduction to five classes per year, any extra time for research would be consumed by endless commitments to new department and divisional committees (appointments, tenure, work-loading, program development) and university-wide planning. And while sabbaticals were now formalized, pressures in small departments to teach remained high in order to ensure the viability of programs and degrees, only relieved by the course-release offered to CURA researchers. On the other hand, for newer faculty (as observed by Lisa Cooke), lower publishing requirements for tenure, in recognition of the weak research culture in place, offered opportunities and the time for community-engaged research that would have been less likely in other universities. In addition, while relationships with community partners differed, for some of us initially they were only "paper partnerships" "reflecting a pragmatic response to funding requirements" (Storey 2010, 157), and even as engagement with CURA projects forged new and stronger partnerships with other community groups, severe time and resource constraints on both sides have limited larger, multi-year research projects—a reality of life in the small university. Nevertheless, a rich and diverse body of work with a Kamloops focus has emerged, which has created the basis for continued research, infused course content and teaching, and opened new possibilities for our students with funding opportunities from the Office of Research and Graduate Studies (e.g., UREAP, Ambassador Program). And despite the "proximity" advantage within UCC/TRU as a small institution, CURA funding and flexible leadership were necessary to empower this proximity and bring together faculty with diverse academic backgrounds to collaborate with each other over an extended period of time.

As the second CURA came to a conclusion, and with no further federal grant support, financial and space limitations at TRU would preclude ongoing institutional support for the continuation of the CURA. However, leftover federal funds and a core leadership unwilling to let this dynamic

Evolution of UCC / TRU as a Knowledge-Support Structure

Community-University Research Alliances Program (CURA)
"The Cultural Future of Small Cities" (2000)

University College of the Cariboo, Kamloops Art Gallery, City of Kamloops, Forest Research Extension Partnership, Kamloops Museum and Archives, John Howard Society, Secwepemc Cultural Education Society, Stuart Wood School, Western Canada Theatre

Additional Partners through CURA (2001-2006)

Kamloops Make Children First Learning Initiative, Comox Valley Art Gallery
Informal Partners – University of New Brunswick, Saint John & University Waterloo as fellow CURA's studying small and mid-sized cities

Community-University Research Alliances Program (CURA)

"Mapping Quality of Life and the Culture of Small Cities" (2006-2012)

Emphasis on Kamloops, Nanaimo, Prince George, Port Moody, and the cities of the Comox Valley

Research team includes 37 community research partners and 26 TRU researchers working in collaboration with faculty from the University of Northern British Columbia; University of New Brunswick, Saint John; and the University of Waterloo

Informal Internal Linkages

Canadian Studies Program

Place Group

Walking Lab

Informal Internal Linkages:

Canada Research Chairs in: Community and Ecosystem Ecology; Rural Livelihoods and Sustainable Communities; Culture and Communities, Children and the Law
B.C .Regional Innovation Chairs in: Aboriginal Health; Cattle Industry Sustainability
TRU / UNBC / UBCO discussions on collaborative research initiatives (accepted in principle)

Post-CURA – Support for "Community-Engaged Research" Model
(Office of Research and Graduate Studies)

Undergraduate Research Experience Award Program (UREAP)
TRU Undergraduate Research Ambassador Award
Community-Driven Research Award (since 2016)
United Way/TRU Community Research Initiative (with shared Knowledge Mobilization Officer)
City of Kamloops/TRU Community Research Initiative (in progress)
United Way / City of Kamloops / TRU - Small City Change Lab (under discussion)

FIGURE 7.3. UCC/TRU as a Knowledge-Support Structure by Terry Kading. Design by Moneca Jantzen, Daily Designz.

wither found strong support and leadership in a local partner—the United Way—whose own national mandate now emphasized poverty reduction, local social issues, and knowledge mobilization to strengthen the capacities of their partner organizations in the community. This opportunity would be combined with the intentional effort to extend the aspirations and principles of the CURA to the university as a whole via TRU's Office of Research and Graduate Studies (with the CURA Director moving into the role of Associate Vice-President).

In 2014 there was the launch of the first Community Research Initiative, in which United Way community partners (many from the Changing the Face of Poverty network) met with interested faculty in a forum to discuss potential collaborative research initiatives (of which the No Straight Lines theatre project was one outcome). This partnership would be formalized in writing, and later, three critical initiatives would be launched from the Office of Research and Graduate Studies.

The first initiative was the Community-Driven Research Award (CDRA), with a total allocation of $25,000 per year for an opening three-year period, offering $2,500 per project to be matched by a community partner (cash or in-kind) for collaborative research endeavours with interested TRU faculty. All funds for the first year have been expended, and second-year funds are being allocated.

The second initiative, intimately tied to enhancing the success of CDRA, was the hiring of a Knowledge Mobilization Officer with a reverse position. Rather than mobilizing knowledge "out from the university," in a shared position in funding, space, and time with the United Way, this officer brings the knowledge and needs of local community organizations to the university. The bases of the successful hiring were deep links to the local community and organizations (as per success in other forms of local leadership) rather than a familiarity with university practices and external funding opportunities.[26]

A forum in late 2016 to mark the official launch of these two initiatives saw brief presentations by 12 potential community partners and 25 faculty—with 4 of the 12 connected and funded and 6 in mediation with the officer to establish sound links with faculty. Combined with "Evaluation Training" funded by the United Way, connections to the broader university network via TRU on Community-Based Research have furthered linkages by our Knowledge Mobilization Officer with the Research Impact Network and the Canadian Association of Research Administrators. From these linkages awareness was brought to SSHRC that the United Way evaluates all community organizations it funds, addressing a reservation on the part of SSHRC about funding particular initiatives due to their own lack of knowledge as to the legitimacy of proposed community partners. As a consequence, SSHRC is now considering partnering with the United Way at a national level for access to their screening practices and results, paving the way for more community organizations to be eligible for research funding across Canada and revealing the power of place-based local knowledge in creating vertical linkages with national impact.[27]

The third initiative builds on TRU's partnership with the United Way by extending formal research ties with the City of Kamloops, and together proposing a social innovation lab / *Small City Change Lab* with a new facility, tentatively planned for the North Shore of Kamloops at the site of a long-abandoned gas station (and within a two-block radius of ASK Wellness, Interior Community Services, Kamloops Immigration Services, the Salvation Army, YMCA-YWCA, Boys & Girls Club, and the Kamloops Foodbank). Modelled on emerging examples in Canada's large urban centres, such as LEDlab and MaRS,[28] the proposed *Change Lab* would support the institutionalization of the learning outcomes and dynamic networks in place (moving from "change makers" to "community change," as per Scott 2004), act as an incubator for new ideas, create new opportunities in the community for students, and, perhaps, generate stronger linkages with surrounding communities in the region.[29] With scaling to highlight the strengths and challenges of small cities, the expectation is that this lab will reinforce community identity, for if it is successful, the definition of success will be that many others are interested in coming to see what this collaborative leadership initiative has leveraged and achieved in becoming a "living lab" for the small city.[30]

As this account has demonstrated, there was no planned and gradual development of this institutional capacity, and at a number of junctures the momentum could have been lost if not for determined leadership within the university (as per Shucksmith 2010). Starting from precarious beginnings, TRU researchers became aware that the standards of Community-Based Research would be hard to meet, observing that a "community-university research alliance, as outlined in SSHRC guidelines, is conceived as an 'entity based on an equal partnership between organizations from the community and the university.' We are working toward equality, but initial differences of perspective, tradition, and purpose preclude any creation of a utopian alliance. Community organizations and universities do not necessarily speak the same language or hold the same objectives and values" (Garrett-Petts and Dubinsky 2005, 4). This has not prevented the emergence of a local model—community-engaged research—in response to the capacities of local organizations and networks, or the generation of important learning outcomes (e.g., *The Small Cities Book* [Garrett-Petts 2005]), that remain as vital touchstones in evaluating the progress of Kamloops in relation to *equality of quality of life* goals. However, and despite two consecutive CURAs and advantages in proximity and face-to-face contact, the challenge of establishing a collaborative administrative structure for both the university and the community has been an arduous task that continues to be explored and tested—much like our efforts in community-engaged research. Thus, as in the larger community of Kamloops, the *natural, human,* and *social capital* continues to develop in TRU, but there is much to be done in achieving the *cultural* and *political capital* that would equalize university and community voices in a process of mutual co-creation on research, projects, and leadership initiatives as a local knowledge-support structure.

This collection represents just one of the numerous opportunities for faculty and students that have arisen from community-engaged research, and exposes the critical role that the university in a small city may have in supporting and inspiring community initiatives—contributing to the local social-creative capital. Most importantly, it reveals how leadership initiatives—with a direct or indirect university role—comprise an important component of the *equality of quality of life* in this small city. It has been recognized of late, that

> at the most basic level, to study leadership in urban and regional development is to be interested in revealing the things that people do to influence other people in these very particular types of settings both formally and informally— openly as well as opaquely—and how they go about doing

what they do. It is also about revealing the types of social processes involved in "making things happen" and in "getting things done" (or not getting things done). Ultimately, the motivation is to understand better how and to what extent the places where we live, work and play are shaped by human relationships and interactions and, specifically, in what ways the meanings ascribed to concepts such as *leader*, *leading* and/or *leadership* can be used to explain how these places evolve (Sotarauta, Beer, and Gibney 2017, 188).

To this end, our individual and collective examinations of leadership initiatives have identified and confirmed the importance of collaborative forms of leadership and learning under the constraints of the new model of governance / "governing through community" and revealed, as best as possible, "who, how and why provides these systems, processes and relationships with future directions" in critical areas of life in Kamloops (Sotarauta, Beer, and Gibney 2017, 188–89). Charles Montgomery's work on *equality of quality of life* furthers this endeavour by providing important standards by which to measure or understand success through transformational leadership, and offers a clear and persuasive "justice-oriented" and "anti-foundational" lens for engaging students and faculty (Butin 2015, 8). His work is also an accessible and compelling way to reimagine physical and social spaces in order to achieve sustainable practices "that foster respect and reciprocity" for the local community (8), and supports "making things happen." This will become more important for small cities as the observed and latent orientations in municipal planning documents and public pronouncements increasingly incorporate the language of *equality of quality of life* ideals, but are weak in community-engaged local content (see Stevens and Mody 2013; and Cleave, Godwin, and Chatwin 2017). Concerted university outreach to the community—via faculty, students, and administrators—will likely reveal numerous local initiatives unwittingly working toward providing content to these principles, and interested in the opportunities and advantages that may arise from engagement with the small university in the small city "to get things done."

Notes

1   Comparisons with Kelowna, Nanaimo, Prince George, and Langley. It was also observed that "when comparing results in Kamloops with other British Columbian municipalities, residents of Kamloops were more likely to say quality of life has stayed the same (71% vs. 57%)" (Trawin 2016, 11).

2   As the survey observed, "Looking at results by age, it was found that younger respondents (age 18 to 34) were significantly less satisfied with alternative forms of transportation in Kamloops such as transit and bike lanes, than were older respondents 55 years of age or older" (Trawin 2016, 16).

3   Examples include the United Way, the Kamloops & District Elizabeth Fry Society, the John Howard Society, the Kamloops Food Bank & Outreach Society (one of the first in Canada), the Canadian Mental Health Association, the Boys & Girls Club of Kamloops, Kamloops Aboriginal Friendship Centre, and the Kamloops Community YMCA-YWCA, Kamloops Food Policy Committee, United Steel Workers union, and various local businesses and property owners—all of which have contributed critical local services and various forms of collaborative leadership in supporting broader initiatives or the emergence of new organizations, e.g., Interior Community Services, ASKWellness, JUMP Program, A Way Home Committee.

4   "I see the same people on the street over and over again. On the North Shore and Downtown. The audience members will see some of the performers in their daily lives after the performance is over. This may have an impact. This wouldn't happen in a big city. If you saw the play in Vancouver and lived in, say, Shaughnessy, would you ever see any of the performers again?"

5   Also, see Dubinsky (2006).

6   "Agencies like Ask Wellness say rental rates are simply too expensive and there hasn't been any construction of affordable units in our community in quite some time and that is leaving people living on a low-income with nowhere to go" (Cronin, 2016, February 10).

7   See *Sustainable Kamloops* at http://www.kamloops.ca/sustainable/index.shtml and *Sustainable Kamloops Plan 2016 Progress Update* at http://www.kamloops.ca/sustainable/pdfs/16-SKPUpdate.pdf.

8   Proposal called for a 1,200-seat theatre, a separate black box theatre, and 350 parking stalls downtown (Klassen, 2015); however, it should be recognized that for the 2015 referendum there was a sense that the "yes" side was not particularly effective in making the case for the project, or in motivating potential supporters to make the time to vote.

9   Based on initial research findings and literature review on adapting "age-friendly" policies to the small city urban context, with Dr. Gilles Viaud, Department of Geography, Thompson Rivers University, and Brayden Wilson, former TRU undergraduate researcher.

10 Dr. Neena Chappell (University of Victoria) reported that while physical health declines, quality of life does not, as the vast majority are psychologically healthier

than younger generations (lower prevalence of mental illness, depression, and mood disorders) with 90% reporting satisfaction with their mental health and 89% satisfied with their lives. Exercise was recommended as the main feature to prevent chronic illness and improve outcomes in later life.

11 As Ginny Ratsoy observed, the "North Shore Community Centre (centrally located and with ample free parking and wheelchair accessibility) is a large apartment complex geared to the senior population with a coffee/gift shop and an impressive array of facilities for activities such as socials, meetings, and exercise classes—an ideal location for making KALS' presence known to the population it wishes to continue to attract." It is also within easy walking, biking, scooter, and driving distance of all the exercise opportunities available at McArthur Island Park.

12 A presentation on local leadership initiatives accepted at the annual meeting of the Canadian Alliance to End Homelessness in the Fall of 2017.

13 The Youth Homeless Manager has been selected at the national level as an advisor to the Homelessness Partnering Strategy (HPS) on youth, and there is now an "A Way Home America" and an "A Way Home Scotland" based on the local A Way Home model.

14 "From 2006 to 2010, it was just a war zone," he (Hughes) said. "You were literally picking up needles off the street. There were, consistently, groups of 10–15 women working, standing in the street" (Brady et al. 2013). See also Lisa Cooke, this collection.

15 On a spatial-locational note, the old Shaw Motel, which was at the centre of considerable problematic activity in the area, was torn down and replaced by an automobile service centre and the Alliance Church—the latter becoming the host for CFP meetings and members offering life-skills programming to local residents.

16 BC Housing will provide loans and funding for the physical construction of housing (in collaboration with incentives from the local government, e.g., development cost reductions, property tax, and utility exemptions), but all ongoing maintenance of the housing facility, support programs, and staffing needs must now be met through agreements with other government agencies or other sources of funding (local, private) established by the community organization interested in providing affordable housing.

17 "Three of the academics (two in Theatre and myself in Sociology) have begun the rehearsal process with the homeless. We have chosen a small theatre in a poor area of Kamloops. Our 'getting to know you' stage of the project takes place in a rather tiny front room of the building which shares it space with a Sushi restaurant."

18 "Concerns were raised about the possibility of the 'non-homeless,' i.e., academics and support workers, outnumbering the homeless participants during the rehearsal process. . . . So far there are approximately ten homeless or recently housed participants (although it's not clear that all ten will remain committed throughout the process) and six academics/students/service workers."

19 See HomeFree Collective organizational chart at http://www.kamloops.ca/ socialdevelopment/homefree/#.WWOd1FGQzX4.

20 Initial results of an ongoing TRU Research Project entitled *After "Housing First"— Creating Employment Opportunities for the Recently Housed*. Principal Investigators— TRU Undergraduate Researchers—Brayden Wilson and Theresa Thoms, Dr. Terry

Kading (TRU) and Bob Hughes (Executive Director–ASK Wellness) (Kading and Hughes 2016–17).

21 Montgomery mentions the research that suggests working with soil boosts serotonin and reduces anxiety, and that retirees who do "environmental" work are half as likely to show depressive symptoms as with the benefits of other forms of volunteering.

22 "Upon returning home from one day in the 'field,' I received an e-mail from the research office at TRU inviting me to a Champagne and Cheese party. The academics in NSL are part of a successful cohort of TRU academics who have been awarded a large grant. The e-mail asks me to extend the invitation to the community partners involved in our research project. I wonder how the NSL front line workers will perceive this invitation—homelessness in Kamloops and Champagne and Cheese at the university—and I am slightly embarrassed about the university's elitist image."

23 The coursework comprised three five-page essays in which students were asked to assess Kamloops in relation to issues of overall happiness, nature and conviviality, mobility, and urban design—and demonstrate familiarity with city's plans and goals in these areas for the last two papers. A further opportunity for interested students to present their insights at the TRU Annual Undergraduate Research and Innovation Conference has always been met with a strong response, followed by robust and extended discussions of life in Kamloops at these sessions. Similar insights are offered in Preface by Ofori-Amoah (2007).

24 Ben Levin, in a discussion paper, "Thinking about Knowledge Mobilization," prepared at the request of the Social Sciences and Humanities Research Council of Canada, provides a succinct definition relevant to our purposes: "Knowledge Mobilization is . . . getting the right information to the right people in the right format at the right time, so as to influence decision-making. Knowledge Mobilization includes dissemination, knowledge transfer and knowledge translation." Levin, borrowing this time from the Canadian Health Services Research Foundation, reminds us of the broad perspective of dissemination that is attached to Knowledge Mobilization: dissemination goes well beyond simply making research available through the traditional vehicles of journal publication and academic conference presentations; it involves a process of extracting the main messages or key implications derived from research results and communicating them to targeted groups of decision makers and other stakeholders in a way that encourages them to factor the research implications into their work; face-to-face communication is encouraged whenever possible.

25 The leadership core comprised Dr. Will Garrett-Petts (English), Dr. James Hoffman (Theatre), Dr. Donald Lawrence (Fine Arts), Dr. Robert MacKinnon (Geography), Jann Bailey (Director of the Kamloops Art Gallery), and Lon Dubinsky.

26 The appointee for the position has lived in the community since the 1980s, and had a private company with contracts from the federal and provincial governments to provide career supports and education for the unemployed from 2000 to 2012, entailing strong contacts and a working relationship with all major community organizations including UCC/TRU.

27   As an aside, our knowledge mobilization officer has been asked to review grant
      applications for a large city-based foundation, as a representative for the "rural"
      perspective.

28   See LEDlab at http://ledlab.ca/about/#approach, and MaRS at https://www.marsdd.
      com/about/.

29   Local examples of initiatives that can be built on are the ASK Wellness Society offices
      established in Merritt (see http://www.askwellness.ca/merritt-ask/) and efforts from
      TRU to establish stronger and deeper collaborative linkages with the University of
      Northern British Columbia (UNBC) in Prince George and the University of British
      Columbia–Okanagan (UBCO) in Kelowna (see Figure 7.3).

30   Through the outcomes of these cumulative initiatives and the activities of the
      Change Lab, with their potential to develop much stronger horizontal and vertical
      capital linkages, it may be possible to better determine the ability of the small city to
      institutionalize the leadership dynamics identified in this collection (as per Scott 2004)
      and their long-term creative impact (as per Florida 2002—see Introduction).

References

Bell, D., and M. Jayne. 2009. "Small Cities? Towards a Research Agenda." *International Journal of Urban and Regional Studies* 33 (3): 683–99.

Brady, S., J. Klymchuk, M. Hendricks, and K. Karcioglu. 2013. *Two Cities: Kamloops.* https://twoworldskamloops.atavist.com/project.

Bryant, C. 2010. "Co-Constructing Rural Communities in the 21st Century: Challenges for Central Governments and the Research Community in Working Effectively with Local and Regional Actors." In *The Next Rural Economies: Constructing Rural Place in a Global Economy*, edited by G. Halseth, S. Markey, and D. Bruce, 142–54. Oxfordshire, UK: CABI International.

Bryant, C., and C. Marois, C. 2010. "The Management and Planning of Communities in the Rural-Urban Fringe." In *The Rural-Urban Fringe in Canada: Conflict and Controversy*, edited by K. Beesley, 337–47. Brandon, MB: Brandon University Press.

Butin, D. 2015. "Dreaming of Justice: Critical Service-Learning and the Need to Wake Up." *Theory Into Practice* 54:5–10.

Carlton, B., and P. Born. 2016. *10—A Guide for Cities Reducing Poverty.* Tamarack Institute. http://vibrantcanada.ca/resource-library/tools-templates/ten-guide-cities-reducing-poverty.

Chappell, N. 2016, June 10. "Keynote Address." *Seniors Symposium* hosted by Oncore Seniors Services, Sandman Signature Kamloops Hotel.

City of Kamloops. 2015. *Food and Urban Agricultural Plan: Harvesting Our Potential.*

City of Kamloops. 2017. *KAMPLAN-Review and Update.* https://www.kamloops.ca/homes-business/community-planning-zoning/official-community-plan-kamplan/kamplan-review-update.

Cleave, E., R. Godwin, and M. Chatwin. 2017. "Cities' Economic Development Efforts in a Changing Global Economy: Content Analysis of Economic Development Plans in Ontario, Canada." *Area* 49 (3): 359–68. doi:10.1111/area.12335.

Cronin, T. 2016, February 10a. "Lack of Affordable Housing Reaches Crisis Levels in Kamloops." *CFJC TV*. http://cfjctoday.com/article/512194/lack-affordable-housing-reaches-crisis-levels.

Cronin, T. 2016, June 7. "'Grow a Row' to Help Feed the Hungry." *CFJC TV*. http://cfjctoday.com/article/529168/grow-row-help-feed-hungry.

CUVIC Conference. 2014. University of Victoria, May 20–22.

Deutschmann, L. 2005. "Kamloops: The Risk Society Is in My Back Yard." In *The Small Cities Book: On the Cultural Future of Small Cities*, edited by W. F. Garrett-Petts, 333–48. Vancouver: New Star Books.

Dubinsky, L. 2006. "In Praise of Small Cities: Cultural Life in Kamloops, BC." *Canadian Journal of Communication* 31:85–106.

Emery, M., and C. Flora. 2006. "Spiraling-up: Mapping Community Transformation with Community Capitals Framework." *Community Development* 37 (1): 19–35.

Etmanski, C., T. Dawson, and B. L. Hall. 2014. "Introduction." In *Learning and Teaching Community-Based Research*, edited by C. Etmanski, T. Dawson, and B. L. Hall, 3–22. Toronto: University of Toronto Press.

Florida, R. 2002. *The Rise of the Creative Class*. New York: Basic Books.

Garrett-Petts, W. F., ed.. 2005. *The Small Cities Book: On the Cultural Future of Small Cities*. Vancouver: New Star Books.

Garrett-Petts, W. F., and L. Dubinsky. 2005. "'Working Well, Together'": An Introduction to the Cultural Future of Small Cities. In *The Small Cities Book: On the Cultural Future of Small Cities*, edited by W. F. Garrett-Petts, 333–48. Vancouver: New Star Books.

Government of BC. 2014. *BC Community Health Profile – Kamloops 2014*.

Kading, T., and B. Hughes. 2016–17. *After 'Housing First'—Creating Employment Opportunities for the Recently Housed*. TRU Undergraduate Research Project. Principal Investigators—Dr. Terry Kading (TRU) and Bob Hughes (Executive Director—ASK Wellness), TRU Undergraduate Researchers—Brayden Wilson and Theresa Thoms.

Klassen, C. 2015. "Brief History of Referenda in Kamloops." *CFJC Today*. Oct. 29. http://cfjctoday.com/article/498982/brief-history-referenda-kamloops.

McCorkell, B. 2011. *Tournament Capital Program*. City of Kamloops.

Montgomery, C. 2013. *Happy City: Transforming our Lives through Urban Design*. Toronto: Doubleday Canada.

Ofori-Amoah, B. 2007. *Beyond the Metropolis: Urban Geography as if Small Cities Mattered*. Toronto: University Press of America.

Schwan, K. 2016. "Why Don't We Do Something? The Societal Problematization of 'Homelessness' and the Relationship between Discursive Framing and Social Change." PhD thesis. University of Toronto.

Scott, M. 2004. "Building Institutional Capacity in Rural Northern Ireland: The Role of Partnership Governance in the LEADER II Programme." *Journal of Rural Studies* 20 (1): 49–59.

Shucksmith, M. 2010. "Disintegrated Rural Development? Neo-Endogenous Rural Development, Planning and Place-Shaping in Diffused Power Contexts." *Sociologia Ruralis* 50 (1): 1–14.

Sotarauta, M., A. Beer, and J. Gibney. 2017. "Making Sense of Leadership in Urban and Regional Development." *Regional Studies* 51 (2): 187–93.

Stevens, M. R., and A. Z. D. Mody. 2013. "Sustainability Plans in British Columbia: Instruments of Change or Token Gestures?" *Canadian Journal of Urban Research* 22 (1): 46–71.

Storey, D. 2010. "Partnerships, People, and Place: Lauding the Local in Rural Development." In *The Next Rural Economies: Constructing Rural Place in a Global Economy* edited by G. Halseth, S. Markey, and D. Bruce, 155–65. Oxfordshire, UK: CABI International.

The Echo. 2017. "Garden Sponsors Gather for Grow a Row." 16 (20): 1–2.

Trawin, D. 2016. "Report to Council from the Chief Administrative Officer on 2016 Citizen Survey." *City of Kamloops.* May 25.

Tremblay, C., and B. Hall. 2014. "Learning from Community-University Research Partnerships: A Canadian Study on Community Impact and Conditions for Success." *International Journal of Action Research* 10 (3): 376–404. http://www.academia.edu/9779830/Learning_from_community-university_research_partnerships_A_Canadian_study_on_community_impact_and_conditions_for_success.

Wellbrock, W., D. Roep, M. Mahon, E. Kairyte, B. Nienaber, M. D. D. García, M. Kriszan, and M. Farrell. 2013. "Arranging Public Support to Unfold Collaborative Modes of Governance in Rural Areas." *Journal of Rural Studies* 32: 420–29.

Williams, A. 2017, June 20. "Affordable Housing Focus of Kamloops Council Workshop." *Kamloops This Week.* https://www.kamloopsthisweek.com/affordable-housing-focus-kamloops-council-workshop/.

Contributors

KENDRA BESANGER holds a master's degree in Media Studies from Concordia University. She has been creating, researching, and contributing to participatory public space initiatives since 2011. She has worked in the not-for-profit, municipal, and university sectors and is currently working as a knowledge mobilization officer for a SSHRC-funded partnership project at Concordia University, in Montreal. Her writing, podcast productions, photography, conference presentations, and other media work have explored topics such as creative storytelling, place making, citizen engagement, food sovereignty, and accessible public spaces.

TINA BLOCK is an associate professor of History at Thompson Rivers University. Her research centres on the history of religion, irreligion, gender, and the family in postwar British Columbia and Canada. She is author of *The Secular Northwest: Religion and Irreligion in Everyday Postwar Life*, which draws on oral history to explore the secular culture of the postwar Pacific Northwest.

LISA COOKE is an associate professor of Anthropology at Thompson Rivers University whose teaching and research interests revolve around Indigenous-Settler relations, contemporary colonial cultural forms, and the anthropology of space and place.

DAWN FAROUGH is an assistant professor of Sociology in the Department of Sociology and Anthropology at Thompson Rivers University, Canada. She is the author of "The Messy Business of Art, Research, and Collaboration: Audience Engagement in Home/Less/Mess," published in the *Journal of Contemporary Drama in English* (2016). She has also published in the areas of wife abuse, gender and mortgage lending, and Canadian/American cultural differences.

TERRY KADING is an associate professor of Political Science at Thompson Rivers University. He teaches and conducts research in the areas of comparative politics, political economy, Canadian politics, and local government. With Dr. Christopher Walmsley, he is editor and contributor to *Small Cities, Big Issues: Reconceiving Community in a Neoliberal Era.*

GINNY RATSOY is an associate professor of English at Thompson Rivers University, teaching Canadian and Indigenous Literatures. In addition to publishing in those areas, she has written about literature in small cities, alternative pedagogies, and the scholarship of teaching and learning. Her articles and book chapters have appeared in *Theatre Research in Canada, The Canadian Journal for the Scholarship of Teaching and Learning,* and European collections published by Editions Rodopi and PIE–Peter Lang, among other places. She is the editor of *Theatre in British Columbia* and *The Small Cities Imprint: The Professional Theatres Issue,* as well as a co-editor of three other books. Ratsoy's recent publications focus on pedagogy and andragogy. In June 2017, *Place-Based Education: An Inter and Multidisciplinary Approach,* which she co-authored with four TRU colleagues, was published by the Society for Teaching and Learning in Higher Education. "The Roles of Canadian Universities in Heterogeneous Third-Age Learning: A Call for Transformation" appeared in *Canadian Journal of Higher Education* in 2016.

ROBIN REID is an assistant professor in the Tourism Management Department at Thompson Rivers University, where she is also a member of the Pedagogy of Place Group at TRU (an interdisciplinary research group). Robin's research interest in cultural narrative, community engagement, and sense of place in urban, rural, and wilderness landscapes has resulted in publications in a wide range of interdisciplinary and pedagogical contexts. She is actively engaged in local community projects and holds board of director positions with a variety of community organizations. Robin is the recipient of the TRU 2014 Teaching Excellence Award and the TRU 2017 Excellence in Internationalization Award.

Index

Numbers in italics refer to figures and tables.

161, 242–43; transdisciplinary academic, 103, 141n1. *See also* Dubinsky, Lon; governance; organic collaboration
Community Advisor Entity, 47
Community Advisory Board (NHI), 40
community capital, 148, 154
Community Capitals Framework (CCF), 148
community entities, 40, 45, 47, 54, 246
Community Gardens, 252. *See also* Public Produce Project
Community Plan Development Process (NHI), 39, 40
Community Research Initiatives, 274–77
Community-Based Research (CBR), 257–58
community-engaged research: Homeless Theatre Project, 261–62; opportunities, 265–67, 271–73; overview, 258–59; power of, 267–68; proximity issues, 259–60; Shower Project, 263–64, 266–67; with UCC initiative, 271–77; value, 264–65. *See also* CURA (Community University Research Alliance); TOHP (Tranquille Oral History Project)
Conquergood, Dwight, 111
Conrad, Diane, 111
cook events, 74, 75–78, 86–89, 94
Cooke, Lisa: on collaboration, 255–56; community-engaged research, 266; culture of giving, 235; Faculty of Arts Colloquium Series, 2013-2017, poster, *176*; Shower Project, 25–26, 65, *65*; on volunteers, 263–64
Cope-Meca program, 139, 142n9
Cox, S. M., 108
creative capital, 6–7, 9, 25, 257
creative class, 6
Crothers, A. Glenn, 213
cultural capital, 7, 95, 137–38, 149, 161, 170, 182, 200, 231, 276
Cultural Future of Small Cities, The, 271
culture of giving, 86–91, 92–93, 94, 96n10, 235

CURA (Community University Research Alliance), 155, 209–10, 212, 223n1, 271–73, *273*, 276
CURP (Community-University Research Partnership), 258–59

D

Dale, A., 148, 154, 160, 168–69
Damer, Enid, 194
Davenport (Iowa), 156
Day of Caring, 155
de Tocqueville, Alexis, 1
Denzin, Norman, 110–11
Derrida, Jacques, 96n10
"Designing Healthy Cities" workshop, 156–57
Deutschmann, L., 239, 249
Diamond, David, 106, 110, 120, 142n5
Diepstra, Stephene, 218
DiMaggio, Paul J., 28n2
Drennan, Laura, 77, 78, 87–88
Dubinsky, Lon: culture of participation, 155; framework for collaboration, 12–13, 94, 101, 106, 131, 178, 241, 255; intersecting pools of capital, 186, 200; on Kamloops, 182, 200, 208; organic collaboration, 73, 161, 216; proximity, 148–49, 169–70, 233; self-interested collaboration, 161; small cities, 175–76
DuPuis, E., 170
Duxbury, N., 147, 148, 156–57, 159

E

ecology of compassion, 26, 73, 83, 86, 96n11
ecosystems: defining, 96n11; urban street life, 26, 73, 78–86
edible gardens. *See* Public Produce Project
Elblag (Poland), 112–13, 142n7
Elias, Norman, 136
Elizabeth Fry Society, 57, 67n7, 101, *102*, 278n3
Emerald Centre (CMHA), 67n6

Emery, M., 148, 154, 170, 196, 231, 247
equality of quality of life outcomes: and
    bonding, 161; Hughes's furthering of,
    249; KALS outcomes, 177, 189, 196,
    200, 244; local capital, 230–34; local
    contributions, 57, 65; overview, 3–5,
    10–11, 19–20, 24–25, 161; Peñalosa
    on, 8; small city advantages, 237; as
    university capacity, 258, 271, 275.
    See also local leadership initiatives;
    Montgomery, Charles
Errington, E., 142n3
ethics boards, 104–5, 260–61
ethnography, 108, 142n4
Europe, 12

F

Faculty of Arts Colloquium Series 2013-
    2014, *176*
failed gift, 78–79, 96n7
Farough, Dawn: audience survey, 142n10;
    collaboration, 249–50; leadership, 65,
    235; reflections on Theatre Project,
    261, 263; Theatre Project Network
    1, *102*; Theatre Project Network 2,
    133; TRU's image, 138–39, 264–65,
    280n22
Fawcett, Kelly, 68n12
Filewod, A., 107, 131, 142n3
financial capital, 148, 154, 240
Five Year Plan to End Homelessness, The,
    245
Flora, C.: bridging social capital, 196, 231;
    North Shore, 239–40; spiraling up
    process, 148, 154, 170, 247
Florida, Richard, 5, 6, 257
*Food and Urban Agricultural Plan:
    Harvesting Our Future*, 252
Food Bank, 252, 253
Formal/Informal Hybrid networks, 90–91
Formosa, M., 180, 189, 192, 199
forum theatre, 124–25, 126
Foucault, D., 136
Freire, Paulo, 109

G

Gagnon, Anne, 182, 184, 186, 194, 195, 198
Galloway, Kim, 68n12
Garrett-Petts, Will, 223n3, 223n6, 235, 266
Garson, Shelaigh, *171*
Gel, Jan, 162
"Genetics on Stage" (Cox, Kazubowski-
    Houston, and Nisker), 125
gentrification, 82, 84, 248–49
Germany, 28n4
Gieseking, J. J., 170
gift giving, 81–82, 92, 96n10
Goodman, D., 170
governance: defining, 13–14, 241, 245;
    forms, 18; impediments, 65; shift to,
    14–16; through community, 258. *See
    also* collaboration
Government of Canada homelessness
    initiatives: ending homelessness
    commitment, 57; *The Power of
    Partnership*, 37–38. *See also* HPS
    (Homeless Partnering Strategy); NHI
    (National Homelessness Initiative)
Green Party, 247
Grow a Row campaign, 252

H

HAP (Kamloops Homelessness Action
    Plan), 101, *102*
happy city principles, 1, 9–11, 157, 170–71,
    177, 189, 192, 195, 199, 219. *See also*
    Montgomery, Charles
Harris, E. M., 165–66
Headline Theatre/Theatre for Living
    (Vancouver), 106, 110, 118, 120,
    124–25, 142n5
Healey, Mick, 217
health performance studies, 125, 127
Heggen, K., 103–4, 132
heritage preservation, 4, 68n11, 199, 223n1.
    See also TOHP (Tranquille Oral
    History Project)
Higham, F., 96n7
HomeFree Collective, 58, 61, 68n9, 246,
    251, 261, 279n19

J

Jantzen, Moneca, *36*, *91*, *102*, *133*, *151*, *183*, *207*, *273*
John Howard Society, 239, 278n3
Johnson, L., 164
Johnston, Caleb, 125
Jonathan, D-J., 199
Joseph, Mark, 213, 216
JUMP (Jubilee Urban Movement & Partners), 56, 101, *102*, 246, 252–53

K

Kading, Terry: Affordable Housing Panel Discussion (October 17, 2017), 68n12; *After "Housing First"—Creating Employment Opportunities for the Recently Housed*, 279–80n20; CFP network, *36*; homelessness focus, 25; on KALS leadership, 182; on Montgomery's urban happiness, 177; TOHP support, 223n3; UCC/TRU as a Knowledge-Support Structure, *273*; on university mission statements, 197
KALS (Kamloops Adult Learners Society): benefits, 189–92, 199–200, 234, 243; community-engaged research, 200–203, 262–63; as independent model, 180–81; leadership, 181–88, 192; organic collaboration, 178; overview, 27, 175–78; third-age learning, 179–81; transformational leadership outcomes, 243–45; TRU-KALS relationship, 184–88, 192–98, 267–68; vision/vision statement, 185, 188, 189; volunteerism, 177, 188, 199
KALS (Kamloops Adult Learners Society) Network, *183*
Kamloops (British Columbia) (profile): city survey 2016, 238, 278n1, 278n2; as community entity, 45, 47; employment profile, 23; location impact, 237; municipal boundaries, *228*; natural capital, 232–33; north-south divide, 239–41; overview, 3–4,

22–23; population, 3, 181; quality of life survey, 233, 278n1; senior population, 182; strengths, 232; trajectory, 231; transportation, 277n2
Kamloops (British Columbia): Big Public Plant-in, 157, 172n5; *Food and Urban Agricultural Plan: Harvesting Our Future*, 252; homeless funding, 45; housing challenges, 238, 278n6; knowledge support systems, 200; network activities locations, *229*; NHI funding, 43, 67n3; and NSL, 101, *102*; public produce budgeting, 167; Scotts Canada grant, 168; small city advantages, 230–38; small city challenges, 238–41; Small City Change Lab, 275, 278n28; small city classification, 28n5; social capital, 241; Social Plan adoption, 149; strengths, 232; as theatre asset, 115–16, 130; types of capital, 231–32, 233–34, 235, 241; youth homelessness pilot program, 54. *See also* North Shore (Kamloops); South Shore (Kamloops)
Kamloops Affordable Housing Needs Assessment, 53
Kamloops Arts Council, 101, *102*
Kamloops Community Committee (KCC): 2003 renewal of funding, 47; concerns, 46–47; funding challenges, 44–45; KWGH, 36, 44–45, 47–49, 58, 61–62; members, 44; progress, 49
Kamloops Community Gardens, 154
Kamloops Community YMCA-YWCA, 278n3
Kamloops Council on Aging (KCA), 202–3
Kamloops Downtown Business Association, 172n5
Kamloops Farmers Market, 236
Kamloops Food Bank & Outreach Society, 278n3
Kamloops Food Policy Committee, 278n3
Kamloops Heritage Society, 223n1
Kamloops Homeless Action Plan, 120–21
Kamloops Homeless Count, 47–48

239; revitalization, 82, 240, 256; Tranquille location, 253–54; as war zone, 249, 279n14

North Shore Business Improvement Association, *72*, 79–80, 81, 82–83, 84, 248

North Shore Community Centre, 187–88, *229*, 244, 279n11

Northern Ireland, 15

NSL (No Straight Lines): background, 99–103; collaborative research process, 108–11; goal, 101–2; health performance study, 261–62; normative/self-interested collaboration, 103–6; power struggles, 112–14; Theatre Project Network 1, *102*. *See also* Homeless Theatre Project

O

Ofori-Amoah, B., 28n5

Ontario, 64

Opp, James, 221

oppressor/oppressed, 110, 142n5

*Orchids (*Cox, Kazubowski-Houston, and Nisker), 125–26

organic collaboration: defining, 13, 15, 28n2; garden project, 161; KALS, 178, 193, 197, 199, 200; KHS, 216; shower project, 73, 94; TOHP, 215, 216

Out of the Cold program, 56

Outside the Rehearsal Hall, *140*

P

Padova. *See* Tranquille (British Columbia)

Passe Muraille (Toronto), 106

peer learning, 185

Peñalosa, Enrique, 8

PGD (pre-implantation genetic diagnosis), 125–26

Philippines, 125

place, 18, 165–66, 232, 277

place-based leadership. *See* local leadership

political capital: defining, 231; KALS location as, 239–40, 244–45; Kamloops weakness, 256, 276; North Shore weakness, 238–39, 240–41; short-term initiatives impact, 247

Politics and Poetics of Giving and Receiving in a Small City, *72*

Powell, Walter W., 28n2

power: conceptualizing, 136; power struggle, 112–14, 139; power struggles, 136–37

Power of Partnerships, The, 37–38

Practicing Democracy, 124–25

Pratt, Geraldine, 125

predicament of proximity, 259–60

pre-implantation genetic diagnosis (PGD), 125–26

Prince George (British Columbia), 278n1

Prince of Wales Fairbridge Farm School (Cowichan Station), 210–11

Project Manager—Housing and Homelessness, 54

provincial homelessness initiatives: BC Housing, 249, 279n16; BC Housing Matters, 43

Provincial Hospital for the Insane (New Westminster), 211

Provincial Housing Strategy, 42–43

Provincial Industrial School (Vancouver), 210

Provincial Lunatic Asylum (New Westminster), 211

proximity: benefits, 63, 73, 115, 202–3, 219, 236, 262, 272, 276; for KALS, 202; to nature, 252; power of, 219, 233, 236; predicament of, 259–60; public garden, 145, 148, 149, 150, 154, 162, 167–69

public history initiative. *See* Tranquille Oral History Project

Public Produce (Nordahl), 147, 156

Public Produce Project: approach, 150–51; challenges, 251–52; community collaboration, 159–61, 251–52; conclusion, 169–72; core working group, 154–55; corporatization,

Shower Project: community-engaged research, 94–95, 263–64, 266–67; cost, 75, 96n3, 96n4; culture of giving, 81–82, 91–93, 96n10; and food, 76–78, 96n6; impact, 84–86; leadership, 73, 86–91; opening, 74–76, 83, 87; overview, 26, 65, 71–74; Shower Project Network, *91*; small city adaptability, 235; transformational leadership, 247–49; urban street-life ecosystem, 78–86

Shower Project Network, *91*

Shucksmith, M., 14, 16–17, 255

Simon Fraser University, 179

small cities: advantages to leadership, 235; creative capital of, 7; defining, 21, 28n5; equality of quality of life outcomes, 276–77; leadership and learning effects, 230–31; as malleable, 170; population, 28n5; proximity, 234–37; social issues, 21–22, 230; as strategic terrains, 147

Small Cities Book: On the Cultural Future of Small Cities, The (Garrett-Petts), *228*

Small City Change Lab, *229*, 275, 280n30

social capital: city sources of, 200, 232, 245; conflict, 138; decline, 5–6, 8–9; defining, 5, 231–32; gains, 256, 276; leadership as basis, 161, 243; spiraling up effect, 148, 154, 170; of steelworkers, 95; types, 10–11; volunteers as, 169

Social Development Supervisor, 49

social isolation, 5, 8

social justice, 105–6, 107, 130–31, 135

social-creative capital, 10–11, 16, 19, 233, 276

Sotarauta, M., 28n4

South Shore (Kamloops): as advantaged area, 239–40; amalgamation, 239; gentrification, 248–49

space: defining, 166; as place, 149–50, *151*; reimagining, 8–9; social, 159, 161–70, 256, 259, 266–67, 277

Space, Place, and Gender (Massey), 149

SSHRC (Social Sciences and Humanities Research Council of Canada), 271, 275, 276

St. Paul's Cathedral, 67n6

Staging Strife: Lessons from Performing Ethnography with Polish Roma Women: (Kazubowski-Houston), 112

Statistics Canada, 198–99

STEM (sciences, technologies, engineering, and medicine), 6–7

Strand, R., 103–4, 132

Strategic Plan, 150

Stuart Wood Elementary School, 155

Supporting Communities Partnerships Initiative (SCPI), 38–40, 45, 46

sustainability, 4, 39, 40, 47, 55, 156–57, 231, *273*

Sustainable Kamloops Plan (2010), 166

T

Task Force on Homelessness, Mental Illness and Addictions, 42, 67n4

'The Cultural Future of Small Cities' project, 28n2

"The Path to Home" poster, 34

theatre. *See* Homeless Theatre Project

theatre (audience involvement): applied sector, 107, 124, 131; discussion, 125–26; focus groups, 125, 126; forum theatre, 124; health performance studies, 125; in *Home/Less/Mess*, 140–41; legislative theatre, 124–25; theatre of the oppressed sector, 124

theatre (popular): defining, 107, 142n3; forum theatre, 124; health performance studies, 125; legislative theatre, 124–25; sectors, 107, 124, 131

Theatre of the Oppressed, 107, 109, 124, 131

theatre project. *See* Homeless Theatre Project

Theatre Project Network 1, *102*

Theatre Project Network 2, *133*

Theatrefront in Toronto (Toronto), 106

third-age learning, 179–82, 199. *See also* KALS (Kamloops Adult Learners Society)

Thompson-Shuswap Master Gardeners Association, 153, 251

Thoms, Theresa, 279–80n20

TNRD (Thompson-Nicola Regional District), 156, 166

TOHP (Tranquille Oral History Project): benefits, 218–19, 222; challenges, 215–17, 253–54; community-engaged research, 265–66; heritage preservation, 210–11, 236; history of Tranquille, 206–9; introduction, 205; MOU (Memorandum of Understanding), 209–10, 215–16; oral history, 220–22; organic collaboration, 215; origin of project, 209–10; overview, 27; service learning, 212–14, 218, 223n8; Tranquille Oral History Project Network, *207*; transformational leadership/potential, 253–54

TOL (Tranquille on the Lake), 208, 209–10, 212, 223n1, 223n2

Toulouse (France), 179

Tournament Capital Centre, 232

Tournament Capital proposal, 240

Tranquille (British Columbia), 27, 206–9

Tranquille Interpretive Centre, 209–10

Tranquille Limited Partnership, 209–10

Tranquille Medical Institute, 206–8, 214, 218, 220, 221, 222, 223n11, 253–54

Tranquille Oral History Project Network, *207*

Tranquille Sanatorium, *206*

Tranquillians, 223n4

transactional leadership, 11, 15, 20, 28, 37, 58, 63, 188, 230, 241

transdisciplinary academic collaboration, 103, 141n1

transformational leadership: defining, 11, 178, 182, 188; Homeless Theatre Project, 249–51; KALS, 192, 243–45; Kamloops potential, 230, 231; Public Produce Project, 251–53; Shower

Project, 247–49; TOHP, 253–54. *See also* CFP (Changing the Face of Poverty) network

TRU (Thompson Rivers University): *After "Housing First"— Creating Employment Opportunities for the Recently Housed*, 279–80n20; *Bridges*, 202; CDRA (Community-Driven Research Award), 274; community engagement, 68n12; Cope-Meca (Career Orientation and Personal Empowerment) Program, 139, 142n9; elitist image, 138–39, 264–65, 280n22; employment profile, 23, 271–72; equality of quality of life outcomes, 4, 271; Interdisciplinary Studies students, 154, 155; Knowledge Mobilization Officer, 274, 280n26; as knowledge-support structure, 178, 200, 201–3, 258, 270, *273*; network activities locations, *229*; and NSL, 101, *102*; Office of Research and Graduate Studies, 272, 274; organic collaboration, 178; origin/profile, 184–85; Public Produce Project involvement, 154, 155, 156; relationship with KALS, 184–88, 192–98, 267–68; relationship with KFPC, 268; as research intensive, 217; Small City Change Lab, 275, 280n20; and TOHP, 209–10; TRUSpace, 223n7; UCC/TRU partnership evolution, 271–75; university links potential, 281n29; view of actors/public, 138–39; Visual Arts students, 154, 155

TRU Arts Colloquium Series, 267

TRU Ethics Committee, 104

TRU Office of Research and Graduate Studies, *72*

TRU Student Union Equity Committee, 68n12

TRUSpace, 223n7

Tsing, Anna, 83

Tuan, Yi-Fu, 149